COLD CASE CHRONICLES
Mysteries, Murders & the Missing

SILVIA PETTEM

LYONS
PRESS

Guilford, Connecticut

An imprint of The Rowman & Littlefield Publishing Group, Inc.
4501 Forbes Blvd., Ste. 200
Lanham, MD 20706
www.rowman.com

Distributed by NATIONAL BOOK NETWORK

British Library Cataloguing in Publication Information available

Library of Congress Cataloging-in-Publication Data available

ISBN 978-1-4930-4455-9 (hardcover: alk. paper)
ISBN 978-1-4930-4456-6 (electronic)

♾️™ The paper used in this publication meets the minimum requirements of American National Standard for Information Sciences—Permanence of Paper for Printed Library Materials, ANSI/ NISO Z39.48-1992.

When you have eliminated the impossible, whatever remains, however improbable, must be the truth.

—SHERLOCK HOLMES (SIR ARTHUR CONAN DOYLE)

Contents

List of Illustrations

Foreword

I was a fan of Silvia Pettem and her writing long before I actually met her. Having grown up in Boulder, Colorado, and being a fan of local and US history, I enjoyed her columns in the local newspaper and purchased several of her books to add to my home library. Her ability to concisely recount a past event and the range of topics she covered captivated my interest.

Thus, when she approached Boulder County Sheriff Joe Pelle in September 2003 and proposed that the Sheriff's Office reopen the investigation of a decades-old homicide, I was intrigued . . . and perhaps a little intimidated.

I joined the Sheriff's Office as a deputy immediately after graduating from college in 1978. I had been affiliated with the agency previously as a member of the Sheriff's Cadet program, and it was there that I decided that I wanted to pursue a career as a peace officer. Through the years I had worked as a deputy on patrol, a detective, a supervisor, and a patrol shift commander. Shortly after Sheriff Pelle took office in 2003, he placed me in charge of the agency's investigative section as detective commander, with the ancillary duty of acting as the organization's public information officer (PIO).

The Sheriff's Office was a good-size agency by Colorado standards but, blessedly, was a relatively uneventful one in terms of dealing with violent crimes. We might handle two or three "who-done-it" homicides a year, on average. While I had worked on a number of homicide cases over the years and had responded on countless death investigations, I had never coordinated an actual homicide investigation, let alone one that had occurred nearly fifty years earlier and involved a victim who was, and remained, unidentified. Where to begin?

Silvia and fellow history buff Alan Cass recounted what they knew of the murder of "Boulder's Jane Doe," providing copies of period newspaper reports documenting the tragic demise of a young, unidentified woman who had been stripped, beaten, and left for dead, in April 1954, along the banks of Boulder Creek in Boulder Canyon, west of town. I was vaguely aware of the case, having read Silvia's previous article about the anonymous murder victim buried in Boulder's Columbia Cemetery, but I knew little else. What I did know was not reassuring: from my prior historical research, I was aware that there were no existing records of the investigation at the Sheriff's Office. Any reports, photos, or evidence had been discarded or destroyed years ago. Given the passage of time, there was little hope of locating witnesses or anyone who had conducted the original investigation. The newspaper articles that Silvia and Alan provided would constitute the basis for our inquiry.

Fortunately, I was accompanied by Detective Steve Ainsworth, our in-house authority on homicide and death investigations. Steve, whose passion was (and is) "cold cases," was intrigued with the challenge of tackling the case. Encouraged by Silvia's evident passion for the victim and Steve's enthusiasm, I briefed Sheriff Pelle and suggested that we pursue the matter. He readily agreed, with the caveat that current cases would take priority. With that, we were off on a five-year odyssey that, through Detective Ainsworth's professional skills, Silvia's dogged persistence and creativity, and forensic assistance from the Vidocq Society, ultimately resulted in the successful identification of the victim, and a plausible (but as yet unproven) case for identifying her killer. Rather than spoil the ending to the story, though, I'll suggest that you read *Someone's Daughter: In Search of Justice for Jane Doe*, Silvia's book that documents the investigation.

Silvia's experience with the Jane Doe investigation and the Sheriff's Office spurred in her a latent, but now consuming, interest in cold cases and missing persons. It has become a new passion that she has pursued as relentlessly as she did the identification of Jane Doe and that resulted in two subsequent books, *Cold Case Research: Resources for Missing, Unidentified and Cold Homicide Cases* (2012) and *The Long Term Missing: Hope and Help for Families* (2017).

I'll wager that if you've picked up this book and you're reading this foreword that you, too, share an interest in probing unsolved mysteries and speculating on the who, why, and how of unsolved cases. What is it about these old (sometimes historically old) cold cases that fascinate—perhaps haunt—us?

From the perspective of a retired cop, personally, the interest is fourfold. First, most people have an innate sense of curiosity; certainly, any good investigator does. We want to know the who, why, where, when, and how of events. Being a cop gives one a front-row seat to the never-ending theater that is the tragicomedy of human existence. As a former colleague was fond of describing the job, "This badge is the ticket to the greatest show on earth."

Second, as a former investigator, I read these stories with a critical eye, evaluating the work done by my professional forebears and contrasting it against my own experience. Did they cover the basics? Were there any clues left unexamined? Did they consider every conceivable option? What would I have done differently?

So, third, I look upon these cases as a means of artificially expanding my own expertise and experience base. What can we learn from their practices? How have techniques, particularly in homicide and missing-persons cases, evolved? In reading these case histories, I was frequently surprised and impressed by what the detectives of years gone by accomplished (albeit in an ultimately unsuccessful effort), given the limitations of the communications and forensic technologies of the time. How fortunate we are to live in the present age, with automated fingerprint identification systems, DNA comparison technology, immediate access to millions upon millions of criminal records, and the ability to communicate with our public-safety counterparts internationally from the convenience of a desktop computer. It also gives me pause: How will we be viewed by our successors fifty years from now? Will they commend our efforts or criticize our incompetence?

Aside from that, the final and perhaps the most important interest is in satisfying the human desire for a sense of closure, both personally and professionally and for the victims and their families. It has been frequently observed by surviving family members (and is documented in a number of the events presented here) that "not knowing" is worse than the finality of death.

I take some consolation in the fact that I'm not alone and that others have faced the same frustration of not being able to resolve every case. There's a sense of personal failure in not bringing them to a successful conclusion. I frequently reminisce about investigations that I handled early on in my career and how I would handle them now, given the benefit of experience and added expertise. Most haunting, of course, are the unsolved homicides and missing-persons cases. Oh, for the ability to travel back in time and to apply the lessons learned through the years.

But of course, that is not possible (and if it were, it would undoubtedly create more problems than it would resolve). However, a well-written history is the closest we will ever come to time travel . . . so sit back, relax, and relive these mysteries of the past . . . and maybe, just maybe, you'll hit upon the final clue that clears the case.

PHIL WEST
OPERATIONS DIVISION CHIEF (RETIRED)
BOULDER COUNTY SHERIFF'S OFFICE

Part 1

Up for Grabs, an Introduction

Fans of the 1977 science fiction film *Close Encounters of the Third Kind* will remember the American officials at an extraordinary landing site for alien spacecraft at Devil's Tower, Wyoming, as they greeted long-missing navy pilots on their return to Earth. "Welcome back. This way to debriefing," stated one of the Americans, who then commented, "They haven't aged at all." If only it were that easy to find missing persons—or solve cold cases.

Cold Case Chronicles can't promise solutions, but, hopefully, it will stimulate thought. This collection of true stories dates from 1910 through the 1950s. The book's focus is on the victims, from men, women, and children who went missing to those who suffered from violent crimes. Some of these individuals even hid parts of their lives, then changed their identities, and were found, but their mysteries remain. In order to understand the victims, we need to view them in the context of their times.

Today's cold case investigators review their cases based on "solvability." What this boils down to are changes in relationships and changes in technology. What if a former spouse of a person who contributed to a murder comes forward, years later, with new information? Or maybe a long hidden but never tested theory is proposed by descendants who are ready to involve others in their family's secrets? Perhaps newly found human remains that include bones or teeth will yield promising DNA comparisons with family members.

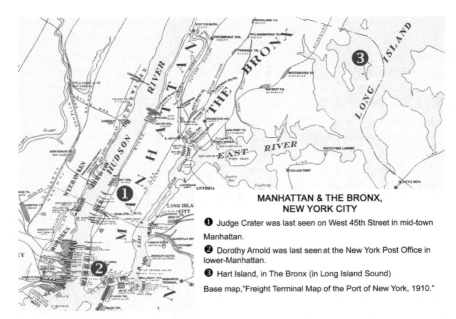

MANHATTAN & THE BRONX,
NEW YORK CITY

❶ Judge Crater was last seen on West 45th Street in mid-town Manhattan.

❷ Dorothy Arnold was last seen at the New York Post Office in lower-Manhattan.

❸ Hart Island, in The Bronx (in Long Island Sound)

Base map,"Freight Terminal Map of the Port of New York, 1910."

Figure O.1. Map of Manhattan and the Bronx.
Judge Joseph Force Crater disappeared in 1930 and Dorothy Arnold in 1910, both from Manhattan. Also within the limits of New York City is Hart Island, in the Bronx. MAP OF THE FREIGHT TERMINAL MAP OF THE PORT OF NEW YORK, 1910, ADAPTED BY AUTHOR, COURTESY OF THE NEW YORK PUBLIC LIBRARY

The following chapters are grouped into categories in order to offer a new look at a variety of old/cold cases. Each individual story is designed to encourage readers to come to their own conclusions. Be forewarned that many of these stories have multiple theories. Readers are encouraged to go back to original sources whenever possible and then think like detectives, weigh the evidence, and see where it leads.

Some accounts of missing persons dwell on the premise that the people who vanished may have arranged their own disappearances, or that a single event, such as an abduction, may have been responsible for the person's death. Rarely, however, is life—and death—that simple. Many cases remain unsolved because they are infinitely more complicated than they initially seemed, and the individuals' disappearances likely were due to a combination of causes.

In part 1 the unsolved and complicated cases of Judge Joseph Force Crater and socialite Dorothy Arnold date from the early twentieth century, only one step away from nineteenth-century folklore and legend. Arnold and Crater were born in 1885 and 1889, respectively, and they vanished twenty years apart, Arnold in 1910 and Crater in 1930, but they lived within walking distance of each other in the borough of Manhattan in New York City.

Mysterious in its own way is Potter's Field on Hart Island, a part of the borough of the Bronx and also within the boundaries of New York City. This enormous, but hidden, cross-section of humanity continues to take in men, women, and children who are indigent and unclaimed, as well as those who died with nothing, not even their names. Chapter 3's "Lost Souls and a Buried Past: Hart Island" is a stark contrast to chapters 1 and 2 and is presented for its historical context and long-overdue acknowledgment as a genealogical resource.

Judge Joseph Force Crater

Cabs and Cabarets

Every day, people disappear. Some are never reported and others not even missed, especially in a metropolis as large as New York City. In August 1930, Judge Joseph Force Crater, a New York State Supreme Court justice with prestige, money, family, and friends flat-out vanished. How could that happen? At the time, everyone had a different theory.

A grand jury was convened in September 1930 and discharged on January 9, 1931. After nearly one hundred witnesses spoke their minds, the jury's members concluded, "The evidence is insufficient to warrant any expression of opinion as to whether Crater is alive or dead, or as to whether he has absented himself voluntarily, or is the sufferer from disease in the nature of amnesia, or is the victim of crime." One of the jurors of the grand jury stated, "If Justice Crater has gone to the great beyond, I hope he is in Heaven." But where he actually was, no one had a clue.

In the years that followed, a favorite gag line among comedians was "to pull a Crater." The reference quickly was applied to anyone who disappeared, and the missing judge became the brunt of jokes in nightclubs and cabarets. People laughed, but underneath they likely felt uneasy as the mystery lingered. A multitude of theories, including one that came seventy-five years later, has kept the judge's case alive for nearly a century.

LOST IN A CROWD

Manhattan, New York, during the 1920s was, and still is today, a throbbing marketplace and financial center. At night theatergoers were dazzled by the "Great White Way," the name given to Broadway for its early and elaborate electronic advertising signs. The country was deep into Prohibition, but

Figure 1.1. Judge Joseph Force Crater.
The mysterious disappearance of Judge Crater, who sat on the New York State Supreme Court, left New York City residents with multiple theories and a wealth of unanswered questions. PHOTO COURTESY OF THE LIBRARY OF CONGRESS, PRINTS AND PHOTOGRAPHS DIVISION, NYWT&S COLLECTION, REPRODUCTION NUMBER LC-USZC2-5842

liquor still flowed, especially in the theater district. As the population hovered at approximately two million people, there was no place to build but up, and the ever-changing skyline continued to climb.

By 1930 the construction of the Bank of Manhattan Trust Building, followed by the Chrysler Building (a striking Art Deco skyscraper), was topped by the Empire State Building. With its 102 floors, it soon would be featured in the horror film *King Kong*, in which the monster gorilla "climbed" to the top of the building but finally succumbed to gunfire from four biplanes. (For more on stunt-flying, see "Daredevil" DeLay in chapter 14.) The Empire State Building remained the city's tallest for forty years. Eventually, it was surpassed by the World Trade Center towers, demolished by terrorist attacks (with airplanes) in 2001.

Meanwhile, many city residents were reeling from the aftereffects of the stock market crash of 1929 that left a surplus of unemployed men. Unemployed construction workers often became cabdrivers, or "cabbies," as they were called, driving automobiles sold right on Broadway by the Checker Cab Company. Affluent New Yorkers, including respectable and middle-aged Judge Crater, preferred to spend twenty cents per mile to hail a cab rather than head underground for the subway or wait on a crowded street corner for a bus.

On Wednesday, August 6, 1930, at 9:15 p.m., Judge Crater was last seen getting into a cab outside of Billy Haas's Chophouse, a restaurant in Midtown Manhattan. (Other accounts claimed he was last seen standing on the sidewalk as his evening's dinner companions got into a cab.) Either way, a cab was involved before he vanished, leaving behind one of the most tangled and convoluted missing-person cases in the twentieth century.

EARLY NEWS REPORTS

Judge Crater's absence was known only to his friends and family for nearly a month. But not until ten days after he failed to appear at the opening of a state supreme court session did news of his disappearance hit, and then explode in, the newspapers. On September 4, 1930, several New York newspapers ran with the headline, "Judge Joseph Crater of New York Supreme Court Absent since Aug. 6."

When newspaper readers finally did learn of Judge Crater's disappearance, they read that he had recently been appointed to the bench by New York governor Franklin D. Roosevelt. Readers also learned that on the day of the judge's absence, he had cashed out his two bank accounts totaling approximately $3,500, and he was believed to have had $1,500 more in cash on his person. (The total would be worth nearly $77,000 today.) Did he make a cash purchase or repay a loan, or was he being blackmailed? Or was he planning to leave the city and start a new life somewhere else? Was he discreet with his money? Or did he end up in the wrong place at the wrong time and get robbed and murdered?

The New York bureau of the *Sun* (a conservative newspaper and competitor of the Democratic-leaning *World*) added new information, explaining that Judge Crater, a Democrat, had been subpoenaed as a witness in an investigation into another judge who was alleged to have paid a ten-thousand-dollar bribe for his (the other judge's) post to the Democratic political "machine," called Tammany Hall. Investigators learned that Judge Crater had discovered the bribe the day before he went missing. Speculation swirled around the possibility that Judge Crater had dropped from sight (either voluntarily or involuntarily) to avoid having to testify.

EARLY INVESTIGATIONS

The *Sun* reporter and, presumably, the police as well, questioned why Judge Crater's whereabouts after his August 6 disappearance had initially remained secret. Was he dead, or was he alive, and, if alive, were his friends and his wife Stella in on a scheme to make it appear that he was dead or missing? The reporter and others wasted no time in looking into the judge's personal life. In doing so, they found a considerable amount of filler for the *Sun's* near daily headline news on Judge Crater.

By most accounts, Judge Crater appeared to have lived a successful but otherwise uneventful life. Born in Easton, Pennsylvania, in 1889, he was educated at Lafayette College and Columbia University. He married his wife, Stella, a divorcee, in 1917. Ten years later he opened his own law practice in Manhattan. The Craters maintained an upscale apartment in Midtown Manhattan, at Eleventh Street and Fifth Avenue, but Stella spent much of her time hours away at their summer home in Belgrade Lakes, seventy miles north of Portland, Maine. The couple had no children, and their marriage was reported as stable. Whether Judge Crater was a faithful husband, however, would be up for debate.

While in the city, the judge lectured on law twice a week at two New York universities. He went to work in the New York State Supreme Court building (formerly the New York County Courthouse) at Foley Square, in Lower Manhattan's Civic Center neighborhood. Although initially appointed to fill a vacancy in the New York court, he was up for election in the fall and was actively planning his campaign. In doing so, he was said to have collected incriminating information, such as the ten-thousand-dollar bribe, on other politicians. During his short time on the bench, he presided over only two cases; one involved a fraudulent conveyance, and the other dealt with an expensive car that was stolen and wrecked by an ex-convict. Did he have enemies? All politicians have enemies, especially when they gather information of corruption on other elected officials.

On September 9, 1930, slightly more than a month after the judge went missing, a writer for the syndicated United Press stated that the Democrats had "exploited the judiciary and formed alliances with criminals and racketeers." Had the judge been approached by criminals? Did he know too much? The newspaper writer explained that the Democrats had filled the pockets of judges "with millions of dollars stolen through fraudulent contracts, payroll padding, and the sale of appointments and special privileges."

Before long, as with nearly every long-term missing-person case, well-meaning members of the public began reporting "sightings." The first sighting of the judge came on September 10. The New York police received an anonymous tip saying that the judge was alive and would show up between midnight and 8:00 a.m. at his summer home in Maine. Newspaper reporters made the nearly four-hundred-mile drive and then waited for a scoop as they huddled overnight in their automobiles. The police patiently waited as well.

The judge never showed up, and poor Stella, reportedly, was on the verge of a nervous breakdown. The police and the press then drove off to their next lead, as the missing judge was "sighted" at a fishing lodge at Tupper Lake in the Adirondack Mountains of upstate New York. Detectives were sent to check out a purported "hideaway cabin" in Nova Scotia, Canada. But the judge was not there.

On the evening of Judge Crater's disappearance, he had dined with an attorney friend, who later testified at the grand jury hearing that the judge had been in good spirits. Most news accounts also mentioned a woman, reportedly a showgirl named Sally Lou Ritz. Apparently, they were the last to see the judge, and neither gave any indication of him being depressed or suicidal. When the police eventually issued a missing-person report, it described him as being in "good mental and physical condition." He was six feet tall, weighed 180 pounds, and had blue eyes (a later report said "brown") and "mixed gray" hair. He also had false upper and lower teeth. According to the police report, the tip of his right index finger was "somewhat mutilated, due to having been recently crushed." But how it was crushed, no one bothered to explain.

Before long, the mystery of Judge Crater's disappearance spread all over the world. In the New York Police Department's Detective Division's "Circular No. 9," the words "Missing Since August 6, 1930" were boldly printed above a then-recent photograph of the "Honorable Joseph Force Crater," shown with slicked-back hair, bushy eyebrows, and a hint of a smile. The police department's commissioner sent the circular (similar to today's missing-person posters) "to police of every city in the United States, Canada, and Mexico; to the consulates in European capitals and northern Africa, and to the leading police chiefs of the Eastern and Western hemispheres." (If true, that would have been a lot of law enforcement agencies!)

Police were said to have methodically checked with every cabdriver in the city, but none admitted to giving the judge a ride. The four-week time gap between the date the judge went missing and the date his disappearance became public, though, gave a cabbie, if involved, plenty of time to come up with a story.

GRAND JURY

The missing-person case took a more organized turn in mid-September 1930, when the New York County district attorney called together a grand jury specifically to investigate Judge Crater's disappearance. The district attorney pulled in anyone and everyone who knew him, even his apartment building's elevator operator. The judge's brother-in-law was called as a witness, and he testified that he had seen him a few days before he disappeared. Of the judge, his brother-in-law stated, "He's not the sort of man who would commit suicide, and I doubt if anyone wanted to kill him." Others weren't so sure.

The brother-in-law also hand-delivered written answers to the grand jury's questions from his sister, Stella, Judge Crater's wife. The district attorney was not pleased, telling newspaper reporters that her answers were "unsatisfactory," especially when Stella was asked for the names and addresses of her husband's most intimate friends. She refused to answer that question at all. To other questions that inquired about safety deposit boxes, life insurance policies, money received, and similar topics, Stella simply wrote, "No." She did, however, explain that during the initial weeks the judge was missing, she didn't contact the police because she had, instead, hired private investigators and relied on her friends. What did she know, and was she covering up for her husband? Her lips, at the time, were sealed.

An Associated Press reporter then turned up "evidence" that led police to believe that the judge deliberately dropped out of sight. First, the judge's court assistant told detectives that before the judge disappeared, he (the judge) destroyed some personal papers. Then, according to the assistant, the judge swore him to secrecy and told him he was leaving. After that, the assistant also disappeared, turning up a few days later.

When the grand jury dug deeper, it discovered a previously unknown bank account from which the judge had, a few months prior to his disappearance, withdrawn seven thousand dollars. Then, a few more days into the investigation, a tall blond woman described in the newspapers as a "scanty" came forward and said that, for five thousand dollars, she would return some (allegedly incriminating) letters the judge had written to her. On top of that allegation, a former law partner testified that he thought the judge had been abducted. Apparently there was no discussion as to who would have been the abductor, leaving open the possibility that he might have been the cabdriver whom no one could find. Had the judge been blackmailed or, perhaps fearing for his life, planned his own disappearance?

In a blatant attempt to sensationalize the story, one syndicated newspaper writer suggested that the judge had a secret life. Of Judge Crater, the writer stated, "There were hints of clandestine affairs and suggestions of mysterious love trysts—none of them in keeping with Judge Crater's known character." The writer further speculated that the judge was more of a man-about-Broadway than ever had been supposed, offering that nightclubs were no more foreign to him than night courts. Apparently, the police believed that there was a woman behind the disappearance and that finding the woman would solve the puzzle. In the newspaper lingo of the times, the process was called "cherchez la femme" or "look for the woman."

The grand jury investigation continued to question women, particularly the numerous chorus girls in and around New York's nightclubs and cabarets. One chorus girl, also interviewed by a reporter, claimed that the judge "had a penchant for the nude shows of Broadway." The judge was said to have frequented Club Abbey, a nightclub at Forty-Sixth Street and Eighth Avenue, just a block from the "peddlers, con men, gamblers, prostitutes and male cruisers" at Times Square. The club was famous for its gay emcees who featured drag queen entertainers known as "pansy performers." Young beautiful "cabaret cuties" came forward and spoke of Judge Crater's "marital freedom." Additional sightings, such as one that stated, "Crater in tropical love junket with cabaret girl" were investigated, but instead of providing leads, the sensational stories only encouraged journalistic competition and helped sell newspapers.

Chorus girls, perhaps seeking publicity, claimed to have attended late-night parties with Judge Crater. One said that he didn't drink much and didn't dance much but that he sat at a table in one of the liveliest of the White Way's after-midnight playgrounds and "watched the fun." Another woman told a reporter that the judge wrote "weird detective stories" and frequented nightclubs for their "local color." She also said that several of his stories were published in the *Saturday Evening Post* under a pen name. If the stories were discovered, maybe they would produce some clues.

During the grand jury proceedings, relatives and friends of the judge speculated that he may have been the victim of foul play. Or, in the hope that he still was alive, they focused on incidents that caused a loss of memory. A newspaper writer also reported that the New York police recently had received a ransom letter demanding twenty thousand dollars in small bills. The letter stated, "We have been caring for Justice Crater since August 14 and believe there is something wrong with his head." As in the case of Lawrence Joseph Bader (see chapter 7), amnesia often is considered in missing-person cases, at least in those from the twentieth century.

In a lengthy interview published by a Brooklyn newspaper, the *Daily Eagle*, one of the judge's male friends tried to defend his character. The friend stated that even though the judge knew dancers and actresses, he, the friend, was "absolutely certain" that Judge Crater's relations were platonic. Of the alleged bribe to the Tammany Hall machine made by a fellow judge, Judge Crater's friend concurred that Judge Crater likely would have been called to testify in the scandal, and his doing so would have been a disgrace. The friend ended his comments by stating, "Or—I'm just conjecturing now—it may have been that he knew something which would injure one of his friends in that inquiry," adding that, "It would be just like Justice Crater to sacrifice himself for a friend."

ONGOING SPECULATION

When the grand jury came to its conclusion that it was unable to determine whether Judge Crater was dead or alive, had disappeared voluntarily, suffered from amnesia, or was the victim of crime, those who testified brought up additional presumptions; they included:

- Suicide
- Abduction
- Accidental death

- Political scandal
- Suspicious money transactions and possible blackmail
- A cover-up carried out by his wife for his benefit
- A cover-up carried out by himself for the benefit of a friend
- Extramarital affairs

As speculation on Judge Crater's whereabouts continued, the nightclub jokes turned into newspaper satire. During the time of the grand jury hearing, an anonymous writer penned a lengthy poem that was published in the *New York Daily News*. The poem began, "Judge Crater, on a summer's day, / closed his desk and slipped away," as if he had become a folk hero who got away with doing something illegal. Then came speculation that the political machine of Tammany Hall "looked the other way." The writer also surmised that, perhaps, the judge simply knew too much. Then the poem concluded with, "O, the mystery is great, but 'twill be far greater, / if they make a mistake, and FIND Judge Crater!"

After the grand jury's proceedings concluded, Stella, the judge's wife (or widow, as the case might be), returned to the couple's swanky Fifth Avenue apartment. There, in a hidden dresser drawer, she found her husband's will (leaving everything to her), along with cash, checks, an insurance policy, and a list of people who owed the judge money. Even so, she fell into financial difficulty. In 1933, after being evicted from her apartment, Stella worked as a secretary to support herself.

In 1938 Stella married electrical engineer Carl Kunz, a widower. Stella had to wait, though, until June 6, 1939, for the completion of her husband's "Legal Presumption of Death" decree before she could receive (on January 10, 1940) Judge Crater's $20,000 life insurance policy. It would be worth nearly $357,000 today.

Stella and Carl were living rather well, and still in Manhattan, in 1940. But they divorced in 1950. At the time, Stella was in poor health. She spent her last six years in a nursing home before she died in 1969 at the age of eighty-two. In her obituary, a reporter for the syndicate United Press International noted that she believed Judge Crater was "the victim of foul play and is no longer alive." Her last words to the press on the topic were, "I, too, could die with peace of mind if I but knew."

THE REST OF THE STORY

The comment of the judge's former wife Stella might have been the last word if it weren't for the discovery, in a safety deposit box, of a long-sealed envelope marked, "Do not open until my death." The envelope, with a handwritten letter inside, was found by the granddaughter of another, completely unrelated, woman named Stella: Stella Ferrucci-Good. To shed new light on a cold case, sometimes all that's needed is the passage of time.

This second Stella had died in April 2005. According to stories published a few months later in the *New York Post*, the *New York Times*, and several other newspapers, the ninety-one-year-old woman from Queens had written that her first husband, Robert Good, had told her, before he died in 1975, what he knew of the judge's disappearance. Robert was a friend of former New York Police Department officer Charles Burns and his brother Frank Burns, a former cabdriver. According to the deathbed confession, Frank was the cabbie who had picked up Judge Crater. The brothers then drove him to Coney Island, where they and a few other accomplices shot the judge and stuffed his body under the boardwalk near West Eighth Street. Whether Robert Good was one of the accomplices is not known. No motive was given for the judge's murder.

In 2005, after the elderly woman's granddaughter found the letter, she turned it over to the police department, whose detectives retrieved the judge's yellowing case file from storage. By then, everyone mentioned in Stella Ferrucci-Good's letter was deceased. The police were able to determine, however, that Charles, the police officer, had been assigned to the Coney Island Precinct when Judge Crater vanished on the night of August 6, 1930.

In "Cops Map Out Dig for Judge Crater" on October 13, 2005, a *New York Post* reporter wrote of the police department's reopened investigation. At the time, detectives were scrutinizing old maps of the Coney Island boardwalk area in an attempt to figure out where to search for his body. Their investigation was complicated (and may have ended abruptly) because, nine years after the judge vanished, the stretch of boardwalk between West Eighth and West Fifteenth Streets had been moved approximately 280 feet. Then, in 1956, the area was compromised again when it was excavated for the construction of today's New York Aquarium, which opened on June 6, 1957.

As anyone who watches old movies of the film noir genre is aware, big-city docks and boardwalks have long been used as dumping grounds for bodies. Finding skeletal remains under the Coney Island boardwalk would not have been unusual. In fact, rumors swirled around five sets of skeletal remains said to have been unearthed in the mid-1950s at the time of the aquarium's construction. However, unless someone was specifically looking for Judge Crater's remains (perhaps identified as a skull without teeth found with Judge Crater's false teeth), he could easily have ended up for burial with thousands of other remains and unclaimed bodies on Hart Island, in the borough of the Bronx, as explained in chapter 3.

Why, according to the press in 2005, did the New York Police Department deem the rumors of Judge Crater's remains "unfounded"? Is a deathbed confession, as written by a dying man's wife, even credible? Maybe a descendant of the cop or the cabbie will come forward to corroborate the story. Or, maybe, like the phrase "to pull a Crater," Judge Crater's disappearance will, again, slip back in time. All that's left, in his case, are multiple mysterious theories and a wealth of unanswered questions. But it does appear that the judge disappeared in a cab, maybe with a glass of Cabernet in his hand.

Dorothy Arnold

As Though She Never Existed

Judge Joseph Force Crater wasn't the only prominent big-city resident to vanish on the streets of Manhattan in the early twentieth century. On Monday morning, December 12, 1910, twenty-five-year-old socialite and heiress Dorothy Harriet Camille Arnold also appeared to walk off the face of the earth. The main points in common between her case and that of the judge were that their families didn't appear to know much about them and no traces of their bodies ever were found. Dorothy was just a carefree young woman (or so people thought) who went out on a crisp December day to buy a new dress and never came home. Did she run away and start a new life, or did something happen to her? Like Judge Crater, maybe her life was more complex than anyone knew and her disappearance amounted to a mixture of both.

UPSCALE AND UPTOWN
Dorothy and her parents, along with her twenty-two-year-old brother Daniel, nineteen-year-old sister Marjorie, and three servants lived at 108 East Seventy-Ninth Street, near its intersection with Park Avenue on Manhattan's Upper East Side. Another brother, John, had married and moved out of the home. Dorothy's seventy-three-year-old father, Francis Rose Arnold, was the well-to-do owner of F. R. Arnold & Company. A census taker described the Brooklyn native as an importer of "druggists' supplies," specializing in French and Russian perfumes. Francis had graduated from Harvard University in 1856, the birth year of his much younger wife, Mary Martha Parks.

Dorothy appeared to do everything expected of her as the oldest daughter in a well-connected family in the old guard of New York society. She had graduated in 1905 from Bryn Mawr College, a private women's liberal arts college

Figure 2.1. Dorothy Arnold.
Dorothy was said to have vanished "as completely as though she never existed," but her private life may have held the key to her disappearance.
PHOTO COURTESY OF THE LIBRARY OF CONGRESS, GEORGE GRANTHAM BAIN COLLECTION, REPRODUCTION NUMBER LC-DIG-GGBAIN-05706

near Philadelphia, Pennsylvania. But her school life may not have been as prim and proper as her parents had anticipated. One notation of her in a Bryn Mawr yearbook was for her performance as a Filipino woman in a class play, a comedy. She and five other college girls sang and danced to a song that included suggestive lines such as "We've lots of beaus; We never bother 'bout our clothes."

Back in New York, Dorothy and her family continued to live in Manhattan. So, too, did a huge influx of immigrants. But the Arnold family's home on the Upper East Side was a world away from the Lower East Side, where Jacob A. Riis (as explained in chapter 3, about Hart Island) walked the streets of the tenements and wrote his book *How the Other Half Lives*. Manhattan's population now tops 1.6 million, yet most readers today are unaware that its number of residents peaked, with more than two million residents, in 1910. Of Dorothy's disappearance, that year, one newspaper reporter wrote, "She was gone from the ken of her whole circle of acquaintances as completely as though she never existed."

Puzzling Investigation
A few days before Dorothy went missing, she had hosted a luncheon with a couple of her female friends, and none had found her to have said anything suspicious or to have alluded in any way to her leaving home. On the day she disappeared, when she arrived downtown, she bought some candy and then charged a book at Brentano's Bookshop. (Bills for both the candy and the book went to her father's accounts.) Dorothy's stated reason for shopping was to buy a dress for her sister's "debut" into society, where the whole family would be on display.

According to the *Brooklyn Citizen*, on January 28, 1911, she had planned to spend the day shopping with "her closest chum," but Dorothy telephoned the young woman that morning and said she was going, instead, with her mother. Then, when her mother offered to accompany her, Dorothy said she would go by herself. Clearly, it was evident that she wanted to be alone that day.

At first Dorothy's parents did not call police, just as, years later, Judge Crater's family wouldn't call them either. Perhaps, Francis and his wife assumed, and hoped, that their daughter would come home on her own. And with the upcoming social event, Dorothy's parents would not have wanted any possibility of a scandal. Maybe they had noted a hint of rebellion in their daughter and were afraid of what they might find.

Like the wife of Judge Crater, however, Dorothy's father, Francis, hired undercover detectives. They worked with two law firms and visited hospitals, asylums, boardinghouses, and morgues. Finally, after six weeks with no leads at all, Francis, nearing desperation, went to the police. Once the story went public, newspaper reporters gave Dorothy full-page coverage. The *Evening World* even drew up a detailed "diagram" of the clothing that Dorothy was wearing when she was last seen.

Dorothy, readers were told, had on an ankle-length, navy-blue serge suit with a black velvet hat topped with two blue velvet roses. Her hair was piled on her head in a "full pompadour," and her hat was held in place with a very long dark-blue hat pin. She wore drop earrings and was carrying a large, black fox muff, tan gloves, and a black cloth handbag. The young woman was five feet, four inches in height, weighed approximately 140 pounds, and had gray-blue eyes. It's not known who provided her description, but she was reported as "pretty, aristocratic, refined, ideally happy in her home, devoted to her parents, and without any serious love affair of any sort," adding that she was "contented" and "absolutely normal in her thoughts and her life." Had someone suggested that she wasn't "normal?" What was being hidden, if so?

The police followed every sighting that came from the public: one person reported seeing Dorothy in a downtown restaurant, while another well-meaning citizen was sure she was living under an assumed name in a boardinghouse in Brooklyn. Then came the possibility of "enforced detention," or abduction. For investigators Dorothy's disappearance (according to the press) had become "the biggest puzzle they ever tried to solve."

DANGERS AND POSSIBILITIES

New York was a busy city, but it was easy to get around. Underground subways had opened in Manhattan in 1904, with trolleys and elevated trains in use even earlier. In 1910 an increasing number of automobiles mixed with horse-drawn vehicles. As far as family and friends knew, however, Dorothy preferred to walk when going out on her own. The newspapers also reported that she was wearing low-heeled shoes when she disappeared, so it's likely that she walked the day she went missing. If so, it would have taken her more than an hour to get to Brentano's at 586 Fifth Avenue, between Forty-Seventh and Forty-Eighth Streets.

During the last week of January 1911, several newspapers published Dorothy's photograph. Immediately, a lead came in to investigators. A riverfront merchant on the Lower West Side was certain that Dorothy was the young woman who, on the previous day, had entered his shop and nervously sought to exchange expensive jewelry for men's clothing. (By then, however, more than six weeks had passed since Dorothy's disappearance.) The reason the woman gave, while averting her eyes, stated the merchant, was that she wanted the clothing for a masquerade party. The merchant also stated that his customer had asked about steamships sailing to European ports from Hoboken, New

Jersey. "I have studied faces," he told an *Evening World* newspaper reporter. "It has been a part of my work as an art student in a night class, and I'm sure that the girl on whom I waited yesterday was Miss Arnold."

The newspaper article failed to state whether or not the merchant's customer made any purchases. If not, perhaps she went to another shop. But the merchant claimed to see the woman walk across the street in the direction of a dock where ferries crossed the Hudson River to Hoboken, New Jersey. After the merchant relayed his information to the police, an investigator telegraphed a French ship that had recently left Hoboken and inquired as to whether an unaccompanied young woman was aboard. Oddly, whoever sent the telegram left out the part about her being disguised as a man.

Dorothy's mother insisted that her daughter was not in love, thus eliminating (in her mother's mind) the possibility that Dorothy ran off with a lover. Instead, both parents publicly stated that they thought she had met with violence, perhaps an attack in a secluded section of Central Park. An editorial writer in the *Brooklyn Eagle* thought it was possible as well. He wrote, "Especially in bad weather there are many places in the large parks at which a couple of strong men might seize, bind and gag even an athletic young woman such as Miss Arnold and force her into a cab. In the writer's opinion, the robbers rarely intended to murder, but the blow from the stuffed club is dealt harder than intended."

Francis, Dorothy's father, told another newspaper reporter, "It was to an act of Providence and not by her own will that my child was lost, and it will be an act of Providence that will restore her to me." Francis then offered a one-thousand-dollar reward for information leading to information on his daughter and was described as a "broken old man" who was "failing visibly and under strain."

FRUITLESS SEARCHES
Once the police had become involved, newspapers reported that police investigators contacted "every hospital, private as well as public, on this continent and in Europe." How was that even possible? The police also continued the work of the initial private investigators by combing through morgues and searching death records, both in the United States and abroad. In January 1911, one of Dorothy's close friends told a *New York Times* reporter, "Something has happened. I don't know what—whether accident or foul play. She always dreaded to do anything that would attract public attention. She would

be the last person in the world to think of disguising herself as a man, as some clue has it. Though she was my intimate friend, she never spoke to me about trouble at home, nor did she seem to regard herself as 'misunderstood.' If she had any romances, I never knew of them."

Even though Dorothy's mother and friends were sure that no man was in Dorothy's life, a zealous reporter revealed a previous engagement. The man was George S. Griscom Jr., a bachelor who lived in Pittsburgh, Pennsylvania, but frequently stayed at the Hotel Schuyler at 57 West Forty-Fifth Street, between Fifth and Sixth Avenues. The *Daily News* then came up with a story claiming that three months before Dorothy's disappearance, she and George had been seen together in Boston, Massachusetts, for several days. Perhaps that possibility, and/or other times she was away from home for a few days, was known to her father, who kept her escapades under wraps during the early part of the investigation. Could she have become pregnant?

After Dorothy disappeared, her parents searched her bedroom and found a stack of letters from George, who was in Florence, Italy, at the time. To confront him about any possible involvement, Dorothy's mother and her oldest brother, John, sailed for Europe on January 6, 1911. The *Sun*, whose reporter did more investigating on his own, broke the story wide open by writing:

> He [George Griscom Jr.] became acquainted with Dorothy Arnold two years ago at Nantucket [Massachusetts]. A love affair developed, the girl's first. They corresponded frequently, and as time went on Miss Arnold's affection for Griscom increased. At one time, so friends of Miss Arnold say, Griscom wanted to marry her, but his proposal was not received with favor by Francis R. Arnold, Dorothy's father, or by his own family.

The *Sun* reporter added that Francis's complaint of George was that he was an "idler," living off his father, the former vice president of the Pennsylvania Railroad. Perhaps Francis had read another newspaper story, from December 1909, telling how George once had been engaged to a "very rich" heiress in his hometown of Pittsburgh, Pennsylvania. The night before their wedding, she broke their engagement because he objected to her having too many dogs. Even so, George seemed to have established a pattern of proposing to women from wealthy families.

After Francis objected to Dorothy's relationship with George, she still corresponded with him through the mail. (And, as George later would tell a reporter, they also corresponded with messages in the "personal columns" of New York newspapers.) Instead of having all of Dorothy's mail delivered to the family's home, she received George's letters at the general delivery window of the New York Post Office. The handsome four-story postal building (demolished in 1939) was located at the lower end of City Hall Park, also in Lower Manhattan. As the *Sun* reported:

> *She [Dorothy] called so often at the women's general delivery window at the main post office that the day clerk there came to know her perfectly by sight. Besides, she had given her name to him so that he could forward to Washington (when she went there to visit a girlfriend over Thanksgiving) letters that might come from abroad. Mr. Griscom had sailed with his father and mother on November 5 [1910].*

Figure 2.2. New York Post Office.
Dorothy was last seen at the New York Post Office on Broadway, in Lower Manhattan, New York. PHOTO DATED 1903 COURTESY OF THE LIBRARY OF CONGRESS, B. W. KILBURN, REPRODUCTION NUMBER LC-DIG-STEREO-1S06749

The private investigators and the lawyers who continued to work for Dorothy's father discovered that, in addition to Dorothy's letter writing, she had become disappointed in a literary career. Apparently, she had submitted a short story to *McClure's Magazine*, but it had been rejected. She needed a place to write and told her parents that she wanted to move into a studio apartment in Greenwich Village. The bohemian neighborhood in Lower Manhattan (and, incidentally, closer to the post office), even in 1910, already had become a melting pot of "free thinkers," known for their artistic and literary pursuits as well as unconventional lifestyles. Just as Francis refused to let his daughter marry George, he also refused to let her move out of the family home. Dorothy just didn't fit the mold that was expected of her.

DIGGING DEEPER

In February 1911 George returned to New York and joined in Dorothy's search, saying that he expected to find her and would marry her when he did. After another month, however, he deemed the quest "hopeless." He likely returned to Pittsburgh. Meanwhile, the public continued to report "sightings" of Dorothy. A female doctor said she saw a young woman resembling Dorothy in St. Augustine, Florida. Someone else reported having seen Dorothy entering an automobile with a "strange" man and woman in Philadelphia. She also was thought to have been seen in Idaho. By March 1911, the police had dragged the lakes in Central Park, but they did not find her body. (There was no mention, though, as to whether they found any other bodies.)

A year after Dorothy's disappearance, the *New York Times* summarized her case. Chief William J. Flynn, who had headed the New York Police Department's Detective Bureau at the time stated that it "would go down in police history as one of its deepest mysteries." For months, the chief said that he thought Dorothy would sooner or later return to her home, but he had reached the conclusion (as had her parents by then) that she was dead and "her disappearance would probably never be known."

Then in April 1914 George Griscom's hometown of Pittsburgh was back in the news. As reported in a syndicated newspaper story titled "Hospital for Women Called a Death House," a Pittsburgh "physician" had confessed that a woman named Dorothy Arnold had been among twenty or so patients in his "maternity hospital" who had been cremated in his basement. The story explained that when "illegal operations" resulted in complications, and when the patients died, their bodies were "heartlessly consigned to a monster furnace."

After hearing of this possible connection to what the press called the "house of mystery," one of Dorothy's family's lawyers, along with two detectives, immediately boarded a train for the nine- to ten-hour ride from Manhattan to Pittsburgh. A few days later, newspaper writers reported that "chemists" were "analyzing ashes taken from the large furnace." In retrospect, this forensic procedure was quite remarkable, considering that 1914 was more than seventy years before the knowledge of DNA (deoxyribonucleic acid, the body's carrier of genetic information) made "analyzing" anything a routine procedure. Presumably, these early crime scene analysts were looking for teeth and bones. Also in the news was an announcement that the "physician" had been sent to prison.

So where was George Jr.? According to his US passport application through the American Consulate in Liverpool, he had left the United States on May 10, 1913, for England. During World War I and at the time of his application in 1918, he lived in Liverpool and listed his profession as "consulting engineer and American Red Cross work." The very next year, in 1919, he switched loyalties and became a naturalized citizen of England, where he resided until his death in 1938. Had George Jr. recommended the Pittsburgh facility to Dorothy in case she discovered she was pregnant and decided to get an illegal abortion?

UNCERTAINTY REMAINED

Death was not unusual during an abortion, and the theory of Dorothy dying during an abortion came up again in 1916. At the time, newspapers reported that an inmate in the Rhode Island State Penitentiary gave a statement to his prison warden that, in December 1910, he had been hired to protect "a wealthy man" and to bury Dorothy's body. The inmate related that Dorothy had died after an "operation"—not in Pittsburgh but in New York State.

Under the headline "Dorothy Arnold Mystery Solved," the *Norwich* (Connecticut) *Bulletin*, on April 18, 1916, gave a full report. The inmate, with six months left to serve on a two-year sentence, stated that he had been hired at a Seventh Street saloon to accompany the "wealthy man's" accomplice to a house in New Rochelle, New York, approximately twenty miles north of Midtown Manhattan. Inside the house, with a man called "Doc," was a well-dressed, but very ill, young woman.

"They brought the girl out to the automobile unconscious," the inmate said in his statement. "She wore a blue skirt and a white waist [blouse], with a little wrap about her shoulders," explaining that she was placed in the rear seat next to him. He also noticed a signet ring on the index finger of her left hand, said to have resembled one she had been wearing. When he asked who she was, a "well-dressed man" (likely the "wealthy man") replied, "Dorothy Arnold."

Then the inmate, the other men, and their unconscious female passenger drove back to Manhattan to the Forty-Second Street ferry, which they rode (with the woman remaining in the car) to Weehawken, New Jersey. They then drove north for more than an hour to an old house on the banks of the Hudson River near West Point, New York. The men carried the still-unconscious woman into the residence, and the inmate and the accomplice returned to Manhattan. The next day they were summoned back to "finish the job." When they arrived, they were told that the woman had died and needed to be buried. "A grave had been partly dug," the inmate told a reporter. "We had to make it deeper, and then the body was brought down, wrapped in a sheet, and placed in the hole. We covered it with dirt." For the inmate's two days of participation, he was paid $250, a substantial amount of money for the time period.

A New York Police Department lieutenant who believed that the scenario warranted further investigation stated that he couldn't say if the woman was Dorothy, but he was certain that the story, as a whole, was true. A prison inspector and four detectives, however, weren't so sure after they fruitlessly searched the cellar of the house a few days later. The inmate said they had searched the wrong house, but additional news reports speculated that his story was a fabrication (from earlier news reports) in order to obtain an earlier parole. Perhaps he wasn't taken seriously, but the possibility that Dorothy died of a botched abortion seemed to have been accepted by the police and by the public.

STEPPED INTO OBLIVION

In the years to come, "sightings" of Dorothy continued in various parts of the country, but they became less and less frequent. Then on subsequent anniversary dates of the day she went missing, as well as whenever new missing-person cases came into the news, a new generation of newspaper reporters would reflect on Dorothy's case. In March 1932, when the kidnapping of the twenty-month-old son of aviator Charles Lindbergh stirred up recollections of the high-profile missing woman, a reporter for the *New York Daily News* wrote, "From a New York sidewalk she stepped into oblivion and mystery still persists." And, as we will see, the Lindbergh baby also popped up in press coverage of the Hatbox Baby (see chapter 9).

In 1935 the press swarmed around a Kansas housewife who actually was thought to have been Dorothy (suspected of running away and hiding her identity) until she convinced detectives that she was a few years too young. Apparently, the woman bore a strong resemblance to the missing heiress, right down to a gold inlay in her tooth (obviously what the investigators were looking for in the ashes from the furnace) as well as a mole on her leg.

In the interim, Dorothy's father, Francis Rose Arnold, had died on April 1, 1922, at the age of eighty-six. The writer of his obituary stated, "When theory after theory proved unavailing, he gradually gave up and retired to a life of seclusion." His wife, Mary, was buried beside him in Greenwood Cemetery, in Brooklyn, in December 1928. According to her obituary, "Her health was undermined with grief." Added the writer, "The parents believed from the first that their daughter was dead, but still the uncertainly remained."

Since Dorothy had come from a wealthy and prominent family, one likely scenario might have been that she was held for ransom, but the family never received a bona fide ransom note. Did she commit suicide or suffer an accidental death? Probably not, as her body never was found. Could she have suffered from amnesia, as was suspected of Lawrence Joseph Bader (see chapter 7), or did she simply run away from home? Was she abducted and murdered, as Judge Crater may have been? What would have been the motive, and where was her body? Was she, like the judge, spirited away in a cab?

One tantalizing bit of information was included in the *Sun*'s newspaper report on February 3, 1911. Dorothy's parents had not found any more letters from George Jr. after the one that she had received at Thanksgiving. Dorothy then sent her last known letter to George Jr. a couple of days after the holiday. But maybe she penned something more personal—such as news of an impending delivery—in a subsequent letter, asked him to burn it, but never got a reply.

In a newspaper article titled "Dorothy Arnold Made Secret Visit to Boston," published on February 22, 1911, an "investigator" for the *Boston Globe* reported that Dorothy had told her parents (then vacationing in Maine) that she was going to spend a week with a college friend. But the college friend supposedly never heard from Dorothy. Instead, according to the investigator, on September 19, 1910, Dorothy registered under her own name at the

Lenox Hotel in Boston. That was the week she was seen in Boston with George Jr., who was registered at another hotel nearby. (Two months later he was overseas.) This news was made public soon after George Jr. returned from Italy in February 1911. He then hired a lawyer, who refused to let him talk with the press.

According to the *Sun* reporter, on December 12, 1910, the very day that Dorothy disappeared, "She asked at the general delivery at the main post office if there was a letter from Italy for her. It was 12:30 p.m., and the general delivery clerk made sure that it was Miss Arnold. There was no letter." There was some reason that Dorothy had ventured downtown alone that day. If she was pregnant, perhaps she had made up her mind that without a firm offer of marriage, she would visit the "maternity hospital" herself. Maybe, instead of going home, she got on a train to Pittsburgh.

Lost Souls and a Buried Past

Hart Island

In the 1890s Danish-born police reporter and journalist Jacob A. Riis walked his "beat" through the overcrowded and impoverished tenement neighbor-hoods of Manhattan's Lower East Side. Then he put his observations into his book *How the Other Half Lives.* In it he told the story of a dead baby whose mother went mad as her unemployed husband packed the little corpse in an orange crate half-filled with straw in order to "take it to the morgue for a pauper burial." The baby ended up on New York City's Hart Island in a small, rough pine box, one of a thousand similar babies stacked together in a single mass grave.

At the same time and on the same island, cries for help came from the patients at what the 1880 US Census identified as the "New York City Branch Lunatic Asylum (Hart's Island), Female Department." Whether the deceased baby's mother was committed to the institution is not known, but poor immigrant women made up most of the asylum's population. Under the longtime jurisdiction of the New York City Department of Correction, Hart's (or Hart, as it's more often called) Island became a home for lost souls, burying the sounds of its past under a shroud of secrecy.

This chapter also is set in New York City, but instead of focusing on one specific case, it tells of the final resting places of many of the city's residents, whose lives and deaths are integral parts of the abundant history on Hart Island. Unlike Judge Crater and Dorothy Arnold in the preceding chapters, the missing and the unclaimed people in this chapter didn't make the front-page news. But their lack of prominence doesn't make their lives any less important.

Potter's Field

Most cities have burial grounds for indigent persons. Either their families lack the money to dispose of the deceased's remains, or the men, women, and children die unknown or unclaimed. Many die without family or friends, and some leave this world even without their names. The fate of these people is a "potter's field," a phrase derived from an old use of the word "potter" (meaning a vagrant or an itinerant peddler) that came to mean burial grounds for paupers, or the poor. The largest such burial ground in the United States (and the largest publicly funded cemetery in the world) is on Hart Island, located in the western portion of Long Island Sound in the borough of the Bronx and within the city of New York.

Ever since 1869 the city has buried people, at public expense, on Hart Island, where a portion of the northern end of the mile-long island became known both as "Potter's Field" and "City Cemetery." Its burials now number nearly one million, the first having been that of Louisa van Slyke. The twenty-four-year-old had no family and died of tuberculosis (also called consumption)

Figure 3.1. Morgue at Bellevue Hospital.
A Scene in the New York Morgue—Identification of the Unknown Dead, as this sketch was titled, was published in *Harper's Weekly*, July 7, 1866.
IMAGE FROM WIKIMEDIA COMMONS

in a New York charity hospital. Her burial came three years after the city opened its first morgue on the grounds of Bellevue Hospital, at 462 First Avenue in Manhattan, now the oldest public hospital in the United States.

Most of the deceased, like Louisa, came from institutions such as hospitals, insane asylums, and prisons. Those who were listed in early records as "Out Door Poor" were found on city streets. In *The Cemeteries of the Bronx*, by Patrick Raftery, the author outlines the places through which the deceased passed from the morgue to the grave. First, as shown in figure 3.1, unidentified bodies were placed for observation on four slightly slanted marble tables in the hopes that family and friends could identify the deceased. The unclaimed, like Louisa, who had no family, as well as others with no one to pay their burial costs, were taken to what was called a "death house." There the bodies were placed in pine coffins to be loaded onto a boat, identified as a "steamer" in the June 1877 *New York Daily Graphic*. The steamer transported its load of coffins to Hart Island, where prison inmates laid the deceased to rest.

At the time, Bellevue Hospital's Medical College was in need of cadavers. According to Raftery, unclaimed bodies that were considered good subjects for medical training were brought, instead, to the classrooms for dissection. Eventually, along with amputated limbs, the dissected deceased also ended up at Hart Island, but they were in pieces and in coffins labeled "boxes of refuse." These boxes also contained skeletal remains from older burial grounds in New York City. In 1890 reporter Jacob A. Riis often visited Hart Island to sketch and photograph the burials.

Figure 3.2. Jacob A. Riis.
In the late nineteenth century, police reporter and journalist Jacob A. Riis sketched and photographed burials at Hart Island's Potter's Field, the largest burial ground for paupers, or the poor, in the United States. PHOTO COURTESY OF THE LIBRARY OF CONGRESS, J. E. PURDY, REPRODUCTION NUMBER LC-USZ62-113814

In addition to pushing for reforms in the Manhattan tenements, he wrote an article for the *Evening Sun* titled "The City's Unclaimed Dead," bringing an increased awareness to the indigent, unknown, and unclaimed. By 1913 the burials were divided into the categories of "Adults," "Infants," and "Limbs."

Hart Island also had a variety of other early uses, and they have been documented by the New York State Office of Parks, Recreation and Historic Preservation, Division for Historic Preservation. In 1864 the island served as a training ground for the Thirty-First Regiment US Colored Troops of the US (Union) Army. In addition, the island was a prisoner-of-war camp for four months in 1865, housing 3,413 captured Confederate soldiers. During the mid-1860s, indigent Union Civil War veterans were buried in a Soldiers' Plot, and a still-standing monument in their memory was erected by the New York City Army Reserve in 1877. (In 1916, however, some of these soldiers' remains were reinterred to the West Farms Soldiers Cemetery at East 180th Street and Bryant Avenue, in the Bronx. In 1941 others were moved to the Cypress Hills Cemetery, in Brooklyn.)

Approximately one-third of the interred are the remains of infants and stillborn babies. Through the end of the twentieth century, an estimated 10 percent were sets of unidentified remains, with closer to 6 percent, so far, in the twenty-first century. Even these "Unknown Males" and "Unknown Females" had familial connections at one time—each was someone's son or someone's daughter. In addition to parents, many of the deceased likely had siblings and/or children. The magnitude of human suffering boggles the mind, and the stories of the deceased are staggering.

THE ISLAND'S ALLURE

Hart Island holds an allure for social historians, especially those deeply committed to researching long-term missing and unidentified persons. Names of many of the other burials are known, however, such as stillborn babies taken from their mothers after birth and hospital patients whose families had no choice but to agree to a "public burial." Years later, as family members and descendants chose to remember and mourn, they discovered that the cemetery, which is *for* the public, was not until recently *open to* the public, and government restrictions tightly controlled limited visitation. That has since changed, due to the dogged determination of Canadian-born New York City resident Melinda Hunt.

In a television interview from 2019, Melinda described herself as a "visual artist" who became interested in Hart Island "because it was invisible." She first learned of the island in 1991, at the time of the AIDS (acquired immunodeficiency syndrome) epidemic and the same year that Jacob A. Riis's nineteenth-century photographs of Potter's Field were reprinted in his book's anniversary edition. During the following years, Melinda produced several exhibitions and public artworks about the cemetery and its burials, and she coauthored a book of photographs. There was no turning back after she was flooded with requests from people trying to navigate city agencies in order to find the graves of their relatives. In 2011 she founded the Hart Island Project, a 501(c)(3) charitable organization registered in New York and New Jersey.

During this same time, the New York State Office of Parks, Recreation and Historic Preservation considered Hart Island's significant contributions in the fields of archaeology, health/medicine, and military and social history and determined that the island met the requirements for a Hart Island Historic District based on both state and federal guidelines. Hopefully, the next step will be placement in the National Register of Historic Places and interpretation and preservation of the cemetery and the island's historic structures.

INSANE AND DETAINED

The correction agency, originally the "New York City Department of Public Charities and Correction," had purchased the island from a private landowner in May 1868. According to a *New York Times* article on February 27, 1869, the purpose of the purchase was to establish "an industrial school for destitute boys." But that would come later. The next use, in addition to the early military operations and after establishment of the potter's field, came in the 1870s, as the previously mentioned asylum. Both the Hart's Island Asylum and another facility on Ward's Island were branches of the main women's asylum on Blackwell's Island, now called Roosevelt Island.

On June 30, 1887, the *New York Tribune* published an article titled "More Room for the Insane," stating that "the new pavilion on Hart's Island has been completed." The still-standing building was described as "a brick structure two stories in height, fitted up with the most approved sanitary appliances for the care of the insane." Before long, the asylum grew to include an entire complex of buildings. At the time of the *Tribune* article, 200 women had been moved from an overcrowded building on Blackwell's Island (in the East River, in Manhattan), while 150 women had been relocated from Ward's

Island, bringing the total on Hart's Island to between 600 and 700 patients. By then many unsavory rumors had begun to swirl around the mental institution and its branches, so Nellie Bly (pen name for a twenty-two-year-old female investigative journalist) asked her editor at the *New York World* if she could go undercover to report on the squalid conditions.

Nellie Bly ended up being sent to the Blackwell's Island Asylum, but the conditions and the treatment were similar to those at Hart's Island and the other branches. With the cooperation of her editors at the *World*, the intrepid reporter practiced "long vacant stares" and "painful grimaces" and then staged a "mad act" that convinced doctors that she was, indeed, insane. Unbeknown to the judge who ordered her commitment, her editors had a plan to have her freed in ten days.

During the 1880s the population of the Hart's Island Asylum had increased, but the 1880 US Census, in its "Schedules of Defective, Dependent, and Delinquent Classes," provides a snapshot in time. The asylum then had sixty-seven "native white" patients, of whom four were restrained with straitjackets and one with a strap. There also were eight "colored" patients, including one in a straitjacket. In addition, there were 226 "foreign-born white" patients. Fifteen of them were restrained in straitjackets and five with straps. No other restraints were documented in the Hart Island Asylum at the time, but other types (as described in the census records) included "muffs, cribs, handcuffs, balls-and-chains" as well as "personal attendants." All this information is preserved by the National Archives and Records Administration and is accessible online through genealogical databases.

In the [Blackwell's Island] asylum, Nellie Bly and the other women were forced to sit on hard benches from 6:00 a.m. to 8:00 p.m. without being allowed to talk and without anything to do. Supper, Nellie Bly reported, consisted of a piece of bread with rancid butter, five prunes, and weak tea. In the evenings each patient was bathed (once a week with soap) in the same bathwater, dried with the same towel, and then put to bed cold and shivering in a wet nightgown. Although Nellie Bly was not classified as "violent," those who were violent were restrained in a "rope gang." Nellie Bly wrote, "The attendants seemed to find amusement and pleasure in exciting the violent patients to do their worse" (or, as we would say today, their "worst").

On the tenth day, as promised, Nellie Bly's editor sent his lawyer, who managed to convince the asylum's doctor that he, the lawyer, would take Nellie Bly under his personal care. "Freedom," she wrote, "was sweeter to me than ever," and she immediately asked for a decent meal. In her two-part series of newspaper stories titled "Inside the Madhouse," she stated that the "bad food and harsh treatment" would make any woman a mental and physical wreck within two months. Her reporting prompted an investigation that resulted in three million dollars being allocated for reforms to improve the asylums' facilities.

Unfortunately, the reforms didn't last. In a *New York Tribune* article titled "Pitiable Insane Paupers," another writer, on March 23, 1892, explained that the patient population on Hart's Island had reached 1,350. "The beds are close together," the writer stated, "and in the daytime, there being no room whatsoever for recreation even for a sitting room, the patients are huddled together on benches in the center of these pavilions, as they are called, without any comfort and absolutely no ventilation. The plumbing arrangements are simply disgusting." Beginning in 1896, New York City's insane asylums were leased by the state of New York under the Manhattan State Hospital Bill. For the next few years, the institution was called the "Manhattan State Hospital for the Insane, Hart Island."

The insane asylum on Hart Island was discontinued in 1899. Then began the construction of a "workhouse for vagrants, old men, and others who are decrepit and unable to do hard work." Some of the men worked in vegetable gardens, while approximately forty men found uninterrupted employment burying the dead, adding more and more bodies, including babies, to Potter's Field each year.

TWENTIETH-CENTURY USES FOR HART ISLAND

In 1905 the workhouse was expanded to include a detention center (called a "Reformatory for Misdemeanants") for young offenders. The institution was an extension of the prison and almshouse then on Blackwell's Island. A "Dynamo Room," with its prominent smokestack, was built in 1912 and housed a generator that powered the entire complex. At some point one or more of the buildings left over from the asylum/reformatory complex was used as a sanatorium for tuberculosis. A remaining two-story residence likely was the home of the workhouse warden. In 1935 a Catholic chapel was built to replace a former church building. The chapel still is intact, but all that remains of its once-prominent stained-glass window is a large circular frame.

In 1936 some of the workhouse offenders were moved to Riker's Island, in the East River. Then during World War II, while the inmates continued to bury bodies, the US Navy, Coast Guard, and Marines located disciplinary barracks on Hart Island. Even then, the deceased were not forgotten. In 1948 prison inmates, with help from custodial staff, erected a thirty-foot-high memorial with a cross on one side and the word "Peace" on the other to commemorate the New York metropolitan area's indigent.

The northernmost ten acres of the island were used, from 1954 to 1961, as a launcher site for guided missiles. Nike surface-to-air missiles, along with those from approximately two hundred other sites within the continental United States, became the last line of defense against the threat of a nuclear attack by long-range Soviet aircraft. A few foundations and small buildings date from this Cold War era, but these remnants of the past have lost their integrity and, thus, are not eligible for inclusion on the State or National Register. The last noncemetery use was called the Phoenix House, and the former asylum/reformatory buildings were repurposed into a rehabilitation center for drug addicts. The facility included a shoe factory and operated until 1976. The island's multiple uses throughout the years has left several abandoned red brick buildings, all in various stages of deterioration.

MORE ON THE CEMETERY

In 1967 the Department of Correction published a booklet titled *A Historical Resume of Potter's Field, 1869–1967*. In it the agency laid out its then-current protocol for Hart Island burials. The writer explained that the body of a deceased pauper was sent to the county morgue in the county where the person died. If the deceased was unclaimed, the body, along with a burial permit, was sent to the morgue at Bellevue Hospital. There (instead of at the gravesite), clergy would perform a service if the deceased was known to be of the Catholic or Protestant faith. The booklet also stated that, at that time, indigent members of the Jewish faith, as well as those of Chinese descent, were buried by their fellow worshippers instead of being sent to Hart Island.

Preparation of the burials at the morgue were described as follows:

> *The bodies of the deceased are wrapped in shroud paper and sealed in pine coffins which are lined with waterproof paper when necessary. Unknowns are fingerprinted and photographed and are interred with all their clothes and belongings so that they can be identified later. Inside the coffins and on top of them are placed the duplicate and triplicate, respectively, of the burial certificate, chemically treated so that they are legible even after 25 years.*

Figure 3.3. Baby caskets at Hart Island.
Prison inmates were photographed in 1991 as they buried caskets of babies in Potter's Field on Hart Island, located in the Bronx, New York City.
PHOTO COURTESY OF FRED R. CONRAD/THE NEW YORK TIMES

Twice a week prison officials drove a truck called the "morgue wagon," full of bodies in coffins and prison laborers, to the dock on City Island for transport by ferry to Hart Island. At the time they handled approximately 125 bodies per week. Under the direction of the officers, the inmates used indelible crayons to inscribe the coffins with the names of the deceased. Then they dug trenches fifteen feet wide by forty feet long and seven- to eight-feet deep before climbing out of the gaping holes on wooden ladders.

The inmates stacked 150 adult coffins, 3 coffins high, into each mass grave. Before filling the trenches with soil, they sprinkled the pine boxes with chlorinated lime. Coffins of limbs (amputated body parts) were interred along with coffins of babies in the babies' mass graves. Instead of individual grave markers, the plots and sections of each of the mass graves were denoted with individual markers of concrete. Prior to 1960 those who were known to be Catholic were buried in a separate section of the cemetery. From 1985 through the early 1990s, the number of burials spiked due to the AIDS epidemic.

Burials of the unknown and unclaimed continued during the 2020 COVID-19 pandemic but contracted employees, instead of inmates, handled, and continue to handle at the time of this writing, the interments. Along with burials the employees also perform disinterments. Current online information explains that once a burial has been confirmed on Hart Island, family members may request a disinterment and reburial elsewhere, such as in a private cemetery. There is no charge for locating and exhuming the remains, but the process can only be done through licensed funeral directors, who will obtain the necessary permits and will charge fees for their services. First, though, it's up to a family member to obtain a death certificate, necessary to confirm that the burial was on Hart Island and not some other cemetery. For additional assistance families can also contact the New York City Human Resources Administration (NYC HRA), Office of Burial Services (OBS).

FINDING THE DECEASED

Some readers searching for their missing New York ancestors may wish to do the research on their own. Those who do should read on. The New York City Municipal Archives houses death certificates prior to 1949. Death certificates between 1949 and the present, however, can be obtained through the New York City Department of Health and Mental Hygiene (NYC DOHMH).

- Death certificates prior to 1949: The New York City Municipal Archives maintains pre-1949 death certificates from all five boroughs of New York City (Manhattan, Brooklyn, Bronx, Queens, and Staten Island). Access, either in person or online, is through the Genealogy Collection of the Municipal Archives, a division of the New York City Department of Records and Information Services (DORIS). These Archives, along with the New York City Municipal Library and the Records Center, are located in an impressive and historic seven-story building across from City Park, at 31 Chambers Street, in Lower Manhattan.

- Death certificates between 1949 and the present: Death certificates of individuals between 1949 and the present are in two parts. One is called the "standard" part, while another includes "a confidential medical report of the cause of death." Either can be ordered, but there are restrictions as to who can do the ordering. While the standard part can be ordered by a niece, nephew, aunt, uncle, great-grandchild, great-great-grandchild, grandniece or grandnephew, the confidential part that includes cause of death can only be ordered by a spouse, domestic partner, parent, child, sibling, grandparent, grandchild, the informant listed on the certificate, or the person in control of disposition.

Many of the burials on Hart Island were, and are, stillborn babies (as well as miscarriages and fetal remains), and finding their records can be a little more complicated. According to the New York City Department of Health and Mental Hygiene, parents (or aunts, uncles, and grandparents, if the parents are deceased) can order birth certificates of stillbirths after the twentieth week of gestation. But if the child was born with "some evidence of life such as a heartbeat or voluntary muscle movement," the infant will have both birth and death certificates.

- Burial records prior to 1977: With a death certificate in hand, the next step in researching a Hart Island burial is to find the deceased's burial records. The names of some of those buried *prior to 1977* are largely in handwritten ledgers. Unknowns are, not surprisingly, listed as "unknown." Originally, the ledgers were stored on Hart Island in the prison warden's house, where a fire destroyed those from June 1961 to July 1977. Infant records from August 1977 to April 1981 also are missing. The remaining records have been preserved by the New York City Department of Records and Information Services (NYC DORIS) and now are available for the public to view at the City's Municipal Archives, on Chambers Street.

- Burial records between 1977 and the present: Records of those buried in or after 1977 are now available online in a searchable database called the "Department of Correction Hart Island Lookup Service," drawn from logbooks maintained by the Department of Correction. As of 2020, the database contained more than seventy-two thousand individuals, listed—if known—by last name, first name, age in years, date of death, and place of death. (Identities of fetal remains have been redacted to protect the personal privacy of family members.)

Unidentified persons continue to be listed as "Unknowns," and a recent search showed several including a forty-year-old person (sex unknown) who died October 8, 1978, at "pier 42 Morton and West Street." This information would be extremely valuable to a family member searching for a person who disappeared on that date and at that location. Other unknowns died in various other metropolitan New York locations, including hospitals and nursing homes.

ADVOCATE FOR THE ISLAND

Melinda Hunt's many years of advocating for the island made possible the public's online access (hartisland.net/burial_records/search) to many of these burial records. In 2008 a *New York Times* article explained that Melinda had obtained approximately fifty thousand records through a request based on the Freedom of Information Law (FOIL), a New York state law that guarantees public access to New York state and local public records. Although gaining access to the records was a huge accomplishment, family members still could only visit Hart Island when escorted by a prison official. Melinda's goal was to make the island physically accessible to the public, as well. On December 4, 2019, the mayor of the City of New York transferred the jurisdiction of Hart Island from the New York City Department of Correction to the New York City Department of Parks and Recreation.

The mystique of Hart Island can't be whittled down to any single death or disappearance, or to any individual or even any class of individuals. It's not one story but more like a million stories of an unfathomable number of burials—the thousands of "insane" women, the men and boys in workhouses and reformatories and the military installations, along with continual burials—dating from the Civil War to the Cold War and beyond. All this humanity has shaped the island as we know it today.

Equally amazing is that, until very recently, most of the island's activity has been largely out of sight. Jacob A. Riis captured part of the story with his unprecedented look at New York City's poor and suffering in his book *How the Other Half Lives*. But the complete story of the lost souls of Hart Island could, perhaps, be titled *How the Other Half Lives and Dies*.

PART 2

MISSING ADVENTURERS, AN INTRODUCTION

The American West and Southwest are far away from the New York metropolis, not just in distance and demographics but also in the dangers the areas represent. Everett Ruess, Glen and Bessie Hyde, and Joe Halpern likely perished while caught up in the beauty of their wilderness surroundings—from the desert landscapes of Utah, to the rushing waters of the Grand Canyon, to the nighttime skies in Rocky Mountain National Park. All of these spirited souls were young and well educated, they appeared to have known the risks they were taking, and, if it's any comfort to their families, they seem to have spent their final days in places that they loved. With missing persons, it's necessary to use the words "likely" and "appear," as each of these adventurers' deaths is a mystery.

Of the four individuals in the following chapters, Everett Ruess, in chapter 4, is the most well-known. National park visitors and others keep his story alive when they buy notecards of his artwork and walk around in T-shirts bearing evocative block prints of his wilderness scenes. The disappearances of Glen and Bessie Hyde, related in chapter 5, brought the dangers of river rafting, especially for a petite young woman of the 1920s, into the living rooms of the nation's newspaper readers. Joe Halpern's story, in chapter 6, also includes his family's search into the third (and even touching on the fourth) generation.

As more and more information is gathered on these young people of the 1920s and 1930s, questions still linger about all of them. Was enough done in the early stages of their searches to find them? Would there be different outcomes if they disappeared today? Will there ever be any resolution? For the families of the missing, these and other questions do not go away.

Unlike the unidentified persons buried on Hart Island (see chapter 3), Everett, Glen, Bessie, and Joe have names but no graves. A few armchair sleuths have even speculated that Joe, at least, was abducted by extraterrestrials! Actually, the idea is only slightly less far-fetched than the 1902 silent film *A Trip to the Moon* (based on novelist Jules Verne's 1865 novel, *From the Earth to the Moon*), in which Longs Peak, in Colorado's Rocky Mountain National Park and near where Joe disappeared, was used as a launching pad to outer space. Writing of Joe's fate, Jack C. Moomaw (one of the park rangers who participated in his search) later stated in *Recollections of a Rocky Mountain Ranger*, "Some people, including the parents, are of the opinion that the missing boy may have lost his mind and wandered away, but I believe that, somewhere up there on the barrens, the wind is moaning through his bones."

4

Everett Ruess

He Kept His Dream

For a few months in 2009, twenty-first-century forensics seemed to resolve the mystery of the whereabouts of Everett Ruess, missing since November 1934. At the time, the twenty-year-old, accomplished artist from Los Angeles, California, walked away from south-central Utah with food for two months, painting supplies, and his two burros, Chocolatero and Cockleburrs. Many decades later came news of the rediscovery of human skeletal remains that, in 2009, were believed to be his. DNA was extracted, theories were pared down to fit the circumstances, and healing began for a second generation of Ruess family members as well as the young man's large and almost cultlike following. Everett's wandering soul was on its way home. Or was it?

The tables quickly turned as DNA profiles were compared again. And then a third comparison disproved the first two findings. Everett was Caucasian, but the remains were determined to be Native American and clearly belonged to someone else. In the intervening years, Everett's family, as well as new generations in the news media, clung to every clue. Had Everett not vanished in Utah, he likely would have enjoyed a long and distinguished career as an artist and writer. Instead, he became a folk hero. He holds a fascination today because fellow travelers and even armchair adventurers can relate to him. His life was wrapped in an enigma as he followed, and then kept, his dream.

MISSING IN THE DESERT

Missing persons can be divided into several categories. Some may be the victims of murder. Some are suicidal and end their own lives, while others may die natural or accidental deaths. Then there are those who, for a variety

Figure 4.1. Block print by Everett Ruess.
Everett Ruess carved this silhouette of a man and two burros (likely himself with Chocolatero and Cockleburrs) and used the image on Christmas cards he sent from San Francisco in 1933. PHOTO FROM SPECIAL COLLECTIONS, J. WILLARD MARRI-OTT LIBRARY, THE UNIVERSITY OF UTAH, EVERETT RUESS FAMILY PHOTOGRAPH COLLECTION P1194N01_02-012

of reasons, choose to disappear. Two men who did choose to disappear at the same time that Everett was missing in Utah were Robert McCoy and James Cecil Palmer. In the spring of 1935, their sensationalized stories were the first to catch the eyes of newspaper readers.

McCoy, a convict, had escaped from the Utah State Prison, in Salt Lake City, where he had been serving time for murder. Described two months later by a *Salt Lake Telegram* reporter as an "unrepentant evildoer," McCoy was taken into custody in May 1935, more than one thousand miles away, in St. Paul, Minnesota. There he had tried to convince an accomplice-turned-informant to hold up a beer parlor. Utah's newspaper readers got a glimpse into forensics when they learned that McCoy's identification had been confirmed by his fingerprints.

Meanwhile, a posse was hot on the trail for Palmer. Also known as "Two-Gun Johnny," a reporter stated that he allegedly had shot two cattlemen near Blanding, Utah, and then fled the scene with his fourteen-year-old "wife." In July 1935, after eluding Utah officials, Palmer (with his bride) was captured by a sheriff in Texas, where he was wanted for murdering the girl's father.

Attention-grabbing accounts of escaped convicts and fugitives from justice helped sell newspapers, but factual police reports and straightforward news items were published in the papers as well. Tucked away on page 23 of the February 20, 1935, edition of the *Salt Lake Tribune* was a plea to the Salt Lake City Police Department from Mrs. Stella Ruess, Everett's mother, that many readers could easily have missed. Titled "Los Angeles Woman Asks Aid in Hunt for Son," a portion of the story read, "Mrs. Ruess told local officers that her son was traveling in southern Utah when last heard from on November 11. At that time he had about two months provisions with him. The youth is well-acquainted with Indians and knows considerable about outdoor life. He is about five-feet-ten inches tall."

Representing Utah's most populated area, reporters for the Salt Lake City newspapers picked up on Everett's story. At the time, an increasing number of vacationers had begun to brave the bumpy dirt roads of the American West and, like Joseph Halpern's family (see chapter 6), they ventured into the country's newly formed national parks. Motorists in southwest and south-central Utah had already discovered the steep red cliffs of Zion National Park as well as the towering spires, called "hoodoos," of Bryce Canyon National Park. Everett and his burros had passed through Bryce Canyon, too, but the last time anyone had spoken with him was in the ranching town of Escalante, Utah, where he mailed his final letter to his parents.

Winter was approaching, but even so, Everett headed southeast to the harsh and uninhabited area now known as the Grand Staircase-Escalante National Monument. As he had done throughout his trek and on previous excursions, he planned to capture the beauty of the landscape with his watercolors. Only a few years out of high school, he had become a seasoned traveler, having already explored other parts of the West and Southwest, eloquently describing the changing scenes in his letters and diaries.

During this same time newspaper reporters wrote about another young man, New York City resident Daniel Thrapp, also missing in southeastern Utah. The twenty-one-year-old "boy explorer," as he was described by the *Tribune*, was a paleontologist studying prehistoric cliff dwellings and on leave from the American Museum of Natural History, in Manhattan. The museum's brownstone and granite building adjacent to Central Park would have been a familiar sight to Dorothy Arnold during her walks (see chapter 2). Judge Crater (see chapter 1) no doubt passed the museum while taking his frequent cab rides. Daniel's parents had last heard from their son in January 1935.

With both Everett and Daniel missing in the same general area at the same time, Everett's mother's concerns gained traction, albeit slowly, by twenty-first-century standards. Two weeks after her request, a spokesperson for the Salt Lake City Police Department announced that the agency had called upon the "tracking skill of Navajos." Likely, the Garfield County (Utah) Sheriff's Office was involved, as well, but it wouldn't have had the resources of a police department in the more populated area of the state.

Before long the news that Everett was missing was picked up in the Ruess family's hometown newspapers. After reading about the missing young man, fellow Los Angeles resident and gold prospector Neal Johnson contacted Everett's parents, claiming to know the south-central Utah area well and offering his support. The prospector had been in contact with a Utah sheepherder who said he had seen Everett near Fiftymile Mountain, forty-five miles southeast of the town of Escalante. According to the *Los Angeles Times*, Johnson took off on March 3, 1935, to look for Everett, asking only that his parents cover expected expenses for Indian scouts.

Johnson's participation increased the frequency of news reports in the California newspapers. "With three Navajos as his guides," stated the *Times*, "Johnson will comb the canyon territory where [Everett] Ruess was last seen. He [Johnson] hopes to reach him late this week, before the spring thaws begin," adding that melting snows would uncover "poisonous water holes" and would endanger the life of anyone wandering in the canyons. Back in Utah, the *Salt Lake Tribune* moved its most recent article on the search from page 23 to page 3 and published it with the headline, "Miner Goes to Search for Artist."

CONTINUED SEARCHES

Meanwhile, the search was still on for Daniel Thrapp. A reporter from yet another Salt Lake City newspaper, the *Deseret News*, initiated an aerial search of Daniel's expected location, south of the town of Green River, where Glen and Bessie Hyde (see chapter 5) had set off, nearly seven years earlier, on their Grand Canyon excursion. Although the reporter and his pilot didn't spot the missing man from the air, they landed in the town of Bluff, Utah, where, at a trading post, they met a rancher who had camped with Daniel and was buying him provisions.

The fellow camper confirmed that Daniel Thrapp was "alive and well." The man added that the New York resident was resting his horses on the west bank of the Colorado River, below the mouth of the San Juan River, and was unaware that anyone had reported him missing. According to the writer, Daniel's companion was "highly amused at press stories expressing fear that the young scientist was dead." Everett's presumed sighting (by the sheepherder) along with Daniel having been found boosted the spirits of the young artist's parents, who remained hopeful that their son soon would be coming home.

By this time, searching for missing persons was taken less seriously by the press and slipped, temporarily, from news items onto the editorial pages. One *Salt Lake Tribune* writer, in his article, "Searching Utah Mountains," stated, "The rugged mountain ranges of Utah have been crossed and recrossed, over ridges and through passes, along icy streams and down snow-bound trails, from border to border during the past few days, looking for scientists and artists, fugitives from justice and escaped convicts."

The editorial writer added that Daniel Thrapp "had settled himself smugly in a remote corner of the commonwealth to enjoy calm meditation and write results." Of Everett Ruess traveling in Utah, he stated that the young artist "expected to paint landscapes as long as he found the scenery beautiful and interesting. That he has not returned to civilization seems to indicate that he is still making pictures, while a search is being carried on at the request of *perturbed* [author's emphasis] relatives."

Obviously, the *Tribune* writer had little compassion for missing persons and near-contempt for their families. He concluded his editorial by stating,

> *On errands of succor and expeditions of justice, men are combing the hills, camping in the wilds, following snow-covered clues, winding through dangerous trails, looking for fellowmen who, for divergent reasons, have hidden themselves from observation and communication. It remains a strange world, inhabited by strange characters whose actions are a constant worry and surprise to their fellowmen.*

Even before the ink in the editorial had time to dry, the search for Everett took a somber tone. On March 8 the Associated Press picked up the story that cattlemen had recently found two burros starving and floundering in the snow in Davis Gulch, a twisting and tortuous sandstone "slot canyon" along the route where Everett was thought to have headed. Had the men found Chocolatero and Cockleburrs? Apparently, nothing to identify them was found with them, and no one could say for sure. The discovery of the burros,

Figure 4.2. Everett Ruess high on a lonely cliff.
Everett Ruess was photographed high on a cliff with one of his burros. PHOTO
FROM SPECIAL COLLECTIONS, J. WILLARD MARRIOTT LIBRARY, THE UNIVERSITY OF UTAH, EVER-
ETT RUESS FAMILY PHOTOGRAPH COLLECTION P1194N01_01-018

however, forced Everett's searchers to face the very real possibility that the young artist may have become lost, was injured, or was dead. Once again, his parents slid onto an emotional roller coaster.

Unlike the search for Daniel Thrapp that had been backed by the *Deseret News* (which enjoyed a scoop), no similar offer was made to find Everett, whose family lacked the financial resources for an aerial search of its own. However, in early March 1935, while the California prospector and his Indian scouts were still on the trail, a group of ranchers and cattlemen from Escalante set out on a ground search of their own. They traveled for forty miles by car and then set up a base camp, where two of the men continued on horseback through a "raging snowstorm." In Davis Gulch the men were unable to find any signs of Everett. The searchers sent word to the young

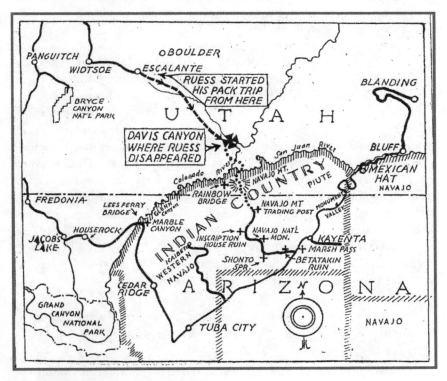

Figure 4.3. Map of Indian Country.
Everett Ruess started his pack trip in Escalante, Utah, and disappeared near Davis Canyon, as shown on this map published in the *Salt Lake Tribune* on August 25, 1935. COURTESY OF THE *SALT LAKE TRIBUNE*

man's parents (most likely by telegram when they got back to Escalante), giving them the news that no parents want to hear, stating, "We fear that your son has wandered into the desolate wastes of the desert and is lost."

EVERETT'S WANDERINGS

Wandering back-country trails had occupied Everett's time even before he had graduated, at the age of 16, in 1931 from Hollywood High School in Los Angeles, California. But he hadn't always craved solitude. On one of Everett's California journeys, he confidently knocked on the door of Ansel Adams and traded the distinguished photographer a painting for one of Adams's now famous black-and-white photographs. When Everett visited Depression-era photographer Dorothea Lange, she sat him down in her portrait studio and took several striking photographs, including two that would figure into the young man's story many years later.

On Everett's last known excursion and before his arrival in Escalante, he had written and painted his way through Utah's Monument Valley, several years before the iconic landscape became the backdrop for director John Ford's classic Western films. Everett had dipped south to Flagstaff, Arizona, and was in and out of Kayenta, Arizona (in the middle of the Navajo Nation), where he had previously worked as a cook and a packer for a team of archaeologists. Sometimes he rode one of his burros, and sometimes he walked alongside. The burros also carried his food and supplies, as well as his camera, some Navajo jewelry and blankets, and cash from occasional sales of his paintings. When Everett knew his next destination, he sent his parents the address of the post office so that their letters (with modest money orders) would be waiting for him.

In addition to writing to his parents and friends, Everett also wrote to his brother, Waldo Ruess, who later shared one of his letters with a reporter from the *Salt Lake Tribune*. It read, in part,

> *As to when I shall visit civilization, it will not be soon, I think. I have not tired of the wilderness, rather I enjoy its beauty and the vagrant life I lead, more keenly all the time. I prefer the saddle to the street car and the star-sprinkled sky to a roof, the obscure and the difficult trail leading into the unknown to any paved highway, and the deep peace of the wild to the discontent bred by cities. Do you blame me then for staying here where I feel that I belong and am one with the world around me?*

STEPPED-UP INVESTIGATIONS

On April 18, 1935, the *Salt Lake Telegram* announced that federal agents, under the direction of the superintendent of Mesa Verde National Park, had entered Everett's search. Despite the discouraging report from the Escalante search party, some still held out hope that Everett simply was holed up in a cave or spending the winter with the Navajos, with whom he was said to be on good terms. Subsequent accounts revealed that Everett's parents held on to that hope, too, especially when Johnson and the Navajo trackers found three dead campfires that possibly could have been made by Everett and two companions.

Building on the attempts of the previous two ground-search teams, the Associated Civic Clubs of Southern Utah sponsored and financed a third search for Everett in May 1935. The *Salt Lake Tribune* announced that ten men on horseback would follow the same route of a party of Mormons who, in the fall of 1879, had left Cedar City (in southwest Utah) and descended from the western rim of Glen Canyon through a steep, rocky crevice known as "Hole in the Rock." The crevice led to a location where Mormon pioneers were able to ford the Colorado River. (Part of this area was flooded in 1963 during the formation of Lake Powell and is encompassed, today, by the Glen Canyon National Recreation Area.)

In May 1935, when an on-the-scene Salt Lake City reporter announced the Civic Clubs' search, he stated, "The people of Escalante have literally been on edge with excitement and the anticipation of solving a mystery that has existed for nearly six months. . . . All members of the party have volunteered their services without pay in spite of the dangers of going into a country that is full of abrupt cliffs and ledges, where one false move means a possible fall of hundreds of feet."

But the clue that everyone was looking for was not in "Hole in the Rock." Instead, it was back in Davis Gulch, where the burros had been found. Inside a cave the men found the letters "NEMO" and "1934" carved on a rock wall. They also found footprints from a size 9 shoe, the same size as Everett's. A few days later, in another cave, they again found "NEMO 1934." No one knew what the inscription meant, but when Everett's parents were notified, it was enough for them to travel to the site to see for themselves.

Everett's parents told the press that their son knew of the character "Captain Nemo" in Jules Verne's book *Twenty Thousand Leagues under the Sea*. They also explained that Everett would have known that Nemo was the Latin name for "no man" (also translated as "no one" or "nobody"), used by Odysseus when his life was threatened by the one-eyed giant Polyphemus in Homer's classic, *The Odyssey*. As another possible explanation, Everett's brother Waldo stated that, in a then-recent letter, Everett had written that he would be "exploring southward to the Colorado [River] where no one lives."

In August 1935 yet another search party (the fourth) took off to look for Everett, this one led by a prolific reporter for the *Salt Lake Tribune* named John U. Terrell. His front-page stories and maps were designed to sell newspapers and covered four successive issues. But, despite the series' title—"S. L. Tribune Expedition into Desert Finds Clues to Fate of Young Artist"—only speculation came out of his investigation when he introduced the possibility of murder. "The united belief of the best Indian and white trackers, traders, [and] wilderness residents of southern Utah and northern Arizona," he wrote, was that Everett "probably met death at the hands of a renegade bad man or Indian in a lonely canyon near the southern end of the untracked Escalante desert." The *Tribune*'s "conclusion"—or perhaps it was the writer's alone—was that Everett had been murdered for his pack outfit.

In the years to come, Everett's legend lived on in the writings of Wallace Stegner, Edward Abbey, and many other authors and journalists. Everett's parents died without ever knowing what happened to their son, as did Everett's brother Waldo. His four children (Everett's nieces and nephews) were left to continue the seemingly endless search on their own. Then, in 2008, only one year after Waldo died, a Navajo man (who had never heard of Everett) came forward with an astonishing story.

A NEW THEORY

In the 1930s the Navajo man's grandfather, Aneth Nez, claimed to have seen a young white man with two burros being chased, and then murdered, by Utes. Decades passed, and in 1961 Aneth told the story to his granddaughter. She then waited thirty-seven years (until 2008) to tell her younger brother, the man who told the story to others. By then, their grandfather had long since passed away. The story filtered down to a wilderness guide in Utah, who called David Roberts, then contributing editor for *National Geographic Adventure* magazine. The guide filled in the editor with this newly discovered information. Could the murder victim have been Everett?

According to the tale that had been passed down through the Navajo family, Aneth had carried the murdered man's body uphill and buried him in a crevice in a rocky outcrop south of Bluff, Utah. In 2008 the grandson, who had heard the story from his sister, went in search of—and found—the remains. Before long, according to David Roberts's account in his subsequent book, *Finding Everett Ruess*, he went to look for himself. As to whether the remains belonged to Everett, no one knew. The major piece of the puzzle that didn't fit was the fact that the burial site was sixty miles east and across the Colorado River from where Everett was last seen and where the burros (thought to have been his) were found. But no one involved in the investigation at the time seemed to be too concerned.

MODERN-DAY FORENSICS

Forensics had drastically changed in the decades leading up to the twenty-first century. In 2009 a rush was on for a comparison of DNA to prove to the world that the use of modern forensics could solve a cold case. But, as a new generation of searchers and family members soon discovered, DNA analysis is not infallible. Author David Roberts stated that the initial DNA comparison to determine if the skeletal remains were Everett's was made between a molar tooth from the remains and a degraded hair follicle from a hair in a hairbrush that had belonged to Everett's late brother. The results did not help to resolve the mystery, as the remains were found to have been contaminated in the lab due to incorrect handling.

Fully committed to either identify or rule out the skeletal remains, David Roberts then brought in Dr. Dennis van Gerven, an anthropologist from the University of Colorado, in Boulder, Colorado. At his lab Dr. van Gerven compared pieces of the unearthed jaw with two portraits of Everett taken by Dorothea Lange. First, he had to reconstruct and photograph the skull. Then when he superimposed his photographs onto those of Everett's, they seemed a perfect match. As noted in *Finding Everett Ruess*, Dr. van Gerven stated at the time, "The odds are astronomically small that this could be a coincidence." To be certain, however, the process warranted a second DNA comparison. This time it was performed between a femur fragment from the remains and saliva samples from all four of Everett's nieces and nephews. The results from that comparison were inconclusive, and Roberts explained that they appeared as a "false reading" due to a "software glitch."

By this time numerous people were following Everett's missing-person case and some, including the Utah state archaeologist, were skeptical. Of particular importance to the archaeologist were the victim's teeth. Several showed "shovel-like" incisors most commonly found among Native

Americans. Although not all of the teeth from the remains had been found, those that were recovered did not match descriptions of the teeth in Everett's more than seventy-year-old dental records. The dental discrepancies and the burial site's unexplained location raised big red flags.

Then Everett's nieces and nephews became concerned and took over making arrangements for a third DNA comparison. This test was performed by the Armed Forces DNA Identification Laboratory (AFDIL) in Maryland. Unlike the previous comparisons, the AFDIL company had the facilities suited to a forensic investigation and compared DNA from both a tooth and a piece of the femur, along with a saliva sample from one of the nephews. These results definitively showed that not only were the remains *not* those of Everett but they actually belonged to a Native American. But who the man was, no one could tell.

As we have seen, three different DNA laboratories produced three different results. Philip L. Fradkin, the author of the book *Everett Ruess: His Short Life, Mysterious Death, and Astonishing Afterlife* states that the first two labs were not set up, as the AFDIL one was, to accurately analyze older DNA samples. He adds that the experts initially approached by David Roberts and Everett's family members should have warned them about the facility's limitations. Emphasizing the fact that they didn't "indicates a certain arrogance or carelessness within the ranks of this particular branch of science."

WILDERNESS SONG

Perhaps the best resolution to Everett's wanderings is that offered in Scott Thybony's *The Disappearances: A Story of Exploration, Murder, and Mystery in the American West*. The author, a travel and exploration writer as well as river guide and archaeologist, followed up on a story he uncovered about a tourist, in the 1970s, exploring for Native American ruins in Davis Gulch. The tourist found human bones wedged within a crack in a rock, and he left notes as to the location of the remains. This site also happened to be the area where Everett and his burros were last seen, and it also was the area where searchers found the "NEMO 1934" inscriptions carved on the walls of nearby caves.

The tourist who had found the bones stated that he left most of them in place, but he gave a few to a National Park Service ranger to give to his supervisor at the Lake Powell marina at Wahweap, near Page, Arizona. Unfortunately, no one today seems to know what happened to the bones. But the discovery site had been well recorded, and decades later, Scott Thybony returned to find the crack, as described, in the documented rock. By the time of his arrival, however, the area had periodically flooded, and he didn't find any more human remains. What he did find, though, above the crack where the tourist had found the bones, was a perfect hideaway in the sandstone and a remote campsite wide enough for a single bedroll.

In an article in the *Durango Herald* on May 13, 2017, writer Andrew Gulliford called Thybony's discovery "perhaps a final conclusion." Gulliford quoted the author as stating, "An ancient juniper had been dragged in for firewood, and a small ring of stones had been placed against the far wall." Thybony added that in his examination of the campsite, there was no evidence of prehistoric use, indicating that it had not been inhabited by Native Americans.

Was this campsite the last place Everett was alive before slipping to his death in the rocks below? It seems very likely. His final artwork and most recent diary may have been blown or washed away, but his letters, his previous years' diaries and his family photographs are now archived in the Everett Ruess Family collection at the J. Willard Marriott Library at the University of Utah. Everett's own writings may be, after all, our best source for solving the mystery of his disappearance. The following lines from his poem, "Wilderness Song," were published during the time of the earliest searches and seem to be prophetic. Everett wrote,

Say that I starved; that I was lost and weary;
That I was burned and blinded by the desert sun;
Footsore, thirsty, sick with strange diseases;
Lonely and wet and cold . . . but that I kept my dream!

Glen and Bessie Hyde

Grand Canyon Honeymoon

Glen and Bessie Hyde were a venturesome couple who spent months planning an unusual honeymoon. On October 20, 1928, long before most newspaper readers had even heard of river running, the newlyweds completed the building of their own flat-bottomed boat, called a scow, and lowered it into the Green River that flows through the town of Green River, Utah. Without any fanfare, they drifted south to the river's confluence with the Colorado River, where they entered Glen Canyon and then pushed on to, and through, the most dangerous rapids of the Grand Canyon, in northwestern Arizona.

If the Hydes had succeeded in reaching their destination in Needles, California, on the Arizona-California state line, Bessie would have been the first woman known to have traversed the Grand Canyon. But neither she nor her husband completed their journey. On December 19, 1928, nearly two months after the Hydes left Green River, searchers found their scow idly floating in the depths of the Grand Canyon, in a quiet pool and still loaded with their belongings. Glen's and Bessie's bodies never were found.

Did they perish in the churning waters? Or did their boat get away from them? If it did, did they try to climb the steep walls of the canyon? Did they die of starvation and/or exposure or, perhaps, from something more sinister? If so, who was the first to die? Accidental deaths for both of them seem the most likely even though, in nearly a century, no remains or even a piece of clothing have ever been found.

To Give Me a Thrill

On November 15, 1928, nearly one month after Glen and Bessie left the town of Green River, the young couple docked their scow at the foot of the

South Kaibab Trail, four thousand feet below the South Rim of the Grand Canyon. According to author Brad Dimock, in his book *Sunk Without a Sound: The Tragic Colorado Honeymoon of Glen and Bessie Hyde,* the couple had passed Bright Angel Trail, which would have led directly to Grand Canyon Village, a small community built around the terminus of the Atchison, Topeka & Santa Fe Railway (AT&SF). Both trails, however, led out of the solitude of the canyon.

Once on the South Kaibab Trail, the couple climbed for several hours, in and out of a snowstorm. After looking down on the rock formations below, Glen wrote that it was "a grand sight." The couple expected to find food and shelter once they emerged on the rim, but instead, they found themselves at Yaki Point, well east of the village. Fortunately, there was a road, and when a solitary motorist came by, he gave the weary travelers a ride.

After arriving in the small settlement, the honeymooners spent a night in Bright Angel Camp, where tents from previous years had been replaced with cabins, and the accommodations (with real beds) were more afford- able than the even more tempting El Tovar Hotel next door. The railroad company had built the luxury hotel in 1905 and catered to wealthy tourists. The Fred Harvey Company, known for its high-quality eating establishments (and hotels) along the route of the AT&SF, was the hotel's chief concession- aire. Both the El Tovar Hotel (now Lodge) and today's Bright Angel Lodge are still in operation. The Grand Canyon National Park was established in 1919 during the presidential term of US president Woodrow Wilson.

The couple's stop in Grand Canyon Village was Bessie's first opportu- nity to mail the letters she had written to her family. In an update to her mother, she wrote that she had just enjoyed a "nice hot bath." It also was the couple's first occasion to interact with other people, and the village's guests particularly were interested in Bessie. A newspaper reporter was there, too, likely reporting on the comings and goings of various guests. His stories were syndicated to several newspapers, and he found Bessie a particularly good subject for an interview. While telling the reporter about the couple's river journey, she stated, "Our main object in this trip was to give me a thrill. It's surely been successful so far. I have been thoroughly drenched a dozen times, and I'm enjoying every minute of the adventure."

Figure 5.1. Glen and Bessie Hyde.
River runner and photographer Emery Kolb captured this smiling image of Glen and Bessie Hyde on the South Rim of the Grand Canyon on November 17, 1928, shortly before they disappeared on the Colorado River. PHOTO COURTESY OF NORTH-ERN ARIZONA UNIVERSITY, CLINE LIBRARY, EMERY KOLB COLLECTION

Figure 5.2. Glen Hyde in scow.
In this photo taken in the Grand Canyon in November 1928, Glen Hyde is stand-ing in his and Bessie's scow—their homemade flat-bottom boat with two twenty-foot oars. GRAND CANYON NATIONAL PARK PHOTO 17190

READERS FOLLOW THEIR JOURNEY

The reporter's story of the Hydes' honeymoon quickly spread all over the country. As readers learned more about the couple, they wanted additional details. Bessie, they soon learned, was born Bessie Haley, a petite twenty-two-year-old who wore her hair in a short flapper-style "bob" that required little care. She had been raised on the banks of the Ohio River, in West Virginia, but was not an experienced river rafter. She did, however, have spunk. In 1926, at the age of twenty, the independent young woman had traveled west to San Francisco, California, where she enrolled in the California School of Fine Arts, now the San Francisco Art Institute. There she painted, wrote poetry, and blended in with other young people in what was called the "bohe-mian crowd," similar to the inhabitants of New York's Greenwich Village (see chapter 2) during and after Dorothy Arnold's time.

In 1927 Bessie boarded an ocean liner that, several nights per week, transported partiers between San Francisco and Los Angeles. National Pro-hibition in the United States was in effect at the time, but unlimited quan-tities of alcoholic drinks were served to willing customers in international waters. Revelers enjoyed the lively jazz bands and dancing the Charleston. Onboard, Bessie met Glen Hyde, the tall son of a Kimberly, Idaho, rancher. This was the same year that a thrill seeker named Clyde Eddy and a crew of college men made national news with their successful river trip through the Grand Canyon. Perhaps over drinks and amid the crowded party atmosphere, either Glen or Bessie mentioned the river runners and discussed the appeal and solitude of a Grand Canyon journey for themselves.

According to the *Twin Falls Daily News*, the slim brunette from the East and the lanky rancher from the West were married in an Episcopal church in Idaho on April 10, 1928. The newlyweds then spent the first months of their marriage on Glen's family ranch, near where he had boated on the Salmon River as a boy. Glen was familiar with scows, particularly the sweep scow, which basically is a wooden box with two twenty-foot oars on either end. While appearing to settle down on the ranch, Glen and his new bride quietly made their own plans. In October 1928, they took a train to the town of Green River, where they built their scow and lowered it into the river.

Newspaper readers also learned more about the first leg of the Hydes' river journey. After leaving the town of Green River, Utah, Glen and Bessie drifted into Lee's Ferry, Arizona (now the standard launching point for rafting trips through the Grand Canyon), on November 7, 1928. The Mormon settlement, nine miles south of the Utah-Arizona border, was named for resident John D. Lee, who had begun ferrying travelers across the river in 1873. When Glen and Bessie passed through, the Navajo Bridge, which was actually a pair of suspension bridges to replace the ferry, was under construction.

Bessie later (at the Grand Canyon Village) said that when she and Glen had stopped at Lee's Ferry, everyone was "very nice" to them. No news reporters were there but she stated, "Several people stood on the bridge and waved to us until we turned a bend in the river as we left in the scow." Bessie added that after leaving Lee's Ferry, the couple stopped again to buy supplies at an Indian trading post.

NEWS REPORTS TURN OMINOUS

Then the rapids began. In retrospect, it's remarkable that neither Glen nor Bessie owned a life preserver, even though 1928 marked the beginning of widespread use of inflatable vests. (These vests came to be referred to as "Mae Wests," named after the then-popular, buxom actress.) Perhaps the young couple was not convinced that they needed them, but Bessie's comments show that they were aware of the devices. If they were concerned, though, why didn't they try to obtain one for each of them at Grand Canyon Village, even if it meant having them sent in by train?

On November 21, 1928, the newspaper reporter in Grand Canyon Village quoted Bessie as saying, "We carried no life preservers. I admit I was scared to death. I can't remember very clearly all that happened. All I know is that I managed somehow to hang on to the sweeps by which the boat is guided and managed to keep the boat as straight as possible in the current until my husband could grasp the sides. Then I helped pull him aboard."

The reporter also wrote of the couple's upcoming plans, calling their journey "daring" and "dangerous." In an article titled "Dares Rapids for Thrill," the writer (whose articles were syndicated and published all over the country) described Bessie as "slight" and Glen as "a rancher, not a professional river man." But the media's focus definitely was on Bessie, as shown in the following two stories: "Idaho woman on perilous journey in a boat" and "With her rancher husband, Mrs. Glen R. Hyde is floating from Green River, Utah, to Needles, Cal." The fact that a woman, especially one so petite, was making the journey, was breaking news. Once newspaper readers were aware of the Hydes' journey, they read every report they could find and made their own comments as well.

As the newspaper reporter continued, "One veteran river man said today that the rancher and his wife will be lucky to reach Needles." The reporter then added, "Many men have drowned attempting the same trip. It is not one to be undertaken lightly by those unfamiliar with the Colorado [River] and its perils or unprepared with the best possible equipment." Was this in reference to Glen and Bessie's lack of experience, their lack of life preservers, or the fact that Bessie was a woman?

The reporter also wrote that men had always managed the boats in the past and emphasized that the rugged terrain of the Grand Canyon created a tremendous risk. "For the greater part of its length, the canyon walls are all but unscalable," he stated, "and even if a shipwrecked adventurer should manage to clamber up the precipitous sides, he could be in great danger of death from starvation before finding his way across the plateau desert land."

On November 23 a writer for the *Needles Nugget*, in Needles, California, again played on the dangers for a woman river runner in an article titled "Woman Dares Raging River." Reading these stories and fearing the worst were the families of Glen and Bessie: William and Charlotte Haley in Parkersburg, West Virginia, and Glen's father, Rollin C. Hyde, in Kimberly, Idaho.

(Glen's mother, Mary, was deceased.) According to a story in the *Salt Lake Tribune* on February 4, 1929, only Glen's father had known, beforehand, of the couple's plans. What a surprise the news must have been for Bessie's parents, although Bessie must have laid out their plans in the letter she wrote from Grand Canyon Village.

DISAPPEARANCE AND INITIAL SEARCH

After Glen and Bessie's overnight stay in Grand Canyon Village, the couple hiked back down the trail, ready to tackle the canyon's most difficult rapids. With them was A. G. Sutro, a man identified by the press as a "San Francisco capitalist." He rode with the Hydes to another trail, then hiked back up to the Village, and was the last person ever to see the couple alive. By their own calculations, they expected to arrive at Needles, California, by December 11. A December 20 newspaper report called them "long overdue." The same day's issue, updated by United Press, reported that the US War Department had commissioned an aerial search and sent, from March Field in Riverside, California, two army airplanes whose pilots had located the scow with most of the couple's baggage intact.

The small wooden boat was stranded on a sandbar in a shallow part of the river near what is called Separation Rapids. For those familiar with the canyon, this was 232 miles downstream from Lee's Ferry and approximately 144 miles from the South Kaibab Trail that directly connected the river with Grand Canyon Village. On December 21 a Pittsburgh, Pennsylvania, newspaper report read, "Man and wife lost is feared; relatives here believe couple that tried to shoot Grand Canyon rapids has perished."

The same day's United Press report stated that aviators from the search planes dropped two messages: one to a ground search party out looking for the Hydes and another near their boat. The first note apprised the searchers of the boat's location, and the other was dropped so the Hydes, if they were in the vicinity, would know that rescuers were nearby.

Stated the syndicated reporter, "Searchers [now] believe that Hyde and his wife abandoned the boat and now are trying to make their way to civilization through Diamond Canyon, a lateral gorge which leads to [the town of] Peach Springs, Arizona." This canyon led south, from the South Rim of the canyon through pine-clad hills to the area inhabited by the Hualapai Indians. Bessie's twenty-third birthday was December 29, 1928, but no one knows if she lived to see it.

Search parties spread out in different directions, to different areas of the canyon. One team, led by experienced river runner Emery Kolb and Chief Ranger Brooks of the Grand Canyon National Park, was the first to reach the scow and found the couple's bedding, clothing, provisions, and undeveloped films, as well as Glen's gun and Bessie's notebooks and sketches. All equipment on the stranded boat, including its oars, appeared to be intact. Bessie's last entries had been made three weeks earlier, on November 30, 1928. Glen's thirtieth birthday was during the interim, on December 9. In a follow-up newspaper story, a reporter stated, "The baggage gave evidence that they [the Hydes] either had died in the swift waters of the river or had abandoned everything but their scant supply of food in a forlorn hope of scaling the canyon walls and reaching civilization."

Another search group included P. P. Papraw, a Grand Canyon National Park official who surmised that he had found Glen's footprints along the river's edge near Diamond Creek. Searchers were encouraged by the footprints, as the discovery indicated that Glen and Bessie had passed the Diamond Creek Rapids, considered by many as the most dangerous on the river route. By then, Bessie's father, William Haley, was there, too, after making the long journey (probably by train) from West Virginia to Grand Canyon Village and down into the canyon's depths.

When Bessie's father was interviewed by a reporter, the reporter explained that there were only a few smaller rapids between the location of Glen's footprints and the cove where the scow was found. From studying maps of the surrounding topography, the searchers concluded that *if* the Hydes' boat had gotten away from them, they could have escaped the river on foot, that is, south through Diamond Canyon to Peach Springs.

A third search was headed by Glen's father, Rollin C. Hyde. According to Associated Press stories on January 1, 1929, he went, initially, to Peach Springs where he set out with a cattleman as his guide and eight other men on horseback toward the Grand Canyon, on the chance that Glen and Bessie were headed in his direction. Glen's father also appealed to the Bureau of Indian Affairs, an agency within the US Department of the Interior, which enlisted the help of residents of the Tuba City and Canyon Diablo reservations, in Arizona. As in the search for Everett Ruess (see chapter 4), it made sense to employ the locals, who knew the territory.

Glen's father also went back to Peach Springs, alone, to search again. At age sixty-nine he must have been in excellent shape, as a news report stated, "He drove his car as far as he could. Then, packing his own provisions, he climbed 4,000 feet back down the canyon wall and spent a week scaling the river shore up and down. On Sunday, January 20, the elder Mr. Hyde climbed out of the canyon to come home with the mystery unsolved." In early February newspapers stated, "Parent of ill-fated adventure seeker at last gives up all hope."

A newspaper writer in 1930 added a few more scenarios to the mystery by asking, "Were they by some freak accident drowned, did their scow break its moorings and did they fall victim to wild animals as they trekked out, did they start out afoot and lose their bearings, or were they murdered?" The writer then added, "Every one of these solutions is within the range of possibility."

THE HYDES' PREDECESSORS

Had there been a precedent for successfully escaping the canyon on foot? The answer is both yes, to getting out of the canyon, and no, to surviving the escape. Nearly sixty years had passed since Major John Wesley Powell's excursion of 1869; he was the first river runner to follow the Colorado River through the Grand Canyon. But hiking to civilization held more dangers than starvation and exposure.

Powell and his nine-man crew of mostly Civil War veterans, trappers, and frontiersmen had packed themselves and their supplies into four wooden boats. Along the way three of the men were convinced that the rapids had become too dangerous, so they decided to abandon the mission and hike north out of the canyon toward the North Rim. Before they left to climb the thousands of feet in elevation from the river, they announced that, if they made it, they planned to walk across more than one hundred miles of barren desert to reach a Mormon settlement in southern Utah. They never made it.

On September 8, 1869, the Mormon newspaper *Deseret News*, published in Salt Lake City, stated, "We have received a dispatch through the Deseret telegraph line from [the town of] St. George [Utah] of the murder of three of the men belonging to the Powell expedition." Although the disappearance of Powell's men has been scrutinized by numerous historians and blamed on Native Americans, author Jon Krakauer, in his book *Under the Banner of Heaven*, wrote that he believes Powell's men were killed by Mormons instead.

Powell and another group of men returned to the Grand Canyon again, in 1871, to head a more scientific expedition that included mapping and photography. His expedition was followed, also in 1871, by a group of explorers and adventurers who accompanied Captain George M. Wheeler of the US Army Corps of Engineers. During the late nineteenth and early twentieth centuries, parts of the river also were traversed by trappers, miners, and Native Americans.

The first group to run the river for pleasure were members of the Stone expedition, in 1909. They included Julius Stone, who financed the trip, along with Nathan Galloway, who designed their flat-bottom skiffs and developed the stern-first rowing technique still used by whitewater rafters. The men also wore life vests made of cork. Inspired by the success of the 1909 expedition, brothers and pioneer photographers Ellsworth and Emery Kolb set out in 1911 and 1912 to take their own pleasure trip—with a movie camera. After the brothers' successful return, they showed the film to tourists at their photography studio in Grand Canyon Village on the South Rim, at the top of Bright Angel Trail. Emery Kolb stayed in the Grand Canyon area for many years and was one of the searchers who found Glen and Bessie's scow.

A few, but not many, other adventurers and explorers passed through the canyon in the early twentieth century. In 1927 came Clyde Eddy, whose expedition Glen and Bessie likely followed while they were in California. Eddy was a college-educated pharmacist and a World War I veteran who recruited willing college men to accompany him, in replicas of Powell's boats, from Green River, Utah, to Needles, California. In a syndicated newspaper report published in the *Charlotte Observer* on September 7, 1927, after the crew's return, Clyde was interviewed about the danger of a boat, or boats, slipping away. "To lose the boats," he wrote, "meant that we almost certainly would die of thirst trying vainly to climb the precipitous walls that hemmed us in."

Mystery or Mishap?

Little progress on finding any trace of the Hydes was made in 1929. Then another search was begun in 1930 by the two fathers—Rollin C. Hyde, at age seventy-one, and William L. Haley, not much younger at age sixty-five. Whether they completed their plan is not known, but they arranged to travel with a guide from the last point where Glen and Bessie were seen and then explore all of the riverbanks and ravines that extended from the Colorado River. A full-page newspaper story in the *Ogden Standard-Examiner* on June 15, 1930, focused on Bessie. Titled "Who Can Solve the Mystery of

This Vanished Bride?" the question put forth to readers was whether Bessie and her husband were overtaken by "mystery or mishap."

LATER THEORIES

The story of the missing honeymoon couple didn't go away. On a rafting trip in the Grand Canyon in 1971, an older woman actually claimed to *be* Bessie Hyde, saying that Glen had been abusive to her, so she stabbed him and escaped on her own. She later recanted her story. Another theory, that both Glen and Bessie climbed out together to start a new life, was equally preposterous. Unlike several other missing-persons cases profiled in other chapters, there weren't any legitimate "sightings"—or at least none that made the news. In 1976 a man's skull with a bullet hole was found on property that had belonged to the since-deceased Emery Kolb. Some thought maybe the skull was Glen's, but it was determined to have belonged to a suicide victim from 1933.

The most romantic theory was that Bessie had been washed overboard and Glen died trying to save her. After all, Bessie had told the reporter in the Grand Canyon Village that, at one point on their journey, she had to pull Glen out of the swirling waters. In 2000 river guide Brad Dimock re-created the Hydes' journey through the Grand Canyon. He and his bride built their own scow to gain insight into Glen and Bessie's experiences. After the publication of his book, *Sunk Without a Sound*, the author stated in an interview with the *Arizona Daily Sun* that the only reasons he and his wife survived were that they had a friend with a motorboat, they had life jackets and helmets, and they were familiar with the route.

"At the end," as author Dimock was quoted, "We had really good feelings about them [Glen and Bessie] and just a great sadness for how quickly and violently they probably died after almost making it. They were so close."

6

Joseph Laurence Halpern

Reaching for the Stars

In the summer of 1933, Joseph "Joe" Laurence Halpern, his parents, and a college friend camped in Rocky Mountain National Park near the town of Estes Park, Colorado. On August 15, the third day of their stay, Joe and his friend left their camp for a day hike. Late in the afternoon, only the friend returned. He had turned back while Joe, who wanted to go a little farther, asked a fellow hiker for directions. Like Everett Ruess (chapter 4), and the Hydes (chapter 5), Joe sought and found beauty in the natural landscape. His passion was the night sky, and he went missing at night on a mountaintop.

A few months prior to Joe's ill-fated high-country hike, the University of Chicago graduate student was working on his doctoral degree in astronomy. On track to becoming an astronomer, Joe had the North Star to guide him and likely was anticipating the annual Perseid meteor shower that peaks in the Northern Hemisphere every August 11 through August 13. If the weather had been clear on the nights preceding his hike, he would have seen some of these "shooting stars" from his family's campsite—a real treat away from the city lights of Chicago, Illinois.

High above the timberline, however, where trees no longer interfered with the expansive sky, the meteors would have been spectacular. Did Joe wait for darkness and then linger too long and lose his step on the way down? In the immediate days of searching that followed, there didn't seem to be any other explanation. Initially, Joe's parents tried to accept this likely outcome. As time went on, however, the parents clung to possible new leads and new hope, but no trace of Joe has ever been found.

Figure 6.1. Joseph, Fanny, and Solomon Halpern.
Joseph Halpern, left, a graduate student in astronomy, posed with his parents
Fanny and Solomon Halpern a few months before he disappeared on a mountain-
top in Colorado. PHOTO COURTESY OF ROLAND HALPERN

THE ROAD TRIP WEST

Joe Halpern was twenty-two years old in August 1933 when he, his parents Solomon and Fanny Halpern, and his schoolmate Sam Garrick packed
their camping equipment into Joe's Ford sedan and left the paved streets of
Chicago. Solomon, a Russian immigrant, was on vacation from his job as
an engineer at the Western Electric Company. Joe's older brother, Bernard,
remained at home, but Solomon and Fanny sent him frequent postcards.
Two flat tires didn't dampen their enthusiasm for the rugged mountains
that Fanny wrote "are beyond description." The Halperns had taken previous
summer road trips in the East and the Midwest, but their road trip west was
a first for the family.

Moviegoers familiar with the 1967 film *Bonnie and Clyde* will recall the
outlaw couple's 1934 Ford sedan. Joe's Ford was a similar make and model

but a year older. Joe did all of the driving, following winding mountain roads through the Black Hills of South Dakota and then continuing west through Wyoming cattle country to Yellowstone National Park. According to a ranger's report filed eight days after Joe was reported missing, the college student's only mountain-hiking experience had been on the trip in the Black Hills and in Yellowstone.

New, too, for all, was driving southeast through Wyoming and then entering Colorado and four-hundred-square-mile Rocky Mountain National Park. With seventy-seven mountain peaks more than 12,000 feet high, the park had become a major tourist attraction since its opening in 1915. The Fall River Road, completed in 1920, gave motorists their first opportunity to climb to Fall River Pass at 11,797 feet, where even the most seasoned travelers felt as if they were on the top of the world. In 1929 the newly opened Trail Ridge Road took flatlanders even higher. The eastern portion of this road opened to motorists in 1932, and the western portion continued on to the town of Grand Lake, Colorado, beginning in 1933; the Halperns arrived that summer.

Publicity on the new road was, no doubt, a drawing card for the family and other vacationers. The National Park Service's "Circular of General Information," published in 1932, stated, "As one looks [from Estes Park, Colorado] at the mighty array of peaks, it is hard to believe that in two hours one can easily drive to a snow bank on a mountain crest." That would have been very alluring on a hot August day, even with a speed limit of twenty-five miles per hour on open stretches and twelve miles per hour on grades and curves. Access roads, as well as campgrounds, hiking trails, and other improvements, had made the park a coveted destination.

TEMPTATION TO LINGER

August 15 was a Tuesday, but the Halperns were on vacation, and one day probably seemed like any other day. The family had pitched their tent, or tents, in the Glacier Basin Camp Ground, one of five free public campgrounds in the park and located just off Bear Lake Road. Joe's mother, Fanny, had taken along her paints and brushes and may have tried her hand at capturing the campground's spectacular view of Hallett Peak, Tyndall Glacier, and Flattop Mountain.

While the parents stayed at the campground, Joe and Sam planned their hike up the Flattop Mountain Trail. The weather was sunny and clear. Joe put on a white shirt with blue stripes, khaki trousers, and heavy shoes that his father later described as "clodhoppers." Joe packed four or five sandwiches, one orange, two bananas, and a 1933 *Rocky Mountain National Park Motorists Guide Map* into a small, gray knapsack. No mention was made of whether Joe had a canteen, and he did not take a jacket.

From Glacier Basin, Joe and Sam drove the 4.7-mile distance to the Bear Lake trailhead and then set off on the trail. Round trip from the trailhead to the summit of Flattop Mountain was measured at 8.8 miles, with an estimated round-trip time of six hours. According to the Park Service booklet, Flattop Mountain is on a direct line between the towns of Estes Park, to the northeast, and Grand Lake, to the southwest. The mountaintop is one of several on the roughly north-south Continental Divide, often called the "backbone of the continent," separating drainage to the Atlantic Ocean, to the east, from drainage to the Pacific Ocean, to the west.

The Park Service booklet gave a vivid description of the route up 12,300-foot Flattop Mountain, explaining that it "zigzagged up the eastern slope," then "passed under and over enormous boulders," and, at one turn, "the traveler looks perpendicularly down 1,000 feet into Dream Lake." The eloquent, and no doubt experienced, hiker who wrote of the trail continued:

> *For a while, the trail skirts the edge of Tyndall Gorge and looks across the vast bed of the glacier to the rugged peak of Hallett. It rounds the perpetual snows topping the cirque of Tyndall Glacier, a favorite resort of ptarmigan. It looks backward and downward upon the flat mile-wide top of the mighty moraine of ancient days, in the middle of which Bierstadt Lake shines, jewel-like, in a setting of pines. It bewilders with its views of exquisite Forest Canyon and the bold heights of Trail Ridge.* Great is the temptation to linger *[author's emphasis] on the inspiring ascent of Flattop, but one must not, for the journey is long.*

At 11,500 feet the woodlands turned to tundra, and Joe and Sam found themselves above the elevation where trees can grow. Several hundreds of feet higher, on the top, the Flattop name became clear, as the summit once was part of a vast, flat erosional surface called a "peneplain," which had been uplifted over eons of time. Then glaciers, including the nearby Tyndall Glacier, carved huge U-shaped valleys on the eastern side of the peneplain.

If Joe and Sam had stayed together, all that can be said today is that the outcome of their hike would have been different. Maybe they both would have returned. Or maybe, if one was injured, the other might have been able to return for help. But at 2:30 p.m., Sam said he was tired and was ready to turn back, and the two parted on the trail. According to Sam's statement, which he later provided to a park ranger, Joe and Sam were "west of the summit of Hallett Peak and about one-half mile south of the Flattop Mountain trail." There they met an unnamed camper who reported that Joe and Sam "were in a friendly argument as to whether to turn around or go on." The camper told the ranger that Joe had asked him for directions to 13,150-foot Taylor Peak, which was also on the Continental Divide and south of Hallett, Otis, and the Sharktooth Peaks.

At 6:30 p.m., after hiking down the steep Flattop Mountain Trail for four hours, Sam arrived back at Bear Lake and waited for Joe. By 9:00 p.m., after the sun had set, Sam alerted an officer at the Bear Lake Ranger Station

Figure 6.2. Flattop Mountain.
In August 1933, Joseph Halpern was last seen near the top of Flattop Mountain (at 12,362 feet), in Rocky Mountain National Park. PHOTO COURTESY OF ROLAND HALPERN

that his friend was missing. Meanwhile, Joe's father, Solomon, also concerned, began walking (and then got a ride) from the campground toward the trail-head at Bear Lake. By 11:00 p.m. two park rangers with electric headlamps headed back up the trail, flashing their lights and yelling and listening, until 3:00 a.m. The search for Joe resumed the next morning at 9:30 a.m.

That same morning, the ranger, with Sam and the unnamed camper, hiked up the Flattop Mountain Trail to the location where Sam and the camper had last seen Joe. It was only then that the ranger realized that the camper had given Joe incorrect directions. Instead of Taylor Peak, the camper had pointed out Chief's Head Peak, even higher and considerably farther away.

As the ranger later wrote in his report, "It should have been apparent to the most inexperienced that it would have been impossible to reach Chief's Head by night fall." Meanwhile, Sam debated as to whether Joe may have, instead, headed toward Andrews Glacier, an alternate route down from the Flattop Mountain Trail. By then, no one knew which way Joe had gone, so crews were sent searching everywhere, from mountain peaks to glaciers to precipitous canyons below.

INITIAL SEARCH

Not knowing if Joe was lost or injured or had plunged to his death off a cliff, park rangers and at least 150 volunteers, including many Civilian Conservation Corps members pulled away from their public service jobs, combed the mountainous terrain by foot and on horseback. Three days into the search, the rangers set up a high-elevation "fly camp," where they had food and supplies hauled in by horseback. The camp was considerably higher and closer to the search area than the base camp near the ranger station, below, at Bear Lake.

Meanwhile, Joe's father and one of the rangers carefully examined the area, on horseback, to the west of the Continental Divide, where the search-ers had set up another fly camp. Solomon and Sam joined the search as well. By the end of the week, Solomon wrote to his other son, Bernard, "Four days of helpless agony and no end to it. There is slight hope that he is only lost and cannot find his way out. Let us hope so."

For a total of five days, park rangers tramped through rugged gorges and across windswept slopes. They followed all possible trails between the Glacier Basin Camp Ground, east of the trailhead, all the way to the town of Grand Lake, west of the Divide, while also scaling the summits of the surrounding peaks. Beginning in 1915 (and continuing until 1990), the Colorado Climbers Club maintained summit registers on the state's highest mountain peaks, where, in weatherproof canisters, hikers recorded their names, addresses, and dates of ascent. As part of the search for Joe, rangers checked the registers on Taylor, Hallett, Otis, and other nearby peaks, but none showed the young man's signature. The searchers also picked up every piece of clothing, "lunch paper," and similar items, which they took to Joe's mother to see if anything belonged to her son, but none did.

The Rocky Mountain National Park's own newsletter, on August 18, 1933, was the first to break the news of Joe's disappearance to the public with a story titled "University Student Lost on the Snowy Range." That day and the next, a syndicated story out of Estes Park followed with additional reports of the search crews. One story stated that footprints, believed to have been Joe's, were found on Andrews Glacier. Another story, however, stated that Park officials "were certain Halpern was either seriously injured or had been killed in a fall from a cliff." Continued the newspaper writer, "So carefully has the region been hunted, in spite of heavy fog and rainstorms Saturday, that if Halpern was still walking about, he was almost certain to have encountered one of the searchers."

On Sunday, August 20, five days after Joe and Sam climbed Flattop Mountain, the park superintendent announced that the rescue portion of Joe's search was over. Quoted the following day, he stated that there was "virtually no hope" that Joe was alive, but that his searchers would make every effort to find his body. There was no mention, however, of sending in an airplane, as was done in the aerial searches that followed the disappearances of Everett Ruess and Glen and Bessie Hyde (as described in chapters 4 and 5).

The following day the *Denver News* reported that the national park authorities were trying to obtain bloodhounds. In subsequent correspondence, Joe's father stated that he left one of his son's shoes "in case dogs could be used." Then a follow-up letter explained that the park's chief ranger had contacted the Denver Police Department, the Colorado Springs Police Department, and the Colorado State Penitentiary to inquire about search dogs, but the only dog available was at the penitentiary, in Cañon City, Colorado. However, without the approval of the prison warden (who was "out of the city"), the dog was not available.

Halpern Family Goes Home

Neither Joe's parents nor Sam knew how to drive Joe's sedan, so they had to depend on other people to get them back to Chicago. On Monday, Solomon, Fanny, and Sam repacked their camping gear into Joe's Ford, and a fellow camper at the Glacier Basin Camp Ground drove them to Denver. The next day, they secured another driver to drive them home. Before they left, Fanny wrote to her son Bernard, "Take good care of yourself, my dear Bernard, you are all we have." The return trip must have been a somber one. While in Denver, Sam mailed a letter to his family, stating, in part,

> I've got some tragic news. Joe Halpern disappeared in the mountains last Tuesday and nothing has been heard of him since. Everyone has lost hope of ever finding him alive. The last four days Mr. Halpern and I have averaged fifteen miles of mountain climbing in our search. Yesterday, we walked and climbed twenty miles, then a terrific wind, rain, and snow storm with no results. It is almost impossible for anyone to remain alive for five nights, without shelter and food, in a climate so cold and stormy. . . . The past couple days have been miserable out here, with a deadly gloom prevailing. Mrs. Halpern cries all night long. It is my belief that Joe is not lost in the mountains but must have seriously disabled himself. It's pitiful, but—Well, I'll be seeing you. So long, Sam

Meanwhile, an Estes Park reporter interjected a bit of optimism that, at least, Joe's remains might one day be found. He wrote that, during the previous year, a trail crew had stumbled upon the skeletal remains of a Texas man who had been missing for seventeen years. The man had started from Grand Lake to cross the Continental Divide from the west and had broken his leg. The trail crew found his bones under a ledge where the injured man must have crawled to find shelter.

The Halpern family received Park Superintendent Edmund B. Roger's latest theory when they opened his letter of September 18, 1933. He wrote,

> It is our opinion, or rather conjecture, that Mr. [Joe] Halpern decided to return by a short cut and descended by one of the steep chimneys [narrow vertical passages in a rock or cliff] into Chaos Canyon or

Loch Vale. With the sense of direction he should have had, there is little reason to believe that he completely lost his way. Rather, we are inclined to believe (and most of the park's veteran guides agree) that he took a short cut for the sheer joy of adventure or he lingered too long on the slopes of Taylor Peak and, in order to avoid the approaching darkness, he went over the precipitous east face of Taylor Peak into Loch Vale.

There are hundreds of these rock chimneys he could have chosen for a descent. A very few of them are passable for the ordinary climber with the ordinary equipment, and in any one of them the danger of rock avalanches is always present. If we advance on this theory, and since searching parties were on Taylor Peak by noon the next day, the indications are that Joe was killed instantly, in all probability, by a fall or an avalanche. The fact that no trace whatever of Joe was found makes this theory even more plausible. As you know, all of the chimneys scalable by ordinary means were searched.

ONGOING INVESTIGATIONS AND THEORIES

The wandering-away theory alluded to by the park ranger became more relevant four months later, when Joe's father, Solomon, wrote to the superintendent that he had filed a missing-person report with the local police in Colorado, in the event that Joe had "wandered away due to some injury having affected his reason or memory, or for some other reason." A possible other reason was hinted at in excerpts of Joe's letters that the family reread after he vanished. In one of Joe's letters to a friend, in 1930, he had written, "And so I stare face out at a cruel, harsh, economically depressed world and am waiting for the day when I'll be a hobo."

Another of Joe's letters tied in with work that he did prior to the opening of the 1933 Chicago World's Fair. In correspondence from a family friend and still in the possession of the family, the writer stated that Joe had been "singled out for the distinction of astronomically computing the precise moment for the opening of the World's Fair." Before the fair did open, on May 27, 1933, four large astronomical observatories, including the Yerkes Observatory (where Joe had been employed), aimed their telescopes on the star Arcturus in order to capture the star's light rays onto photoelectric cells.

The light signals then were converted into energy, amplified, and supposedly used to turn on the machinery and lighting at the grounds of the fair.

During this time, and while working at Yerkes Observatory, Joe had written,

> *The sun falls in the deep northwest, and soon again the stars will be free to shine on me as I harness their feeble rays for the benefit of science. Patiently, I will hold them, minute after minute, hours and hours, and their impression will be preserved for the perpetual future. Enormous volumes of imperfect observations for the use of imperfect observers. Happy is the life of an astronomer! Away, far away, from the banalities of men, detached in the beautiful soliloquies of comprehensiveness and unity. The mortal cares, worries, being, loves—vanish into insignificance before this formidability of nature.*

In November 1934 Solomon wrote several letters concerning Joe's disappearance. By then he and Fanny had moved to a farm in La Porte, Indiana, so it was necessary that he send his new address to anyone who might have new information on Joe. One letter was to the Federal Bureau of Investigation (FBI) asking the agency's help in searching for Joe. After the Bureau searched its Identification Unit's files, it placed Joe's information and a photo into its file of missing persons.

The FBI explained that if Joe was an amnesia victim and was arrested for "vagrancy or some other crime," his fingerprints would be in their files. So Solomon sent the agency fingerprints of Joe's right index, middle, and ring fingers, which were on file in the savings departments of post offices in both Chicago and in Williams Bay, Wisconsin. FBI director J. Edgar Hoover himself, however, stated that his agency couldn't *initiate* an investigation, since Joe's disappearance had not been in violation of any federal laws.

To the director of the Yerkes Observatory, Solomon wrote, "We just found out that it is highly probable that our son, Joseph L. Halpern, is alive." Solomon then explained that a friend of his claimed to have seen Joe begging for a meal at a restaurant in Phoenix, Arizona. Police later confirmed that the man in question, under a different name, had spent three weeks in a transient camp and then left. Added Solomon, "We are sure our son is a victim of amnesia and is helplessly wandering somewhere in the U.S.A. His mother is heartbroken, but the ray of hope we just received helped her a great deal."

Solomon also offered a fifty-dollar reward for information on Joe's whereabouts. On a neatly hand-lettered poster, with the text all in capital letters and a head-and-shoulder photo of Joe, Solomon stated that the University of Chicago graduate was "proficient in French, German, mathematics, astronomy, and chemistry" and that he "is a good chess player, does not smoke, usually goes without a hat, and may travel under an assumed name."

In 1936 the FBI received a letter from a California man named Samuel Greenfield. His motive for writing and how he learned that Joe was missing are not known. But he claimed to have spent his childhood days with Joe, and he stated that their parents "have been rather close friends for the past twenty-five years." The man also wrote that after Joe was "seen" in Phoenix in 1934, he headed to Nebraska with the Civilian Conservation Corps and then worked in Michigan for the Lewis Brothers Circus. None of these "leads" led to any documented information. Solomon, meanwhile, in his frequent letter writing, never mentioned the Greenfield family, and any connection with the "friend" in Phoenix is unclear. In 1942 another seemingly out-of-place letter to the FBI was written by an Iowa resident, Ted Wilson. "[Joe]," the man wrote, "was known to be with a rather rough crowd in 1933."

During World War II, Solomon wrote to the US War Department to see if anyone named Joseph Laurence Halpern was serving in the military. When he was told that no one by that name was in the service, Solomon specifically asked J. Edgar Hoover's help in trying to match Joe's fingerprints with military men, even if Joe had signed up under an assumed name. "All we want to know is that he is alive," Joe's father wrote in 1944. "For the sake of his mother, who is ill from constant worry, we appeal to you to help us in locating our son."

Some Resolution

Prior to 1950, the Halperns had moved from their farm in Indiana to Dade County, Florida. There, in April 1950, they went to probate court, where Solomon and Fanny established a "Legal Presumption of Death" for the "estate of Joseph Halpern, allegedly deceased." One purpose of a presumption of death claim is to distribute property, but Joe may not have owned more than the Ford sedan and his savings accounts. Most states, including Florida, required a waiting period of seven years and, by then, Joe had been missing nearly seventeen. At the time, Solomon was seventy-four years old, and Fanny was sixty-seven. They must have felt a need to have some sort of resolution, but it took them a long time to come to grips with the fact that Joe was not coming home.

Ten years later, in 1960, Joe's brother Bernard wrote to J. Edgar Hoover, still the director of the FBI,

When I visited my parents recently, my father mentioned for the first time a circumstance that could possibly lead to some information concerning the disappearance of my brother. He stated that forest rangers were of the opinion that my brother's companion knew more about the disappearance than he would admit at that time. Since he was a friend of my brother's, my father asked the rangers to cease questioning him as he was obviously in an agitated state of mind.

Joe's college friend Sam lived most of his life in the Chicago area, where he attended the University of Chicago and Rush Medical School. In 1937, four years after Joe's disappearance, Dr. Sam Garrick earned his license as a physician and surgeon. He married Bernice Daniels, served in the military during World War II, and had two or three children. Sam died in August 1976 at the age of sixty-four. He and the Halpern family apparently did not keep in contact, and it's not known if the authorities questioned him further about his hike with Joe.

Sam, however, had an older brother, Isadore Edward Garrick. In 1965 Joe's brother Bernard wrote to Sam's brother Isadore and received this reply:

I was sorry and grieved to hear of your parents' deaths. They were wonderful people. In 1933 and 1934, I wrote them when they wanted the one-hundred odd letters of correspondence that I had with Joe to see if there were any leads—and, apparently, there were none. I had not written to them since that time, as I knew the loss of Joe left a wound that would never heal, and my writing would only hurt.

I am sure my brother [Sam] has told the whole story—a case of bad judgment on both his and particularly Joe's part. You state he was visibly agitated. Under the circumstances, how could this be otherwise? Joe persisted in wanting to take a different (and a very treacherous) path down the mountain than they had taken up. Sam persisted on the same path since he was bushed. They didn't agree and went their

separate ways. That, unfortunately, is the simple and whole story. I
need not tell you that Joe was my closest and dearest friend, and that
I think of him often.

Into the Next Generation

Both Solomon and Fanny went to their graves without ever knowing what
happened to Joe. Fanny died in 1963 at the age of eighty-two. Solomon
died in 1964 at the age of eighty-eight. Son Bernard was left in charge of
the family's mystery. Then, after Bernard's death in 1998, his son, Roland
Halpern (Joe's nephew), picked up the threads of the search. At first Roland
appealed to the National Park Service and asked for any advice or assistance
the agency could provide.

In the twenty-first century and armed with new technological advances
that included the internet and DNA comparisons, Roland contacted sheriff departments in counties bordering Rocky Mountain National Park. He
asked about unidentified remains, but at the time, none were known to exist
from the time period. In 2009, when the National Institute of Justice inau-
gurated the National Missing and Unidentified Persons (NamUs) system,
Roland entered Joe as a missing person. The National Park Service is listed as
the contacting agency, and Joe's identifying information, as well as a profile
of Roland's DNA (as a family member), is now on file, to be matched to any
suitable unidentified remains that may, someday, be found.

A few years later Roland contacted the Jackson County (Colorado)
Sheriff's Office and learned that unidentified human skeletal remains had
been found in the vault of the county's 1913 courthouse. There was no
accompanying information as to where or when the remains were found
(or who put them there), except for a note saying that they might be those
of "an old prospector."

The Jackson County (Colorado) Coroner's Office sent the skull for
DNA testing to the University of North Texas Health Science Center, which
was able to obtain mitochondrial DNA (mtDNA), traceable through mater-
nal lineage. Hoping to at least make a comparison, Roland sent, for similar
DNA testing, envelopes with stamps likely licked by Joe's mother. Unfortunately, no usable DNA was obtained. The bones, however, were inspected
by an anthropologist who had been asked to determine if they were Native
American, but they were not.

Roland also pursued two federal sources of information—the Rocky Mountain Region of the National Archives and the FBI. In the National Archives he found an "Accidents in National Parks" file that contained "A Report on the Disappearance of Joe Laurence Halpern." It was written on August 23, 1933, by John S. McLaughlin, former chief ranger of the Rocky Mountain National Park, and contained information on the initial search, the photo of Joe submitted by his parents, and a detailed colored map of six days of search routes. In recent correspondence with the author, Roland stated that he was amazed at what he has been able to uncover.

In order to obtain the FBI's missing-person file on Joe, Roland had to file a federal Freedom of Information Act (FOIA) request. That file included some, but not all, of the Halpern family correspondence as well as the correspondence on the "sightings" that suggested the possibility of Joe walking away from the park and starting a new life. The FBI file also included Joe's fingerprints from his postal savings accounts.

In the summer of 2010, a few months before the one hundredth anniversary of Joe's birth, Roland took his then-eleven-year-old son on a hike up the Flattop Mountain Trail, extending the search for Joe into the fourth generation of his family. Roland's hope is that with today's resources, his son won't have to wonder what happened to Joe. And, while going through papers of his father's estate, Roland came across the burial records of his grandparents, who were laid to rest in the Mount Nebo Cemetery, in Florida. Roland contacted the cemetery and was able to purchase an available nearby plot in the hope that if Joe's remains were found, they could be interred there, finally reuniting him with his mother, who had never recovered from the loss.

PART 3

CHANGED IDENTITIES, AN INTRODUCTION

Joe Halpern's missing-person case (chapter 6) included speculation that the young man could have walked away and taken on a different "life" under another name, giving his family hope that he was still alive. In looking back, years later, the likelihood of Joe walking away from a loving family and a promising career doesn't make much sense. However, some missing persons do walk away and live for years under changed identities. The story of Lawrence Joseph Bader's dual lives, in chapter 7, may or may not have been his choice and will leave most readers scratching their heads. Perhaps, as in so many unexplained cases, there is no definitive answer.

Twylia May Embrey, in chapter 8, definitely chose to disappear, but how did she do it so easily, and how did she get away with it for more than a half century? Did she have any idea that, back in the 1950s, she had left behind some clues that would catch up with her after her death? Twylia, far from her roots in Nebraska, is buried in Massachusetts with her second family. Lawrence, also deceased, rests forever with his first family in Ohio.

As shown in chapter 9, Sharon Elliott (the "Hatbox Baby") also had different identities during her lifetime, but her choices had been made for her. She had a birth name and an adopted name, which isn't unusual in itself, but at the time of her birth in 1931, she was widely described by the press as a "foundling," defined by the Merriam-Webster dictionary as "an infant found after its unknown parents have abandoned it." Today, after an extensive search by a team of researchers, the identity of her parents is known, but speculation continues to swirl around the circumstances of their child being found.

Sharon's story began on the Arizona desert. It ended there, as well, with the scattering of her ashes and the remembrances of those who had become her extended family. They were the ones who helped her find her own identity. (Later, part 5 will introduce yet another person with dual identities: William Desmond Taylor, in chapter 15. As an actor and movie director, he lived under his assumed name for fourteen years before his tragic demise.)

7

Lawrence Joseph Bader

Gone Fishing

In 1957 Lawrence Joseph Bader was a thirty-year-old salesman from Akron, Ohio, who went to Cleveland, Ohio, on business and then disappeared while fishing on Lake Erie. He resurfaced in Omaha, Nebraska, as John "Fritz" Johnson, a local television personality, and he lived and worked under that name for seven years. Lawrence/Fritz was thought to have suffered from amnesia (defined by the Mayo Clinic as a loss of facts, information, and experiences), which often comes up in missing-persons cases but, in reality, is quite rare. In the 1940s and 1950s, amnesia was a common plot device in movies and radio and then television shows, but it was more prevalent in fiction than in fact.

The *Akron Beacon Journal* broke the story of Lawrence's disappearance on May 17, 1957. The previous day, at 4:30 p.m., the married father of three children had rented a fourteen-foot motor boat at a marina in Rocky River, Ohio, a lakefront suburb of Cleveland. He had brought his own life preserver, and he had another that came with the boat. When Coast Guard personnel on patrol saw him head out on the lake, they advised him of an upcoming storm and later stated that he had ignored their warnings.

The next day, the boat, slightly damaged but with both life preservers still intact, was found on a sandy beach a few miles east of the marina and within the city of Cleveland. Search teams, looking for Lawrence's body, sent out dredging patrols, but they came back empty-handed. The missing man, described as a "husky 200-pounder" and an "excellent swimmer," was nowhere to be found.

Mary Lou Bader, Lawrence's wife, was five-months pregnant with the couple's fourth child. She remained at the couple's home in Akron, an hour's drive from the lake. When interviewed the next day by a local newspaper reporter, she said her husband had gone to Cleveland to see about some "bad checks." He also had told her that if he went fishing, he would be home late. According to the article, Mary Lou asked him to forgo the fishing trip. His reply was, "Maybe I will and maybe I won't. I'll see."

PRESUMED DROWNED

The US Coast Guard didn't hold out much hope of finding Lawrence. Its personnel believed that, without his wearing a life preserver, there was no way he could have survived. (For more on the subject of life preservers, see chapter 5, on Glen and Bessie Hyde.) And although no one verbalized it, at least, to the press, the obvious consensus was that if Lawrence *was* alive, he would show up. Presuming that Lawrence drowned, a Coast Guard spokesman stated, "In some cases a body will wash ashore. In other cases, drowned bodies disappear. There is nothing to do but wait for the body to come to the surface."

Lawrence, however, *did* survive. Could he have faked his disappearance and planned to escape his home, family, and job? News reports did indicate that he was delinquent on his income taxes, had incurred some debts, and had taken $350 with him. Or did he hit his head on the side of the boat or on one of its oars and then fall overboard as he tried to navigate the choppy waters of the lake? If so, amnesia, caused by brain damage, was possible, as it can be triggered by trauma to a person's head. Sometimes people and events of the past are forgotten, but new memories can be formed.

If Lawrence did suffer from amnesia, he still would have had to swim through stormy waters. Where along the southern shore of Lake Erie would he have reached dry land? Wouldn't lake currents have taken him in the same direction as his boat? Had anyone seen an exhausted-looking man emerge out of the water? There was no mention in the press of search parties other than those assembled the following day by the Coast Guard. Was Lawrence visibly injured? Where did he go? Unless there was an accomplice either waiting on land or in another boat to assist him, these are questions that probably never would be answered. Lawrence later would claim that he didn't remember anything of his former life, except that he had served in the US Navy.

Home and Family

Lawrence was born in 1926 in Akron, Ohio, and was raised in Akron as well. The son of a well-respected dentist, he was the fourth of six children and attended St. Vincent High School during World War II. But as soon as he turned eighteen, he left during his senior year to join the navy. From December 1944 through 1946, Lawrence served on the USS *Amphion*, a repair ship that was equipped with a wide variety of shops that included pipe fitting, sheet-metal work, and welding. The ship was tasked with cruising along the eastern coast of the United States and mooring alongside other navy ships at sea, allowing its skilled personnel to perform needed repairs. What types of repairs Lawrence might have done, if any, is not known, as records from the National Archives show him with the rank of "hospital apprentice second class." He completed his high school education in 1946, after he returned home.

In 1952 Lawrence married his high school sweetheart, Mary Lou Knapp, in a Catholic ceremony in Akron's St. Sebastian Church. Mary Lou, also born and raised in Akron, worked as a secretary at the time and later would become a special-education teacher. She, too, came from a Catholic family with long ties to Ohio. Mary Lou and Lawrence settled into a 1940s-era suburban home in a quiet neighborhood, a few blocks from the Fairlawn Country Club. Lawrence got a job selling cookware for the Reynolds Metals Corporation and was said to have been doing well.

Lawrence appeared to be a devoted husband and father. Life was good as the Bader family grew to include one, two, and then three children within the couple's first four years of marriage. A news report would later state, "He and his wife were getting on well, [and] he had a future with his company." Lawrence also purchased three life insurance policies. His then most recent policy, from the New York Life Insurance Company, came with a $14,000 double indemnity that would pay double in (and only in) the case of an accidental death. The policy also included mortgage protection on the family's home. In today's currency, the dollar amount would be equivalent to more than $250,000.

When Lawrence didn't return from Cleveland, Mary Lou called the Akron Police Department and reported him missing. Meanwhile, on a routine patrol, the Coast Guard found the boat that Lawrence had rented, along with fishing tackle positively identified as his. According to an *Akron Beacon Journal* article, after the Coast Guard said there was nothing it could do, its search-and-rescue team actually did continue to look for Lawrence's body for at least six weeks before declaring the mission a "failure."

On August 9, 1957, less than three months after Lawrence's disappearance, Mary Lou filed a claim with the Social Security Administration for death benefits for her children. The next month, the couple's fourth child was born, thus creating an even greater need for financial assistance. Initially, however, Mary Lou's claim was turned down, as government investigators soon discovered that Lawrence had not filed income tax returns from 1952 (the year the Baders were married) through the time of his disappearance in May 1957. What that meant was that even if his body had been found, he hadn't paid enough funds into Social Security for his survivors to qualify for full benefits.

LEGAL PRESUMPTION OF DEATH

Like spouses of other missing persons, Mary Lou was left in a murky legal limbo. Was her husband dead or alive? None of the three life insurance policies could be paid until the Summit County (Ohio) medical examiner was able to issue a death certificate. She soon learned that without a body, obtaining a death certificate usually requires a seven-year waiting period, even before a probate judge files a document called a "Legal Presumption of Death." According to Ohio statutes, however, the waiting period can be less if the missing person is, or was, "exposed to a specific peril of death," such as an accident. In the fall of 1958, Mary Lou appeared in Summit County (Ohio) Probate Court to begin formal legal proceedings.

In trying to decide whether Lawrence was dead or alive, members of the Akron Police Department, along with the police in Lakewood, Ohio, west of Cleveland, assisted investigators from both the Social Security Administration and the individual insurance companies. As one of the investigators testified, they "left no stone unturned."

Somehow, perhaps due to the "specific peril" clause, Lawrence was legally declared dead in 1960, three years after he went missing. The New York Life Insurance Company holding the double-indemnity policy agreed to pay in full, but not until May 15, 1964, after the total waiting period of seven years. Meanwhile, newspaper reporters noted that Mary Lou was able to collect on one of the other two life insurance policies. As the children entered school, she continued church activities as well as dinners and teas for alumnae from her college sorority. Life went on for Lawrence's family, even without him.

Stated one of the life insurance company's attorneys at the time, "I do not believe Bader planned his disappearance but was inclined to be headstrong and overconfident. He wanted to fish in the lake, and he threw caution to the wind." Before the judge's ruling, a court referee stated, "There does remain, of course, the remote possibility that Bader may have voluntarily absented himself for reasons known only to himself."

DOUBLE LIFE

Seven years and nine months after Lawrence disappeared, everything for Mary Lou, her children, and the rest of the Bader family changed. Sightings in missing-person cases are common, but a sighting of Lawrence turned out to be true. On February 6, 1965, the *Akron Beacon Journal* updated its readers in his missing-person case with the headline, "Akronite 'Dead' for 8 Years Found Alive in Chicago?" and continued, "Look-alike denies he's L. J. Bader; Say brothers identify him."

Figure 7.1. Lawrence Joseph Bader. In February 1965 Lawrence Joseph Bader, aka John Fritz Johnson, was photographed leaving an Omaha, Nebraska, hospital after eight days of tests. PHOTO FROM THE AUTHOR'S COLLECTION

Apparently, a Bader family friend had attended a Chicago sporting goods show and said he saw a dead-ringer resemblance between Lawrence and a man exhibiting archery equipment. The friend asked the man if he was Lawrence Bader. Saying no, the man introduced himself as Fritz Johnson, a television announcer from Omaha, Nebraska, with a wife and two children. Even so, the family friend was insistent and persuaded Fritz to talk on the phone with Richard Bader and John A. Bader, the missing man's two brothers. Solely on the basis of Fritz's voice, the brothers flew to Chicago.

Mary Lou, though, stayed home. At a later date she told a reporter that she never doubted that her husband was deceased. If this situation arose today, all that would be needed to confirm the man's identity would be a DNA comparison with one of his brothers and/or children. But DNA testing would not be available for two more decades. And, as in the case of the Hatbox Baby (see chapter 9), genetic genealogy, in which DNA testing is combined with traditional genealogical methods and historical records, was even more in the future.

Fritz (the man from Omaha) still denied that he was anyone other than who he said he was. But he agreed to meet with the Bader brothers and also have his fingerprints taken for comparison with Lawrence Bader's, which were on file from his time in the navy. The following day the Federal Bureau of Investigation (FBI), through the Chicago Police Department, announced that its experts had made a positive identification. "It's one and the same man," stated a police lieutenant, "or else it's something from the beyond." In another comparison, a plaster cast of Lawrence's teeth, made by his dentist (who was his father), visually matched with Fritz's teeth. (See chapter 11, "The Boy in the Box," for the use of a plaster face mask.)

When the Bader brothers met Fritz in person, they were convinced he was their long-missing brother Lawrence, basing their identification on Fritz's voice, his appearance and mannerisms, similar head scars, the coincidence between the date of Lawrence's disappearance and Fritz's arrival in Omaha, the plaster cast of Lawrence's teeth, the fact that both Lawrence and Fritz talked about serving in the navy, and the interest in archery that had brought Fritz to the Chicago show.

Other than Fritz's acknowledged interest in archery and the navy, he continued to deny that he was the missing man. But, according to newspaper reporters, he did admit to being struck by his resemblance to one of Lawrence's brothers, both in voice and his appearance. Fritz claimed, though, that he didn't know anything about his family or of being born and raised in Akron. He had no recollection of his parents or siblings or even of his (i.e., Lawrence's) wife, Mary Lou, and their children. When interviewed in the past, Fritz claimed, without any documentation, to have been an orphan who had been left on a Boston doorstep as a foundling. Even Fritz, aka Lawrence, like everyone else, was at a loss for words.

Records from Fritz's former employer in Omaha showed that he started working as a bartender at an Omaha steakhouse on May 21, 1957—only four days after Lawrence went missing! Neither Fritz nor anyone else had a clue as to how he got from the shores of Lake Erie to downtown Omaha. In one scenario, he could have caught a ride on the closest main road, the Memorial Shoreway (US Route 2). Perhaps he was picked up by a long-haul trucker and then climbed out of the rig eight hundred miles later, in Omaha.

Or since he had money with him, maybe he hitched a ride to the then-new, nearby Burke-Lakefront Airport, in Cleveland. During that time he also would have had to come up with clean clothes before interviewing for, and starting, a new job. And if he had amnesia, did bartending come naturally, or did he need to learn a new skill?

After two years in the steakhouse in Omaha, Fritz began working for a local radio station. While there, newspaper reporters noted that as a publicity stunt, he sat on a flagpole for a month to raise money for polio. After his stint on the radio, he switched to television station KETV. To thousands of his viewers, he was the well-dressed, affable, dapper man who told them about the news and weather and also reported on sports. Remarkably, he was on his viewers' television screens for years without being recognized. He certainly wasn't in hiding. Described as short, dark-haired, and well-muscled, he was a champion archer, and articles that included his photo were frequently published in Nebraska newspapers.

While everyone was still numb from the revelation that Fritz had a former identity as Lawrence, a local newspaper reporter arrived at Fritz's Omaha home. His second wife, Nancy Johnson, a former photographer's model, answered the door, stating that her husband was in the bedroom, under sedation. The reporter described Nancy as "a strikingly attractive brunette." She, too, admitted that she "didn't know what to think" of the man she had married in 1961. Nancy had one child from a previous marriage, and the couple had another child together.

But for Nancy, there had been room for doubt, as she disclosed to an Omaha reporter that her husband had no birth certificate and no proof of the thirteen years he claimed to have served in the navy. Nancy also stated that Fritz had no proof of two head injuries he said he received, one in World War II and one in the Korean War. (According to navy records, Lawrence had only served for two years and only in World War II.) And what about Fritz's head scars that the brothers recognized as similar to Lawrence's? Hadn't Lawrence ever spoken of them?

Back in Akron, Ohio, Lawrence's stunned siblings gathered in their widowed mother's living room to discuss the recent turn of events. All agreed they would do whatever they could to help their brother and also to help Lawrence's wife, Mary Lou. Of Mary Lou, Lawrence's mother stated, "She has always taught his children to love their father dearly and to pray for him. She always told them to remember him and all the good things about him." As a Roman Catholic, she was barred from remarrying as long as her husband was alive. Then, in court, her husband was declared dead. She experienced an emotional roller coaster when, subsequently, he was proven to be alive. It's no wonder that her attorney called her marital situation "confused." For the rest of her life, Mary Lou would remain single.

Untangling both Lawrence's and Fritz's personal situations was complicated enough, but legal problems loomed on the horizon as well. Attorneys representing the Bader family met in Chicago with Fritz's attorney and agreed that Lawrence must have suffered from amnesia. "I certainly don't think any charges should be filed under these circumstances," stated the attorney from Omaha who was quoted in the press. "If there was no intent to do wrong and no recollection of having done wrong, I don't think there was any crime." Still, all agreed that a man couldn't legally have two wives.

While Fritz's wife, Nancy, was reported to be "in seclusion," Fritz entered Omaha's St. Joseph's Hospital for eight days of "physical, neurological, and neuro-psychiatric" tests. Afterward, all that the doctors would say was that there was no evidence that Fritz, their patient, remembered his life as Lawrence Bader. Complicating, or contributing to, Fritz's medical condition was the fact that, within the previous year, he had had a cancerous tumor removed from his brain, resulting in the loss of one eye. Afterwards, he wore an eye patch. Could the tumor have been growing for years and contributed to memory loss? If so, wouldn't the memory loss have been gradual instead of sudden?

As Fritz from Omaha came to accept that he actually was Lawrence from Akron, Fritz and Nancy realized that their marriage was void. To clear the record, Nancy filed for an annulment. Fritz, however, indicated that he wanted to continue to live in Omaha, even though he had moved out of his and Nancy's home. In March 1965 Lawrence's two brothers flew to Omaha to see him, and their visit was followed by a visit from Lawrence's mother. She had already sent his doctors some family photos to use in "memory restoration efforts," but he didn't remember anyone in them.

Meanwhile, Nancy took a job as an airline ticket agent. In an interview in May 1965, she called Fritz an "upset and unhappy" man. By then he had taken up residence in the YMCA, but he often came to his former (Nancy's) home to visit their children and to work in the yard. Instead of continuing his work at the television station, he went back to being a bartender at the same steakhouse where he worked when he first arrived in Omaha. He also mortgaged whatever property he owned in order to pay child support to both his still-current wife Mary Lou (who stayed in Ohio) and his estranged wife, Nancy, who stayed by his side.

And what about Lawrence and Mary Lou's children? At the time, when a Bader family member was asked, the reply was that the children had been told that their father was alive, but they were too young to grasp the situation. Understandably, it had to have been a distressing and emotional experience for everyone involved. And what of Fritz and Nancy's children? Nothing was reported in the newspapers other than the summation that Fritz was very much in love with Nancy and devoted to his family in Omaha. As his attorney stated, "Having no recollection of a previous life, he wants to preserve what he now has. But under no circumstances does he want to shirk any responsibilities in Ohio."

On February 9, 1965, three days after the news broke that Lawrence (as Fritz) was alive, the *Akron Beacon Journal* stated that Fritz's Omaha attorneys had held a press conference. According to the reporter, "[Fritz] smoked a pipe, with his attractive wife Nancy gripping his free hand. . . . Neither said a word, and at one point tears welled in Nancy's eyes." Meanwhile, another *Journal* headline read, "$40,000 Bader Problem: Government, Insurance Investigators Face Big Task." Even though seven years and nine months had passed since Lawrence had disappeared, the insurance companies wanted their money back.

Not only had Mary Lou received the double-indemnity life insurance policy from the New York Life Insurance Company but she had also collected money from the other life insurance policies as well as $254 per month (for several years) in Social Security payments. And although Lawrence's reappearance in life had come after the required seven-year time period, the insurance company tried to foreclose on her home in efforts to recoup its money. The tug of war was still continuing a year later, when Mary Lou filed a lawsuit to reinstate the policy.

Fritz, meanwhile, remained in Omaha with Nancy at his side. Then his brain cancer spread to his liver. He died at the age of thirty-nine, in September 1966, still insisting that he had no memory of his life in Ohio. A memorial service for "John Fritz Johnson" was held in Omaha, and then his body was transported to Akron, where he was buried at the Holy Cross Cemetery as Lawrence Joseph Bader. He was interred near his father, with Mary Lou and the children in attendance. Lawrence's small, flat stone simply reads, "Lawrence J. Bader 1926–1966," and its only decoration is a Roman cross. In the preceding year, news reports stated that Mary Lou and the children had met with him in Chicago, but they kept away from reporters.

VOLUNTARY DISAPPEARANCE OR AMNESIA, OR BOTH?

The last known person to see Lawrence (as Lawrence Joseph Bader) in 1957 was the man who rented him the motorboat. According to "Bader News No Surprise to Boatman" (a United Press International article reprinted in the *Lincoln Star* on February 11, 1965), the boat owner said he had explained his reasoning to detectives, at the time, saying that he never believed that Lawrence had perished on the lake. Lawrence, he said, had left the dock at 4:30 p.m. and insisted on running lights, after indicating that he intended to be gone only two hours. The boat owner said the gas hose to the outboard motor had been disconnected, and that it couldn't have happened on its own, even in a storm.

Was the boat owner's implication that Lawrence had disconnected the hose to allow the boat to drift, according to the wind and the lake's currents, while he, Lawrence, made his escape in another direction? Did he get to the shore even before the storm hit? Added the still-angry boat owner, "He [Lawrence] owes us a boat, motor, and equipment." Could it be that Lawrence left voluntarily, as was speculated in the courtroom "for reasons known only to himself"? And then, over time, could his growing brain tumor have brought on a true case of amnesia? If so, the double identity of Lawrence Joseph Bader and John "Fritz" Johnson might have been a combination of both, but no one, at least publicly, ever came to any firm conclusions.

Twylia May Embrey

Don't Fence Me In

Twylia May Embrey was the only girl in her 1952 high school graduating class in Maywood, Nebraska. There were seven other seniors, and all of them were boys. One, in an interview in 2005, remembered Twylia as "adventurous and pretty." The farmer's daughter was slim and approximately five feet, three inches tall, with soft, curly, light brown hair. Like other schoolgirls of her day, she wore skirts with blouses or sweaters and crew socks with loafers or saddle shoes. Even decades later, Twylia's classmate still recalled that she loved to dance to the song, "Don't Fence Me In," popularized, at the time, by singer and guitar player Roy Rogers:

> I want to ride to the ridge where the west commences,
> Gaze at the moon till I lose my senses,
> Can't look at hobbles and I can't stand fences,
> Don't fence me in.

Another high school friend, a girl who was in her junior year when Twylia was a senior, exposed a darker side of the seventeen-year-old's life. That friend, many years after high school, said that Twylia had confided in her that her father had raped her. Twylia then told her father that the day after she graduated from high school, he would never see her again. She kept her promise. It was as if Roy Rogers had sung "Don't Fence Me In" directly to her.

That year, 1952, Twylia left home. She then changed her first, middle, and last names, traveled around the country with her new identity, got married, got divorced, and then married again. After living as "Twylia" for seventeen years, she spent the next fifty-four years as "Theresa," without so much as a phone call to her Nebraska family. When she died halfway across the country at the age of seventy-one, she was unaware that, for five decades, three generations of her family had been searching for her. Her oldest sister, Mildred "Midge" Garner, remained in the same house for more than a half century in the hope that her little sister Twylia would one day come home.

TWYLIA'S NEBRASKA YEARS

Twylia's parents, Charles and Adeline "Addie" Embrey, already had four girls and two boys when Addie gave birth to her seventh child, Twylia May, on October 15, 1934. The family lived on a rented ranch in the Spotted Horse Precinct of Arthur County, in the sand hills of north-central Nebraska. The grass-covered hills and sandy soil were unfit for farming, but the land was good for cattle. As mentioned in a family history (written circa 1987 by a daughter-in-law), the Embrey family lived near a trailhead, where Charles built or dug large cisterns so drovers could water their stock.

Arthur County was, and still is, rural, with only one small town, also named Arthur. Both the county and town were named in honor of Chester A. Arthur, twenty-first president of the United States. Oddly, the president, a New York lawyer, didn't seem to have a connection with the town. Or if he did, no one could remember it. The county's entire population peaked in 1930 with 1,344 people, and forty-one-year-old Charles, thirty-year-old Addie, and their large and growing family were among them. By 2010 its population had dwindled to 460 people, including 116 men, women, and children in the town.

In 1937, when Twylia was three years old and the aftermath of the Great Depression made life difficult for many residents, Charles Embrey moved his family to a rented farm between the towns of Wellfleet and Maywood, off US Highway 83, thirty-six miles south of North Platte, Nebraska. There, where the undulating and open prairie sprouted a few cedars, Charles raised cattle, hogs, and chickens and planted corn and pinto beans. Twylia's sister Midge remembered that the family couldn't afford peanut butter, so their mother squashed beans to put in sandwiches for the children to take to the Maywood School for lunch.

The Embrey family had horses, too, and Twylia loved to ride and also to sketch. Delphia June, the eighth and youngest child, was born in 1940. Midge, the oldest, married in 1942 and moved to Wellfleet, where she settled into her longtime home. Midge never claimed to know the details, but, in an interview in 2005, she said she was aware that Twylia and their father had had a falling out. After an "incident" while Twylia was in high school, Twylia moved in with another sister who lived in Maywood, near Twylia's school. Graduation day was the last time anyone in her family saw her, and then Twylia moved again—to North Platte. There, her family was told, she got a job as a waitress at the Little Lemon Café, near the busy railroad depot where passengers and freight were hustled on and off the mainline trains that crisscrossed the country.

As the Embrey family's history is remembered, Charles stopped at the café a few months later, asked for his daughter, and was told that she had hopped a train for California. Meanwhile, a North Platte resident who claimed to have been a former boyfriend told a different story. He later recalled that he had reluctantly watched as Twylia willingly got into a large, yellow Cadillac convertible with Nevada license plates. The distinctive car even had bull horns mounted on the hood, and a man was at the wheel. Whether Twylia knew the man or simply was hitchhiking no one knew, but it seemed obvious, with either story, that Twylia was headed west. When her former boyfriend was interviewed, he couldn't help but add, somewhat wistfully, "She sure was pretty."

Twylia's family never knew, exactly, when she left North Platte. She could have left in the summer or fall of 1952 or early in 1953. The Embreys didn't reported her missing, as they just assumed that she would come back on her own. Unlike today, when most police departments will take a missing-person report as soon as a family member deems a person is missing (without requiring a wait of twenty-four hours), some families, in the early 1950s, didn't think of involving the police at all. If they had the financial means, as did Dorothy Arnold's parents in 1910 (see chapter 2), they could have contacted private investigators. In the 1950s, investigators would have searched telephone directories and public records, but even they had few resources when a missing person traveled out of town or out of state.

In 1954 a writer for the *Denver Post* interviewed the owner of the Tracers Company of America, an agency based in New York that prided itself as "specialists in the field of tracing lost persons." At the time, the firm defined lost or missing persons as "husbands, wives, teenagers, debtors, heirs and witnesses," with a few "love swindlers" and "amnesia" persons thrown in. Teenage boys were reported missing more than twice as often as teenage girls. Twylia fit into the rather vague category of teenagers who were said to have "desired to be free of parental discipline and those who just take off to be alone and far from usual surroundings."

In 1957, after the Embreys' youngest child, Delphia June Embrey, usually just called "June," graduated from high school, Charles and Addie auctioned off their farm implements in Nebraska and drove to California. According to family legend, their purpose was to look for Twylia. However, Addie's mother as well as Addie's sister, Marvel Withers, previously had moved from Nebraska to San Bernardino County, east of Los Angeles, California, so it's likely the Embrey parents stopped to see them as well. Little did any of them know that Twylia had already been married and divorced and had settled in the eastern United States—and was not in California after all.

Figure 8.1. Twylia May Embrey.
Twylia May Embrey posed for this high school graduation photo before disappearing from North Platte, Nebraska, either in the summer or fall of 1952 or early in 1953. PHOTO COURTESY OF JENNIFER KITT

A Sister's Search

In March 1981, Twylia's mother Addie, then eighty-one years old, was widowed, nearly blind, and confined to a wheelchair in a nursing home in Curtis, Nebraska. Out of the blue, she received a letter from a man named Bill Wederski. He wrote that he had seen Addie's name in a telephone book and was writing to ask if Twylia was her daughter. If so, he wanted to contact her "to see how she [Twylia] is." He stated that he had met Twylia more than thirty years earlier, adding, "She may have been my first girlfriend."

Anxious for any information on Twylia, Addie referred the letter-writer to Midge (Twylia's oldest sister). Bill then called Midge and followed up with another letter, explaining that as a traveling carnival worker, he had met Twylia in Maywood, in 1948, when he was nineteen years old and Twylia was

Figure 8.2. June Embrey and Twylia May Embrey.
Sisters June and Twylia Embrey posed on the family's farm before (or after) a horseback ride. PHOTO COURTESY OF JENNIFER KITT

fourteen. According to Bill's letter, he and Twylia had ridden on a gray roan horse together, and she told him she was "having problems" with her father.

From Midge, Bill demanded a lot of personal information on Twylia, even asking for a clip of her hair or some jewelry he could show to a psychic. He also explained that he once had worked as a private investigator in San Bernardino County, California. He didn't mention the family members already living there (he may or may not have known about them), but he wrote that he was certain that he could find Twylia.

One document that Twylia's family had carefully tucked away in an old tobacco tin was Twylia's original Social Security card. That same year, in 1981, referencing the Social Security number, Midge wrote a heartfelt letter to Twylia in care of the Social Security Administration. Midge asked the agency to please forward the letter to Twylia's current address on file. "Wherever you are, won't you please get in contact with me?" begged Midge in her letter. She explained that their father had died, and their mother didn't have many years left. "We desperately want to know how you are," added Midge, closing with, "We all love you." A return letter from the Social Security Administration formally acknowledged that the agency had no work history or any record of her. Twylia had no paper trail at all. (In 2014, the Social Security Administration discontinued its letter-forwarding services.)

Meanwhile, Bill Wederski's frequent letters continued for nine months. During that time Midge did share some photos of Twylia as well as Twylia's Social Security number. Then Bill's letters suddenly stopped without any explanation. Had he been trying to steal Twylia's identity? Was he preying on a vulnerable family? Was he writing on behalf of Twylia herself? No one knew, but the family never heard from the now-deceased man again. Later research revealed that he was married and working as a truck driver during the time he was writing to Twylia's family.

Back in the 1950s, when Twylia first left home, her parents were the ones who searched for her. In the 1980s Twylia's sister Midge took on the job herself, on behalf of her siblings and her ailing mother. By 2004 Midge's granddaughter, Twylia's grandniece Jennifer Kitt, shifted the quest into another generation, just as Joe Halpern's nephew had done for the missing astronomy student (see chapter 6).

Was Twylia Murdered?

Meanwhile, and also in 2004, others (including this author) were involved in another search—for the name of an unidentified woman found murdered in 1954, near Boulder, Colorado. At the time, the author had partnered with the Boulder County (Colorado) Sheriff's Office and the Philadelphia-based Vidocq Society to identify "Boulder Jane Doe." A syndicated newspaper reporter picked up on the story and ran it all over the country, including in North Platte, Nebraska. Jennifer then contacted the author to ask if Twylia could have been Boulder Jane Doe. (For more on the Vidocq Society, see "The Boy in the Box," chapter 11.)

By the time Boulder Jane Doe was exhumed in 2004, DNA had become a legal form of identification. The process involved developing profiles from DNA extractions from unidentified remains and keeping them on file in the hopes that a relative would come forward and serve as a family reference for DNA comparison. The sheriff's office had similar hopes for finding a potential family member so that Detective Steve Ainsworth could identify the murder victim.

Midge, as Twylia's sister, became that potential family reference. Detective Ainsworth drove from Boulder to North Platte, where he met with Midge, swabbed a small amount of saliva from her mouth, and sent the sample to a lab to be compared with DNA extracted from one of Jane Doe's femurs. Meanwhile, both Midge and Jennifer waited anxiously to see if Midge was related to the murder victim. If so, Boulder Jane Doe would be identified as Twylia May Embrey.

The results came back negative, but the suspense continued. Investigators believed that the femur used in the DNA comparison might have been contaminated, so they tried another DNA comparison of Midge's saliva with DNA from one of Boulder Jane Doe's teeth. Stated Jennifer, through tears, at the time, "I want to find Twylia, just not this way, just not this way." After more interminable waiting that dragged on for months, DNA again ruled out Twylia as Jane Doe. So, where was Twylia? This author, still searching for the identity of Boulder Jane Doe (identified in 2009 as Dorothy Gay Howard), pitched in to find out. Joining in, too, was Micki Lavigne. The preschool teacher, who volunteered her services as a private investigator for family and friends in her spare time, had answered a query the author had posted on a genealogical website about Boulder Jane Doe.

The first step was to compile lists of women named Twylia, from all over the country, with her same (or close) birth date. Searching for missing persons had come, full-blown, into the internet age. Instead of relying solely on locally published and public records (such as telephone directories and courthouse records), people-searching all over the country had become a lot easier. Although published and public records still are essential, researchers now can tap into the aggregated information in online databases. Jennifer, Micki, and the author all worked from their homes, in different parts of the country and on our own computers, and corresponded by email. Jennifer and Micki did most of the calling. Hundreds of surprised, sometimes annoyed, and occasionally sympathetic women answered their phones, but none admitted to being Twylia May Embrey.

In the meantime, Detective Ainsworth had contacted the Social Security Administration about the Social Security number for "Twylia May Embrey." But the detective was told, as Midge had been, that Twylia's number had no recent activity. (In the 1950s, Social Security numbers were not assigned at birth, as some are today, but they were assigned to individuals, usually as teenagers, when they entered the workforce and were hired by employers who paid into the Social Security system.) For Detective Ainsworth, the "no activity" classification easily fit the scenario that Twylia, who was given her number when she started her first job, either never worked another job, or that she was deceased and no one had contacted the Social Security Administration to collect on a death benefit.

Then, one evening in April 2006, one year and four months after Jennifer initially learned of Boulder Jane Doe, Micki sent out an email to her fellow researchers that read, "I think I might have found something."

TWYLIA AS THERESA

In a series of hastily written emails, Micki explained that she had started using search engines to come up with various combinations of Twylia-related words, including places she had lived and her family names. In one search, Micki entered only Twylia's parents' names, along with several counties in Nebraska. Suddenly, up popped an online obituary of a woman named Theresa "Teri" Naimo who had died, three weeks previously, in Massachusetts. The woman, however, had been born in Nebraska, and the names of her parents (although slightly misspelled) were Charles and Adeline Embrey! Included in the obituary was a photo of an attractive, but aging, woman who bore a resemblance to Twylia, but her birth date was a few years off. Could Theresa, who died in 2006, have been Twylia May Embrey?

As part of the Boulder Jane Doe investigation, Detective Ainsworth had opened a missing-persons case for Twylia. When given Theresa's obituary in order to verify its information, he called a person identified in the obituary as a "dear friend." In doing so, the detective learned, and passed on, the startling news that Twylia had been living as "Theresa" for more than fifty years! When Jennifer was put in contact with Theresa's friend, as well as members of her second family, and they compared notes, Twylia's story began to emerge.

No one knows whether, in 1952 or 1953, the man in North Platte with Nevada plates on his Cadillac actually drove Twylia to Nevada or, perhaps, California. Apparently, Theresa (as Twylia was known in Massachusetts) never discussed her past. Rumors, however, had placed her in Albuquerque, New Mexico, and perhaps, briefly, in California, before she surfaced in Jacksonville, Florida. In 1954, going by the name "Theresa Trende" and without a Social Security card, she got a job in a Jacksonville nightclub or bar. There she met a marine named William "Bill" R. Keeley, from Somerville, Massachusetts. Although it's not known what credentials Theresa presented in order to get a marriage license, she married Bill in Florida and became Theresa Keeley. When Bill finished his tour of duty, the young couple moved to his family's home in Massachusetts.

According to Bill's sister, who was a teenager at the time, Bill got a job as a bellman at the Statler Hotel, while Theresa worked in the offices of the John Hancock Mutual Life Insurance Company, both in downtown Boston, Massachusetts. Then, on August 12, 1955, after Theresa started working at the insurance company, she applied for a Social Security card—her second one. According to records provided by the Social Security Administration after her death, there was a box on her application form following a question that asked, "Have you ever before applied for or had a Social Security or Railroad Retirement number?" As "Theresa Jonne Keeley," she clearly checked "No."

Theresa then was given an entirely different Social Security number. No wonder neither the Boulder detective nor the Social Security Administration had found any activity under Twylia's name or number. Twylia was alive and well and working, but she had changed her identity, or most of it, to Theresa. She correctly stated that she worked, at the time, at the John Hancock Mutual Life Insurance Company. But instead of giving her correct date of birth (October 15, 1934), she added nearly four years to her age by stating she was born December 3, 1930. (Perhaps she had used this date in Florida as well, in order to be over the age of twenty-one and thus be permitted to work in the bar.)

For her birthplace, instead of Arthur, Nebraska, Theresa wrote Luverne, Minnesota. She slipped a bit into her past, however, by stating her father's name as "Charles Edward Trende" instead of his correct name of Charles Edward Embrey. For her mother she also gave the correct first and middle names, but she used her grandmother's last name to come up with "Iva Adeline Keys," instead of Iva Adeline Cowman.

In the late 1950s, while Twylia's parents were searching for their daughter in California, Theresa and Bill Keeley divorced. For a short time, Theresa continued to work at the insurance company. Then, in 1959, she met Joseph "Joe" Naimo on a blind date and married him. Joe came from a large Italian family and ran a civil engineering firm. Joe and Theresa Naimo moved to a comfortable home in the suburbs. After their wedding Theresa occasionally worked at her husband's firm, sometimes filling in as a clerk. Mostly she stayed at home, doing crafts. She never had children, but Theresa's obituary from March 30, 2006, states that she was close to her nieces and nephews.

Jennifer's search for her long-lost great-aunt was partly to bring resolution to her grandmother, Midge, who had taken on the search after her parents had died. Midge, by the time of Twylia's death, was in her late eighties and longed for a reunion, even though she had once expressed her frustration by stating, "If I ever find her alive, I'll kill her." Little did Midge or anyone else in her Nebraska family know that Twylia (as Theresa) told her husband, Joe, that she had changed her identity. Joe died two years before her, but on his deathbed, he relayed Theresa's carefully guarded secret to his nephew. And on Theresa's deathbed, she revealed her Nebraska roots to her "dear friend," the informant for the obituary.

After Theresa's death, Joe's nephew made several phone calls in hopes of making contact with Twylia's Nebraska family, but the people he called were unable to refer him to Midge or to Jennifer or to other family members. "Theresa J. Naimo" was laid to rest with her incorrect name but correct birth and death dates of 1934 and 2006 beside her husband in Lindenwood Cemetery, in Stoneham, Massachusetts. Their joint gravestone reads, "We love you, but God loves you more."

After Micki's research uncovered the surprising news that Theresa and Twylia were one and the same, newspaper reporters jumped on the story. The *World-Herald*, from Omaha, contacted both the Nebraska and Massachusetts families. Those in the Boston area who knew Twylia as Theresa called her "a generous woman who looked like the actress Faye Dunaway." Another friend described her as "an elegant woman who loved to entertain, liked folk music, and organized trips with friends and neighbors."The friend added that Theresa could "create grapevine wreaths and dried-flower arrangements like Martha Stewart" and that "she had the beauty of a movie star—slim, with a preference for high heels and low-back dresses."

Twylia fit the mold of the runaway teen who had taken to heart the old cowboy song, "Don't Fence Me In." One wonders if she had missed her horses and the wide-open spaces of her youth. One thing for certain, though, is that her family, especially her sister Midge, missed her. And three weeks after her death, when her successful change in identity was brought out into the open and the search was over, the final ending for her Nebraska family was bittersweet. Midge no longer worried about whether her little sister was a murder victim or if she had lived on the streets. As Theresa, she had been well-loved and had lived a comfortable life.

But Midge's dreams of seeing Twylia were over, and she no longer needed to sit by her phone. Mildred "Midge" Garner died peacefully in her sleep in 2019, at the age of ninety-seven.

9

The Hatbox Baby

A Christmas Miracle

On Christmas Eve 1931 Ed and Julia Stewart were in a hurry to get to their home in Mesa, Arizona, east of Phoenix and now a part of the Phoenix metropolitan area. The young couple had spent the day several hours away with family members, but they were forced to stop on their way back due to a problem with their car. In the dark but clear evening, with forty miles to go, the car's fuel line, supposedly, broke. As Ed worked to repair it, Julia wandered off and heard a cry. It seemed to be coming from a round black pasteboard box—the kind that women's elaborate hats, at the time, were placed in to keep them from getting crushed. Julia called to Ed and, together, they opened the box. Inside, they claimed they found an infant girl, clean and well-cared-for, with blue eyes and red hair.

Who was the baby? Who and where were her parents? Was this an attempt to get an unwanted child a good home, or was she left to die in the middle of nowhere, among the scrubby desert plants and cacti (and home to coyotes, reptiles, and scorpions) that lined the lonely stretch of the oiled gravel, two-lane road? The headline in the following morning's *Arizona Republic*, on Christmas Day, read, "Find Abandoned Babe in Hatbox on Desert." The infant was deemed a "miracle," and her story would be repeated in newspapers across the country year after year.

Fifty-five years later, in 1986, Faith Morrow, an elderly and dying Arizona resident told her fifty-five-year-old daughter, Sharon Elliott, an astonishing story and gave her a large manila envelope full of letters, documents, and old, yellowed clippings. Not only had Sharon been adopted but she had been the center of a 1931 mystery. She was, in fact, the famous "Hatbox

Baby." Sharon had always believed that Faith was her biological mother, so the revelations of both her adoption and the mystery were a lot for her to absorb, leaving her with more questions than answers. Her true identity finally was established in 2017, but the why and how of her being found are questions that still are being debated.

THE FOUNDLING

With Ed driving and Julia holding the baby (and feeding her water from a spoon, as Julia later testified), the Stewarts headed straight to the Mesa (Arizona) Police Department where they handed over the baby to a bewildered police constable, the only officer on duty. Fortunately, he found a nurse-midwife to care for the hungry little foundling. The couple told their seemingly improbable story: after having a problem with their car, Julia heard a cry and then she and her husband discovered the box 150 feet from the roadway.

They were, they said, in a hurry to get home, as they had left their own eight-month-old baby in the care of Julia's mother. In the days to come, an initial investigation and search for the "Hatbox Baby's" birth mother turned up no new information, and the little girl remained unclaimed. According to an article by senior reporter John D'Anna and published in the *Arizona Republic* on December 25, 2018, both Ed and Julia were summoned, in January 1932, to the Pinal County (Arizona) Superior Court, where a judge questioned the couple and declared the baby abandoned.

During Julia's sworn testimony, she mentioned that she was a nursing mother who had been "in torture" because she had not fed her baby that day. An intimate topic such as breastfeeding (and the results of not breastfeeding) would have been difficult for an eighteen-year-old woman to discuss in the male-dominated courtroom of the 1930s, so perhaps Julia was too embarrassed to admit to giving the baby anything but water, if she did. But there was no explanation for deviating from her testimony when, a few months later, she told a reporter for the *Kansas City Star* that the car problem was a flat tire, not a broken fuel line.

Also during the court hearing, Julia stated they had driven straight through the Arizona mining towns of Miami, Globe, and Superior, but when Ed took the stand, he said they had made a fifteen- to twenty-minute stop along the way. No one questioned the discrepancies.

On Christmas Day 1931, even before the court hearing, newspapers and a local radio station announced that the little girl would be available for adoption. Faith Morrow, then Faith Stieg, was listening to her radio and heard the news. The twenty-eight-year-old Phoenix-area housewife rushed to the Mesa police station and put her name on the list of people offering to adopt the baby. Several other families had indicated that they wanted the baby as well, but heavy rains washed out a bridge on the day of the adoption proceedings and few could get to the courthouse. In addition to Faith and her husband, Henry, only one other set of prospective parents showed up.

The other couple who hoped to adopt the baby already had a child, so the court favored Faith and her husband, who were childless. Many years later, in 1986, Faith filed a "Motion to Open Adoption File" with the Pinal County (Arizona) Superior Court to unseal the baby's adoption records. In her hand-written statement, reprinted in the *Arizona Republic* on December 26, 2018, Faith had stated, "The [former] Judge asked me our reasons for wanting to adopt, and I told him I loved children and had miscarried many times and I thought maybe it was God's way to have people like me who loved all babies to make loving homes for homeless and abandoned babies." She also wrote that she and her husband had asked previous Arizona governor W. P. Hunt (from Globe, Arizona) to recommend them as adoptive parents.

Faith and her husband Henry, a grocery store manager and head of a seemingly stable home, were awarded the child on February 15, 1932. They named their new daughter Sharon Elizabeth Stieg. As reported in the *Tucson Citizen* on that date, "When the baby was placed into the arms of the new mother, everyone in the courtroom burst into tears. Judge Green's comment was that the baby was most fortunate in being welcomed into such a lovely home as awaited it."

In D'Anna's article, titled "Sharon Elliott Found Out She Was the 'Hatbox Baby' Just before Her Mother Died" and published in the *Arizona Republic* on December 24, 2018, the reporter reflected, "It was two years into the Great Depression, and people were desperate to find something good to hold on to." Reporter D'Anna played, and continues to play, an important role in the Hatbox Baby saga. In addition to contributing more than thirty years of his own detective work and writing articles along the way, he wrote a series of ten individual articles to document the story's progress. D'Anna's articles ran in the *Arizona Republic* from December 23, 2018, through January 1, 2019 (see "For Further Reading").

THE SECRET

Obviously, friends, family, and neighbors knew of Sharon's adoption and joined in the parents' joy. But as Sharon grew up, Faith insisted that Sharon never be told that she was adopted. Even though Faith did change her mind when she was dying, keeping the circumstances of Sharon's adoption under wraps had been very important to her for more than half a century. Why? Had the adoption been arranged? Had the governor overstepped his boundaries? In the early days, keeping the "Hatbox Baby's" secret had been hard to do.

In March 1932, when Sharon was nearly three months old, the twenty-month-old son of aviators Charles Lindbergh and Anne Morrow Lindbergh was abducted from his crib in the family's New Jersey home. The Lindbergh baby still was missing when a nationally syndicated newspaper reporter tied in the boy's story with that of the "Hatbox Baby." At the time, adoptive mother Faith was interviewed by a *Kansas City Star* reporter, and she begged for privacy. "Oh, please don't print anything about us," Faith stated. "I mean, please don't tell who we are and that the child now has our name."

"The baby is growing so nicely," Faith added, "but already she is a sensitive little thing, and with this queer start she would be doomed to unpleasant attention all her life. We don't know anything about her real parents, and we don't care. Nobody can ever take her from us now. We love her so, we'd do anything for her. We don't want her to be told (when she's in school) that she has no mother and daddy really, but was just thrown away on the desert. We don't want her ever to know it."

Faith even told the reporter that, if it became necessary, she and her husband would change their names and move "far away, to give the baby a fair chance in life," adding that they would even move to a foreign county if they had to. Meanwhile, police from two Arizona counties were on the lookout for the mother of the baby, admitting that they had no clues and that the baby seemed to just "drop out of the sky." When a "strange woman" came into the Mesa Police Department asking about the baby's health and welfare, she aroused enough suspicion that two officers ran out after her. According to the *Kansas City Star*, the woman quickly drove off in her car—a car with no license plates. Could she have been the baby's biological mother?

More articles on the "Hatbox Baby" were published the following Christmas, particularly in the local newspapers. "She has found a good home," stated one reporter. "She can walk a bit now. She smiles and gurgles and plays with a kitty. She has the colic only rarely. She is a sweet baby. The kindly judge in the case says so." Sharon later would say that she had a normal upbringing in a middle-class home with the only mother she ever knew.

Sharon did have, however, a turnover of father figures. Faith and Henry Stieg had married in 1928, but they divorced even before Sharon's first birthday. Henry actually had been Faith's second husband. Her first marriage, to Sigmund Ingersoll in 1925, also had ended in divorce, but after marrying in Flagstaff, Arizona, the Ingersolls settled in Prescott, north of the Phoenix metropolitan area. And according to reporter D'Anna, it was in Prescott that Faith worked as a clerk-typist and made some important contacts, particularly at Fort Whipple, a former army post that had been turned into a veterans hospital.

After Faith and Henry's divorce, she (with Sharon, then a toddler) moved from the Phoenix area back to Prescott, where Faith resumed her work at the hospital and married her third husband, Charles Cook, a widowed plumber with a young son. A year later, Charles died of tuberculosis. In 1939, when

Figure 9.1. Sharon Elliott, "Hatbox Baby."
Sharon Elliott is shown, in 2003, holding an issue of *Parade Magazine*, from 1951, with the story, "Where Is the Hatbox Baby Today?" BY PERMISSION OF THE ©
USA TODAY NETWORK, PHOTO BY MICHAEL CHOW/THE REPUBLIC

Faith was thirty-five years old, she married again, to Arthur Morrow, a carpenter. Sharon was eight years old at the time. According to the 1940 federal census (accessible via Ancestry, ancestry.com), the family, including Faith's stepson, then lived in Los Angeles, California.

Arthur, Faith, and the two children settled down in the metropolitan area, where Sharon attended the Westridge School for Girls and Inglewood High School. In 1951 the nationally published *Parade Magazine* ran a story titled "Where Is the Hatbox Baby Today?" Little did the readers know that she was alive and well, would marry and have a family, and would work as an administrative assistant for an aerospace company.

UNBURDENING HER SOUL

In 1986, after the adoption records had been unsealed, Faith, then age eighty-three, called Sharon and asked her to come and see her. By then, Faith was widowed and had moved back to Arizona, to the small town of Cottonwood an hour or so from her former home in Prescott. Sharon was considering a move from California to Arizona as well. Faith may have needed to unburden her soul, or perhaps she was concerned that there was someone still alive who might reveal her closely guarded secret.

When Sharon arrived at her mother's home, Faith handed over the large manila envelope that contained Sharon's adoption records and old newspaper clippings as well as family photos and mementos. Faith died the following year, 1987, leaving Sharon with unanswered questions. In 1988 Sharon called the *Mesa Tribune*. John D'Anna worked there at the time, as a reporter, and he happened to answer the phone. As D'Anna wrote in a story published by the *Tribune* on December 25, 1988, Sharon's visit with Faith was the first that she, Sharon, had learned that she was adopted and was the "Hatbox Baby." With the help of D'Anna, Sharon spent the rest of her life—thirty more years—searching for answers to her identity.

After D'Anna's first article on Sharon, he was contacted by a private investigator who helped adoptees find their birth parents. The investigator's interest led to a "Hatbox Baby" story in 1989, on the television show *Unsolved Mysteries*. As with the *America's Most Wanted* coverage of the "Boy in the Box" case (see chapter 11), tips poured in. Suddenly, the mystery of the Christmas miracle was back in the news.

Afterward, the private investigator wrote to Ed and Julia Stewart and asked for additional comments. Everyone wanted to know how the couple had had so fortuitously come across the newborn baby that Christmas Eve night on the desert. The Stewarts, in a curt reply, refused to give any information, perhaps fearing, or knowing, that they had perjured themselves in the court proceedings. Ed died in 1992, followed by Julia in 2002, without either of them ever providing more information.

In 2003 D'Anna tracked down and interviewed the Stewarts' daughter, who claimed that her parents had never talked with her about the "Hatbox Baby." On Reddit (reddit.com), in a much more recent (2019) internet discussion forum, D'Anna stated that the Stewarts' daughter called her parents "honest, hard-working folks." Of their possibly having helped facilitate the "finding" of the baby, D'Anna added, "That said, it's not hard to imagine scenarios that may have led them to shade the truth. They were young and probably financially stressed during the Depression. They had a small child of their own. It may have been a way for them to make some quick money but then got overwhelmed by the publicity and were ashamed of their involvement.'"

SIFTING THROUGH THE DATA

Ever since 1988, when D'Anna first talked with Sharon on the phone, until her death in 2018, he helped her put together the missing pieces of her life. D'Anna had help from several highly skilled researchers and genealogists, but the trail they followed was long and convoluted, with numerous twists and turns. Sharon eventually would learn the names of her birth parents and thus her own identity, but only a theory—albeit a good one—surrounded the mystery of how she was placed in the desert. And it went back to Faith's days in Prescott.

But we're jumping ahead. First came Sharon's discovery of her identity. In 2016, when Sharon was nearing her eighty-fifth birthday, D'Anna mentioned to her the exploding new field of genetic genealogy. By then, he had been a reporter for the *Arizona Republic* for more than two decades. As indicated in his article of December 30, 2018, Sharon agreed that the idea was worth a try and sent a swab with her saliva to one of the direct-to-consumer DNA testing companies, which in her case happened to be Family Tree DNA. In theory, as other people with similar genetic characteristics also sent in swabs, they were put in contact with each other. Then their family trees were compared for their most recent common ancestors. In genetic genealogy, the phrase "most recent common ancestor" is the key to unlocking the person's identity.

After going back (sometimes several generations) to the most recent common ancestor, genetic genealogists then follow different lines of the family tree down to the present, to the person whose identity is in question—in this case, Sharon's. The process has a vocabulary of its own, but skilled genetic genealogists trace the family linkage to see where they intersect on branches of other trees, thus leading to more common ancestors. But the tests only produce results when someone with similar genetic characteristics has sent in a DNA sample.

Sharon's first two tests indicated only third or fourth cousins at best. Third cousins, for instance, share a single set of great-great-grandparents, and their family history charts can get unwieldy. But Sharon's initial discouraging results only meant that not enough people, or, more specifically, not enough of those in her family, were in the database. Bonnie Belza, the genetic genealogist working with D'Anna, submitted Sharon's DNA again and included additional databases.

According to D'Anna's *Arizona Republic* article on December 31, 2018, Bonnie settled on the Strackbein, Roth, and Kautz family lines. A woman who had been unknown to Sharon before the DNA comparisons was found to be related both to Sharon and to the Roth family, thus tightening the family relationship. The newly researched family lines belonged to German immigrants who had settled near Davenport, Iowa, in the 1850s. Bonnie refined her research to a redhead named Freda Strackbein (Roth), born in 1908, and to Walter Kautz Roth. But how did these people from Iowa have a baby found in Arizona? And why would a married couple abandon a baby?

FAITH'S LOVE

Sharon's adoptive mother was eighty-three years old when she filled out the "Motion to Open Adoption File." As she wrote, "I could better tell her [Sharon] she is adopted than to have some other person, well-meaning or otherwise, tell her after I'm gone." But Faith didn't tell Sharon that she may have been in on the adoption from the beginning. At least that was the conclusion floated by D'Anna and his fellow researchers, as he revealed in his *Arizona Republic* article on January 1, 2019. D'Anna and his team looked again at Faith's work history in the 1920s, and then again at her 1930s employment at the Fort Whipple Veterans Hospital in Prescott, Arizona, and came up with a plausible scenario.

Through DNA, the reporter and the genetic genealogist knew that Sharon's biological parents were Freda and Walter Roth. The newspaper announcement from their wedding, on August 1, 1931, stated that, for their honeymoon, the couple would take "an extended trip to Sioux City and points west." Freda would have been four or five months pregnant at the time and starting to loosen her clothing, but given the events that followed, it's obvious that she concealed her condition.

D'Anna found that, at the time, a family member of the Roth family had been convalescing at the Prescott veterans hospital. The patient was being cared for by his niece, a public health nurse with maternity experience who worked primarily with unwed mothers and placed babies for adoption. Faith and the nurse were approximately the same age, so it's likely that the two of them, both staff in the same hospital, may have become acquainted or even friends. (D'Anna even tracked down and interviewed the nurse's then-elderly daughter, who said the scenario made sense to her.)

It has been well documented that Faith desperately wanted a baby. And Sharon's biological mother, Freda, while newly married, likely chose to avoid the scandal that she believed would follow if people did the math and learned that the baby was conceived out of wedlock. In reflecting on the past, it is important to observe people in the context of their times. Freda and her husband must have done their own soul-searching and then decided that a private adoption would be best for their child, that is, to see that she got a loving home.

Word may have filtered back to the nurse in Prescott who placed babies for adoption. And as speculated by D'Anna and his researchers, the nurse and her patient were family members of Walter Roth, father of the baby. Meanwhile, Freda and Walter Roth definitely did head west. On December 9, 1931, and with a birth certificate to prove it, Freda gave birth to a baby girl in Angelus Hospital, in south Los Angeles, California. The December 15, 1931, issue of the *Los Angeles Times* listed recent births including, "Roth, Mr. and Mrs. Walter. Daughter, Angelus Hospital, December 9."

In those days new mothers spent a week or more in the hospital. As soon as Freda was released and ready to travel, though, Walter likely drove her and the baby to Prescott, where the newlyweds could easily have handed their firstborn child to the nurse. Was there a lot of emotion? No one knows. But that was where the "setup" for the adoption may have begun. At that point the Roths could have simply given the baby to Faith, but perhaps all parties involved wanted the adoption to proceed legally through the court system.

As part of D'Anna's scenario, Ed and Julia Stewart may have been in on the plan as well. Their job was to open the hatbox, lift out the baby, and testify in court, even though they may have been given the baby in Globe or Superior or at some prearranged meeting place along the way. Julia Stewart did, however, comment on the baby's red hair, which turned out to be the same color as the hair of her biological mother.

SHARON'S STORY CAME FULL CIRCLE

Sharon died on December 1, 2018, just short of her eighty-seventh birthday. Her daughter and family were unable to pay for a funeral, so D'Anna, along with the investigator and the DNA genealogist, took it upon themselves to handle the financial arrangements for Sharon's cremation. Then, with a minister, who also had been touched by her story, and a small group of dedicated researchers and friends, they commemorated Sharon's life and scattered her ashes on the desert, west of the town of Superior, in the same place that her story began.

In 1988, when Sharon first met D'Anna, she also visited with the former Mesa constable who took her in on that Christmas Eve so long ago. The retired lawman was ninety-five years old at the time of their meeting. Sharon always remembered his words and said that they comforted her for the rest of her life. As quoted on December 24, 2018, by D'Anna, the former constable had said,

> *Was somebody hiding in the sagebrush and watching to make sure you'd be found? Was that good-hearted couple who brought you in telling us the whole story? Nobody knows for sure, but this much I am certain of. The baby put into my hands that night was clean and well-cared-for. You were meant to be found and given a good home.*

PART 4

TEN AND UNDER,
AN INTRODUCTION

Chapter 9 on the "Hatbox Baby" is more than a good Christmas story. Sharon Elliott's adoption was so unusual that the details still are being unraveled. Had there been some illegal activity in procuring the infant from her birth parents and/or a transfer of funds in facilitating her being found? That part of her story is undetermined. But throughout the Great Depression and into the 1950s, baby brokers across the country bought—and also stole—babies and young children for adoption on the black market.

The following section continues the topic of young children, including, in chapter 10, the nonfamily abductions of Marjory West, Steven Damman, and Freddie Holmes. All were grabbed when their families weren't looking and, like many others, may have been put up for adoption with illegal operators raking in large profits. Childless couples willing to pay exorbitant fees for healthy, good-looking babies and young children often were unaware, or unconcerned, that the little ones they brought into their homes had been procured on the black market.

The story of Philadelphia's "Boy in the Box" is told in chapter 11. The unidentified boy may have been purchased prior to his being abused and then found deceased in 1957. There are two big mysteries in this case. One is the boy's identity, and the other is the name of the person or persons responsible for what the medical examiner, at the time, declared a homicide. Investigators are well aware that the place to begin in solving the murder of an unidentified person is to determine the person's name and that quest, so far, has taken more than sixty-three years.

Chapter 12 tells the story of Connie Smith, a Wyoming girl who vanished from a summer camp in Connecticut. While teens frequently run away and young children are prone to abduction by family members, neither was the case for ten-year-old Connie. According to information and statistics from the National Center for Missing & Exploited Children (NCMEC), the closest category of missing children to describe Connie's disappearance is very rare and is called "lost, injured or otherwise missing." This classification further is defined as "a child who has disappeared under unknown circumstances, or a child who is too young to appropriately be considered an endangered runaway. [The classification] ranges from a child wandering off and becoming lost, to a child who may have been abducted, but no one saw it happen."

Tragically, a few of these "otherwise missing" cases end up in murder. That was the case with nine-year-old Walter Collins, missing from his Venice, California, home in 1928. At the time, his mother was a telephone operator, and his father, a former streetcar conductor, was serving time in San Quentin Prison. Meanwhile, an eleven-year-old runaway boy (very young by today's standards) was picked up in DeKalb, Iowa. The boy answered yes when he was asked if he was Walter Collins from California.

As the story was presented in the newspapers and in film, the runaway boy wanted to see his favorite movie star, Tom Mix. When police turned the boy over to Walter's mother, she explained that he wasn't her boy. But the police were anxious to close their case and told her to keep him anyway! In 2008, the story was made into a Hollywood movie, *The Changeling*. The gripping and powerful period piece portrays the true stories of the victims—the runaway child, the missing child, and the distraught mother.

Young Child Abductions and Black-Market Babies

Similar to chapter 3, about Hart Island, this chapter discusses a topic rather than one specific case. But first, we'll take a look at three young missing children: Marjory West, Steven Damman, and Freddie Holmes.

MARJORY WEST

On May 8, 1938, four-year-old Marjory West was enjoying a Mother's Day picnic with her family in the White Gravel Creek area of the Allegheny National Forest, in northwestern Pennsylvania. With her hair curled into long ringlets, Marjory resembled, and even dressed like, Shirley Temple, the child actress who was Hollywood's number-one box office draw at the time. Suddenly, little Marjory was gone.

Marjory (often misspelled as "Marjorie"), her older siblings Allen West and Dorothea West, and their parents had attended church in their hometown of Bradford, in northwestern Pennsylvania near the New York state line. After the service was over, they drove southwest approximately forty miles to a picnic area in the national forest. Marjory's father and brother went fishing.

Then, as Dorothea later recalled, she and Marjory were on a search for wildflowers and were attracted to some violets. For a short time, Dorothea left Marjory and carried the girls' bouquets to their mother who was seated in the family's car. When Dorothea returned to where she and Marjory had picked the flowers, Marjory was gone. One newspaper account mentioned that her mother and sister thought, at first, that she was playing the game "hide-and-seek." When she didn't return, her father, brother, and other picnickers in the area immediately started to search, and then someone drove seven miles to a telephone and called the police.

As soon as the police arrived and the news got out, the whole community turned out to help. During the next few days, men from the National Guard, Pennsylvania State Police, and the Civilian Conservation Corps were joined by merchants and professionals, who temporarily closed their businesses and offices. The searchers (using miners' lamps at night) stretched out four feet apart in mile-long lines and started through a densely wooded twenty-square-mile area said to be populated by rattlesnakes and bears. The New York State Police sent in bloodhounds and their handlers but turned up nothing. (Later, the local police department bought a bloodhound of its own.)

Meanwhile, a news report quoted a local resident who said that his car "was ditched on the narrow Morrison-Marshburg Road by a speeding car less than a mile south of where the child was last seen only a few minutes after she was said to have disappeared." As it became more and more unlikely that Marjory had simply wandered away, her mother in a news report "expressed the opinion that her daughter had been kidnapped." Marjory's mother publicly appealed to the child's abductor to either take the little girl to any American Legion post or bring her home with "no questions asked."

In June, on the eve of Marjory's fifth birthday, her mother again pleaded, through the press, with whoever may have taken her. "I cannot sleep nor eat until my little girl is returned home safely," she told a reporter. "If you prefer to wait until dark, then drop her off on any street in Bradford, but first give her a note with her name and address on it. Explain carefully what she is to do for she is such a little girl."

Meanwhile, the Bradford Citizens' Reward Committee offered a two-thousand-dollar reward for information resulting in Marjory's safe return, as well as one thousand dollars for the recovery of her body. There were no leads by December 15, 1938, and the committee let the reward expire. Along with the portrait of the pretty, but slightly serious-looking, young child, her description read:

- Age 4 (four) years
- Blue eyes
- Long, curly red hair
- Freckled face
- Wearing red Shirley Temple hat, blue dress, and patent leather shoes
- Talks with a southern accent

In May 1939, shortly after the one-year anniversary of Marjory's disappearance, Bradford residents were on edge when another young girl was reported missing. Local, county, and state police wasted no time joining in the search, and the girl's description was broadcast on the radio and over state police teletype. The local newspapers didn't mention how she was found, but she was discovered, seven hours later, playing in a park. Marjory was not that fortunate, but the newspapers remembered her every Mother's Day for years to come.

TENNESSEE CHILDREN'S HOME SOCIETY

Marjory's mother's gut feeling that her daughter had been kidnapped wasn't as far-fetched a theory as it may have seemed. Between the years 1932 and 1951, the Memphis branch of the Tennessee Children's Home Society was run by an unscrupulous and stern-faced woman named Georgia Tann. She seemed to be the most notorious of the baby brokers, but many young children passed through the doors of other so-called adoption agencies in states that included Pennsylvania, Delaware, New York, Texas, and Montana. In recent years, Georgia's story has been revived. According to the *New York Post* on June 17, 2017, she was the mastermind behind thousands of black-market adoptions while she "stole from the poor to give to the rich," receiving up to five thousand dollars per adoption.

Georgia Tann was said to have had various means of procuring babies and children for her wealthy, but unsuspecting, clients. She got newborns by bribing nurses and doctors to tell new parents that their babies were stillborn. Also, her agents grabbed young children such as Marjory, Steven, and Freddie off the streets. Afterward the children were told that their parents had died, while a complicit judge falsified their records and adopted them out for large profits, mostly to couples in New York City and Los Angeles. Before the law caught up with Tann, movie stars including Joan Crawford and June Allyson were said to have adopted children from her agency.

Thousands of illegally acquired babies and young children passed through the Tennessee Children's Home Society's doors. Some of the less marketable children were neglected or abused and allowed to die. Nineteen of them, names unknown, were buried years ago in an unmarked mass grave in the Elmwood Cemetery in Memphis, Tennessee. In 2015 the cemetery erected a monument in memory of those children and hundreds of others. Its inscription reads, in part, "In memory of the 19 children who finally rest

Figure 10.1. Tennessee Children's Memorial.
Decades ago, nineteen of the numerous children who died at the home of the
Tennessee Children's Home Society were buried in an unmarked grave in the
Elmwood Cemetery in Memphis, Tennessee. In 2017 the cemetery erected this
monument in the children's memory. IMAGE FROM WIKIMEDIA COMMONS

here unmarked if not unknown, and of all the hundreds who died under the
cold, hard hand of the Tennessee Children's Home Society. Their final resting place unknown. Their final peace a blessing. The hard lesson of their fate
changed adoption procedure and law nationwide."

Fortunately, adoption laws *were* changed after the Tennessee governor,
upon receiving reports that children were being sold for profit, launched an
investigation in 1950 into the Tennessee Children's Home Society. The *Nash-
ville Banner*, on September 12, 1950, stated that one thousand babies and
one million dollars may have been involved. Charges were filed against the
Society, but Georgia Tann was critically ill and unconscious at the time. Three
days later, she died of cancer at the age of fifty-nine.

The post–World War II era of the early 1950s was full of promise and
prosperity for young families, but the geopolitical tension of the Cold War
between the United States and the Soviet Union foretold of dangers that
lay ahead. While schools held "duck-and-cover" drills that were supposed to
protect children and staff in case of a nuclear attack, some families built fall-
out shelters in their basements and backyards. And when more illegal baby
brokers followed in the footsteps of Georgia Tann and made the news, new

parents held their babies a little closer. This was especially true following the disappearance of Steven Damman.

Steven Damman and Freddie Holmes

Like Marjory West, Steven Damman and Freddie Holmes also were taken from their families. Steven, a handsome two-and-a-half-year-old boy, was kidnapped from outside of a grocery store on Long Island, New York, in 1955. That same year, Freddie Holmes, a one-year-old, was snatched from the driveway of his parents' home in New York's Catskill Mountains. Both boys had blond hair and blue eyes. Their abductors only had to look for children who would bring a good price, pick them up, and then carry them away. No traces of Marjory, Steven, or Freddie, or hundreds more, have ever been found, although they still could be alive with different, but unknown, names. Their abductors remain unknown as well.

On October 31, 1955, Steven's mother left her son outside of a grocery store while she stepped inside to make a purchase. With Steven was his seven-month-old sister, in her baby carriage. When the mother came out of the store, both children had disappeared, but the baby (still in her carriage) was found behind the store. Little Steven was gone, and everyone agreed that he couldn't have strayed far on his own. Despite extensive searches by police and volunteers, as well as hundreds of airmen brought in from nearby Mitchel Air Force Base, no one was able to locate him.

A shopper in the store that Halloween day saw a man pick up the boy, while a woman wheeled the baby in the baby carriage behind the store. At the time, the shopper didn't think much about the incident and merely assumed that the man and woman knew the mother and were caring for the children. But the next day, when the shopper learned that the boy was missing, she called police. Searchers went out in droves, looking for the toddler last seen wearing a blue shirt, a red sweater, and dungarees (blue jeans). By then, the kidnappers, with little Steven, had made their getaway. According to a November 4, 1955, article published all over the country, the resulting publicity surrounding the boy's disappearance reminded parents, once again, to carefully guard their little ones from what a reporter termed "a black-market ring in young children."

Like Steven, one-year-old Freddie also had blue eyes and blond hair and also was abducted in New York State in 1955, as noted above. The toddler's family last saw him on May 25, 1955, playing in the driveway of their rural home near Grahamsville, in the Catskill Mountains. Freddie wore faded brown corduroy overalls and a long-sleeved pullover shirt. In the author's correspondence with Freddie's sister, the sister told of busloads of men from a nearby Air Force base scouring the woods for any scrap of Freddie's clothing or human remains.

Freddie's family was large and loving. Without much money and without a television, the boy's sister said that Freddie was the family's source of entertainment, as they taught him to sing, dance, and say clever things. After his sudden disappearance, his sister remembered sheriff officials ripping up the floorboards of the family's farmhouse and then digging up her mother's newly planted garden. Her parents were considered suspects in the boy's disappearance and given polygraph tests. A decade or so later, her father died, a victim of suicide. Her mother had a sudden heart attack and had often told her family that she had "a hole in her heart related to the loss of her baby son."

Steven and Freddie are still missing. In February 1957, a young, unidentified boy who would have been approximately Steven's age was found deceased in Philadelphia (as discussed in the next chapter). Philadelphia police wasted no time sending footprints of the Philadelphia boy to investigators in Nassau County, New York, but the prints didn't match. Then in 2003, in order to confirm the Philadelphia investigator's earlier results and to keep up with changes in technology, DNA from their boy was compared to Steven's sister's DNA to see if there was a familial connection. The comparison conclusively ruled him out. Meanwhile, Steven's parents moved back to their native Iowa, taking with them a huge emptiness they could never fill.

Steven's story returned to the news yet again in 2009, when a fifty-seven-year-old Michigan man came forward saying he thought he was the missing boy. According to the *Des Moines Register*, the man believed that he had been adopted. "As I got older, I realized how different I was from my mother and father, and that something wasn't right," he told a reporter. Then the man saw a photo of Steven's mother and believed there was a family resemblance. The Michigan man contacted Steven's sister, and they appeared together on the *Today* television show to discuss their possible family connection. But DNA disproved the man's theory. He wasn't Steven and, at the time of this writing, Steven is still missing. So, too, is Freddie.

Could Steven and Freddie have fallen victim to illegal baby broker Bessie Bernard? According to the 1940 federal census, when Bessie was thirty-eight years old, she was no longer living with her husband, Stuart Bernard. Instead, she and her child lived in Manhattan with Bessie's parents, Isadore and Fanny Weiner. On that year's census form, the space for Bessie's "occupation"

(c) Report a sighting

Share this poster

MISSING

HELP BRING ME HOME

NCMEC: 1149544

Steven Damman

Age Progressed

Missing Since: Oct 31, 1955
Missing From: East Meadow, NY
DOB: Dec 15, 1952
Age Now: 67
Sex: Male
Race: White
Hair Color: Blonde
Eye Color: Blue
Height: 3'2"
Weight: 32 lbs

Steven's photo is shown age-progressed to 65 years-old. He was last seen on October 31, 1955, outside a grocery store. He was wearing dungarees, a blue shirt, red sweater, and brown shoes. Steven has a small scar on his chin and a mole on the back of his right calf.

DON'T HESITATE!

ANYONE HAVING INFORMATION SHOULD CONTACT

CALL 911 OR

1-800-8435678 (1-800-THE-LOST®)
Nassau County Police Department (New York) 1-516-573-7000

Figure 10.2. Steven Damman poster.
The National Center for Missing & Exploited Children's missing-person poster for Steven Damman shows his photo at the time he was missing, in 1955, as well as an age-progression image of what he might look like today. COURTESY OF THE NATIONAL CENTER FOR MISSING & EXPLOITED CHILDREN

was left blank, but the census-taker had written "yes" under a column titled "other income." This other income, no doubt, came from Bessie's illegal baby-trafficking scheme that stretched up and down the American East Coast. Eventually, the law caught up with her.

On January 15, 1950, the *New York Daily News* reported on Bessie's initial arrest after she allegedly assaulted a detective while he was searching her apartment for her business records. Bessie, described as six feet, two inches tall and weighing 240 pounds, was charged, along with her attorney, with "conspiracy and illegal placement" of babies. As stated in the *Daily News*, "It was the first information, or indictment, under New York State's new adoption code, and the prosecution will be watched with interest by all persons and organizations concerned with ending the racketeering in babies."

A subsequent court trial revealed that the attorney had procured the babies in Miami, Florida, and then hired accomplices to fly with the babies to New York City. There, after Bessie recruited adoptive parents, she would meet them either at the Newark Airport or New York City's Pennsylvania (railroad) Station or on a designated New York City street corner. Each time she handed over a baby, the new parents would pay two thousand dollars, equivalent to more than twenty thousand dollars today.

As stated in another *Daily News* article, on November 1, 1950, Bessie and her attorney were convicted in June 1950 for violating a public health law that prohibited the procuring of infants and privately placing them for adoption. The attorney was sentenced to one year behind bars, but Bessie avoided her prison term by paying a $2,500 fine. Although Steven and Freddie's abductions came five years later and the two boys were older than infants, Bessie reportedly remained in New York City, where she was said to have remained in business as late as 1970 under her maiden name of Elizabeth Weiner.

UNWED MOTHERS AND THEIR NEWBORNS

From the 1930s through the 1950s, there was a ready supply of newborns and a constant demand for them as well. To understand why, it's necessary to delve into the context of the times. In the beginning of the Depression-era days of the 1930s, it was not unusual for unwed girls and young women to be faced with unplanned pregnancies, or be "in trouble," as their situations were called at the time. Contraceptives were neither as accessible nor as effective as they are today. Abortions were dangerous and illegal. Even when financially caring for a child was possible, an out-of-wedlock baby brought shame upon an unmarried mother's family. Some unplanned pregnancy situations, of course, were resolved when the mother married the baby's father, but marriage wasn't always possible.

Ready to help these vulnerable and unwed mothers were charitable and religious agencies, including the Salvation Army, the Florence Crittenton Mission, and the Child Welfare League. These legitimate agencies observed adoption laws and didn't charge fees to their patients, but not all who needed their assistance made it to their doors. Some women and girls ended up in illegally run maternity homes, or "hospitals," as they were often called. These businesses took advantage of the mothers while making hefty profits on their babies. Usually housed in residential areas of cities and towns, most of the "hospitals" were unrecognizable to passersby. If they were recognized, their owners moved to other locations.

One such facility was run by Dr. Jerome D. Niles, in Middletown, Delaware. In the 1930s and 1940s, in addition to his private practice and serving, for a time, as the president of the Delaware Medical Society, the outwardly respectable doctor ran his own "maternity hospital" for unwed mothers while quietly trafficking their babies. In later years, some adoptees who had been born there and were researching their births found that normal adoption procedures had not been followed and parents' names on the birth certificates were false or inaccurate. Meanwhile, forty-five miles away, the Veil Maternity Hospital, in West Chester, Pennsylvania, advertised for unwed mothers, while assuring couples in search of babies that "the whole legal procedure is conducted without publicity, and all correspondence is confidential." What that meant was that the adoptions were not done through the courts, and no legitimate records of the adoptions were kept.

Unwed mothers usually entered these facilities when their pregnancies started to "show." An exposé of the Veil "hospital," titled "Traffic in Babies" and published in the September 16, 1939, issue of *Collier's* magazine, told the story of a typical pregnant young woman who mopped hallways for months to pay for her room and board. Believing she had no choice, she had signed a release form for her then-unborn child at the time she entered the hospital. After giving birth she never saw her baby and never was told if it was a boy or a girl. Her baby was then sold to a childless couple for five hundred dollars, all pocketed by the management.

The Veil hospital had a second Pennsylvania location, as well as branches in New Jersey, Missouri, and Kansas. All through the 1930s, these "hospitals" were denied licenses, but, as *Collier's* reported, "Girls continued to go through the front door, and babies went out by the back."

The article also gave statistics provided by the US Children's Bureau, a federal agency formed in 1912 that maintains its involvement in children's issues and is operated under the US Department of Health and Human Services. According to the Bureau, in 1938 (the year previous to the *Collier's* article and the year that Marjory West went missing) only one-third of the seventeen thousand children adopted in the United States went to their new homes through reputable child-placement bureaus. The others, more than eleven thousand, were, in the magazine author's words, "cash commodities sold by commercial nurseries and bootlegged by private individuals, mostly doctors." Tracking down the babies was difficult if not impossible. Unwed mothers had been instructed to register under fictitious names, and they frequently were moved from one facility to another.

HELP AND HOPE

Today there is a lot of available information and statistics on missing children, especially from the National Center for Missing & Exploited Children (NCMEC; see missingkids.org). "Stranger or nonfamily abductions," which would have included the black-market abductions of the past, now make up only 1 percent of missing children. And for them, according to the NCMEC, the most common lures are offering a child a ride, candy, or money, and using an animal to catch the child's interest. Also in the "nonfamily" category is infant abduction, in which babies under one year of age usually are taken by a female of childbearing age. Another category of missing young children are abductions of minors made by a member of a child's family (or someone acting on behalf of a family member) who takes a child from, or fails to return a child to, the child's custodial parent.

And what trends have changed the face of adoptions, at least in the United States, in recent years? According to the Institute for Family Studies (a 501(c)(3) organization focused on research and public education), the domestic supply of adoptable infants has declined due primarily to dramatic reductions in pregnancy and birth rates among teenagers. When unmarried young women do give birth, more of them are attempting to raise their babies on their own, or with assistance from grandparents or other relatives, rather than putting the child up for adoption. Meanwhile, an increasing number of infertile couples, or those who have put off trying to have children of their own, are adopting children from other countries, particularly from Asia.

Steven and Freddie, and maybe even Marjory, could be living under adopted names, unaware that they were stolen from their biological parents. The good news is that now, with genetic genealogy (see a brief explanation in chapter 9), there is new hope for them and many others whose true identities are unknown. There also is hope for the parents who are seeking answers regarding their long-missing children. At the time that the man in Michigan took a conventional DNA test to determine if he could have been Steven Damman, the missing boy's father was seventy-eight-years old. When interviewed by a reporter, the father stated, "This has not been easy for me. It wasn't easy back then. We still don't know what happened to our boy."

The Boy in the Box

America's Unknown Child

The preceding chapter discusses missing young children, but what happens when someone *finds* a child? In 1957, thirteen-year-old Philadelphia resident William L. "Bill" Fleisher walked into a supermarket with his mother and was startled to see a poster, in the store window, that showed a deceased unidentified little boy who quickly became known as the "Boy in the Box." Decades later, Fleisher stated, "I had never before seen a photo of a dead child."

Fleisher credits the poster with leading him into a career in law enforcement. He's a former Philadelphia Police Department officer and Federal Bureau of Investigation (FBI) special agent who later became an assistant special agent in charge of the US Customs Service in Philadelphia. He's also a cofounder of the Vidocq Society, an international organization of crime-solving experts based in Philadelphia. And from the organization's founding in 1990 to 2020, a total of thirty years, he served as the Society's commissioner. The image of the boy's photo has never left Bill's memory, and he and his colleagues in the Vidocq Society still are determined to identify the boy, whom they have since renamed "America's Unknown Child."

If ever there was a child crying out to be identified, this is the one. Even when the case appeared impossible, police, medical examiners, and Vidocq Society members assembled (and some still do) every year on November 11 at the boy's grave. Today, as most of the original investigators have, one by one, passed away, the old guard has become considerably smaller. But sometimes the passage of time can be helpful as people once afraid to speak out are more likely to come forward, and new advances in technology bring new hope.

At the time of this writing, the boy's identity is still unknown, but a Philadelphia CBS television reporter who attended the November 11, 2020,

Figure 11.1. Police at the scene, "Boy in the Box."
On February 26, 1957, officers of the Philadelphia Police Department searched for clues after an unidentified boy was found deceased in a cardboard box. The Good Shepherd School is in the background. COURTESY OF THE SPECIAL COLLECTIONS RESEARCH CENTER, TEMPLE UNIVERSITY LIBRARIES, PHILADELPHIA, PENNSYLVANIA; PHOTO FROM THE *PHILADELPHIA BULLETIN*

gravesite gathering announced that "the Vidocq Society is closer than ever to figuring out who this boy is." The Society's members work with law enforcement, so they have to keep the details close to their chests. But stay tuned.

DISCOVERY AND EVIDENCE

Susquehanna Road, between Verree Road and Pine Road in the Fox Chase neighborhood of Northeast Philadelphia, is, today, a paved city street with a tidy string of nearly identical brick duplexes on the south side. But in the 1950s, before the residences were built, Susquehanna Road, near Pennypack Creek, was a narrow country lane. The occasional dump site for locals was bordered partly by woods and was choked with thick underbrush. On a cool and drizzly February day (or night), someone, still unknown, thought it was isolated enough to discard the body of the little boy.

On the north side of the road, through the woods that led to a creek, was a driveway up to the buildings of the Good Shepherd School for Wayward Girls. The Catholic institution housed girls and teens who had been emotionally disturbed and/or were victims of abuse. (Sadly, today, many of these likely runaways are called "thrown-away teens.")

On February 25, 1957, a twenty-six-year-old Army veteran stopped along Susquehanna Road and got out of his car. The young man, then attending La Salle College a few miles away, later explained to police that he stopped to chase a rabbit that had jumped out in front of him. Some reports, however, say he was in the habit of spying on the girls at the school. Either way, he also investigated some muskrat traps that he found among the debris. And that's when he noticed a large, corrugated cardboard box that looked as if it had been used to ship a piece of furniture.

Inside the box, the young man saw what, at first, looked like a doll, but then he realized it was the body of a young child. Not sure what to do, he drove back to La Salle College (now University), where he confided in two faculty priests, who advised him to notify authorities. The following day, he called the Philadelphia Police Department. He was extensively questioned and voluntarily submitted to a lie detector test that cleared him of involvement in the case. As a result of his call, police in their red Chevrolet police cruisers rushed to the scene, followed by detectives wearing trench coats and fedoras.

The discovery of the child's body was splashed all over the newspapers in the hope that someone would come forward with information that might lead to the boy's identity. "Beaten Boy's Body Found in a Box" was the main headline on the front page of the February 27, 1957, *Philadelphia Inquirer*. When Remington Bristow, an investigator with the Philadelphia Medical Examiner's Office, picked up his morning newspaper, he read the stories and assumed that an identification would be made before he started his midnight-to-8:00 a.m. shift.

Both the *Inquirer* and the *Philadelphia Evening Bulletin* included photos of police combing the site where the "death carton" was found, as well as a photo of the homicide squad captain examining the box after it had been taken to police headquarters. The poster that was viewed by young Bill Fleisher explained that the information had been provided by the *Philadelphia Inquirer* as a public service. Within two weeks, four hundred thousand posters had been distributed, and flyers were included in utility bills sent to

Philadelphia residents. In addition to a description of the unidentified boy, photos of his head were shown from the front as well as right and left profiles. The profiles showed a disturbing distortion in the shape of the boy's head, as if it had been held in a vise.

One of the first tips to come in to police was from a motorist who told of a "strange incident" he witnessed near the spot where the boy's body was found. The man said that, on the previous day, he was driving along Verree Road (approaching the Susquehanna Road intersection) when he spotted a car stopped along the side of Susquehanna Road with a woman and a teenage "boy" standing by the car trunk. The man told police that the woman looked as if she was groping for something in the trunk.

According to newspaper reports, the woman appeared to be between forty and fifty years old, of medium height, heavyset, and wearing a checked cloth coat. Her companion was approximately twelve to fourteen years old and was of about the same height as the woman. The man said he turned onto Susquehanna Road and slowed his car, thinking the woman had a flat tire, and he asked if he could be of any assistance. He told police that both the woman and the teenager turned their backs to him, remained absolutely mute, and seemed to be trying to conceal the license plate of their car. The man thought this was strange but decided they didn't want him interfering with whatever they were doing, so he drove off.

The deceased boy, thought to have been dead for two to three days, was described by reporters as "apparently molested and beaten by a sadist" and between four and six years old. Further descriptions called him slender, thin-faced, and pale-skinned. Police reports noted that the boy, with emotionless blue eyes, had a full set of baby teeth, still had his tonsils, and had been circumcised. His blond hair had been "crudely cut in a crew-cut style," and his fingernails and toenails had been neatly and recently trimmed. He also had scars on his chin, chest, and elbows. Since a search of missing children did not turn up anyone who fit the description, the police sent out radio bulletins to all of its officers. Detectives made visits to hospitals, orphanages, and private welfare agencies all over Philadelphia and southern New Jersey.

News, at the time, traveled quickly as operators typed press releases and bulletins into teletype machines that resembled large manual typewriters. Then the text was sent via dedicated telephone circuits to other agencies that received and spit out the retyped messages on teletype machines of their own. At the Philadelphia Police Department, the chief inspector of detectives used this method to send the boy's description all over the country. The FBI gave the case top priority, and the American Medical Association circulated the boy's photo to its affiliated physicians. Surely, investigators thought, someone would remember treating the boy or, more likely, would recognize a family member, unless the boy (like the children at the Catholic home) was a "thrown-away" child too.

Initially, after the police had removed the boy and the box from the scrubby underbrush, they went door-to-door in adjoining neighborhoods, asking residents for any information they could provide. Two weeks later, they canvassed the same neighborhoods again. The second time, they stopped at the home of a teenage boy who hadn't been at his family's home the first time the police had come by. The teenager told the police that a day or two before the college student's discovery, he, too, had seen the box while walking home from a baseball game. He admitted ownership of the muskrat traps, and he said he stopped to look at them. That's when he saw that a body was inside the box. Terrified, he went straight home and was too frightened to tell anyone, even his parents.

A closer examination of the fifteen-by-nineteen-by-thirty-five-inch cardboard box showed that it had originally contained a baby's bassinet sold by the J. C. Penney Company, but the company had a cash-only policy at that time, so there were no store records indicating the identity of the purchasers. The police did, however, manage to track down all but one of the remaining twelve bassinets and boxes from a nearby store. The box that had held the unidentified boy was sent to the FBI's lab, but its analysts did not find any distinct fingerprints.

After the boy's body was removed from the box, investigators discovered that he had been wrapped in a faded cotton-flannel blanket that had been torn in half. The blanket's design included diamond-shaped blocks of green, rust, brown, and white, and it had been mended with a poor grade of cotton thread. Hoping for a lead on where it had been purchased, the detectives had the blanket tested at the Philadelphia Textile Institute, where it was determined that it had been made either at Beacon Mills, in Swannanoa, North Carolina, or at the Esmond Mills in Granby, Quebec, Canada. Unfortunately, investigators found that thousands of these blankets had been manufactured and shipped to dozens of wholesalers throughout the country, so it was not possible to determine all of the stores where they had been for sale.

Meanwhile, after a medical examiner placed the boy on a cold metal table under a bright light, he called in a physical anthropologist from the Graduate School of Medicine at the University of Pennsylvania. The expert determined that the boy's height of forty and one-half inches approximated the height of a child of three years and eight months, but his weight of thirty pounds equaled that of a child of only two years and two months, indicating severe malnutrition.

The medical examiner told reporters there were "bruises all over the boy's body, particularly on his head, legs, and arms" adding, "The boy's death is definitely due to a homicide, and that's all that I can say at this time." As Bill Fleisher, Vidocq Society commissioner, later articulated in a 2017 Philadelphia televised ABC news story, "The boy was abused and neglected until his little flame went out."

EARLY LEADS AND (FIRST) BURIAL

In February 1957, the day after the news broke, the police began receiving leads. One caller spoke of Steven Damman, the almost three-year-old boy (see chapter 10) who, two years earlier, had been kidnapped from a grocery store on Long Island, New York. Steven was ruled out, however, when his footprint, recorded at birth, failed to match the footprint of the "Boy in the Box." In addition, the missing boy had a broken wrist, but when medical examiners X-rayed the Philadelphia boy's body, they didn't find any evidence of previous fractures.

Then came a steady stream of people who asked to view the boy's body in the morgue. One was a US marine who said he was "reasonably sure" the child was his brother. The marine was one of eighteen children and had been out of close touch with his family for some time. During the previous year, his parents and most of his siblings moved to California, leaving one daughter and one young son in Philadelphia with an older brother. When the family was found, the young son was still alive.

Another morgue visitor was a Camden, New Jersey, woman who claimed to have seen the boy in a restaurant where she worked. The child was with a short stocky man whom the boy identified as his father. Several more people from Camden went to the morgue and said that they, too, had seen the boy tagging along with his father, a handyman doing roof repairs. Two weeks later, police found the man and the boy, alive and well. Leads kept coming in, but hopes turned to frustration, and the "Boy in the Box" continued to lie in the morgue.

One police detective drove all the way to Thornton, Colorado, to question a then recently arrested woman who had thrown the body of her three-year-old daughter in the trash. According to news reports, neighbors claimed that the woman's son was malnourished. When asked about her son, she replied that he was in Philadelphia. Then the boy was found hiding under a bed. Meanwhile, police compared similarities between the "Boy in the Box" and a young girl found deceased in a park in New York. The police even got a letter that read, "I know my sister must have had an illegitimate baby, and she's the kind that would kill it."

A few months after the unidentified boy's discovery, on a hot muggy day in July 1957, the police and medical investigators laid him to rest in grave number 191 in the Philadelphia City Cemetery. As in previous years at the Hart Island Cemetery in New York (see chapter 3), inmates from a nearby prison helped transport bodies and dig graves for burials of the indigent, unclaimed, and unknown, so inmates likely assisted with the boy's burial, as well. The solemn group gathered for what a reporter called "simple and touching rites." The Philadelphia Homicide Squad had raised enough money to buy the boy a small gravestone—the only gravestone in the entire cemetery, and it appeared that the bleak burial ground would be the boy's final resting place. Under a few stylized flowers edged into the stone, the unknown child's inscription read:

Heavenly Father
Bless this Unknown Boy
February 25, 1957

KEEPING THE STORY ALIVE

At the time, Remington Bristow was one of several investigators in the Philadelphia Medical Examiner's Office, and his assignments were alphabetical by the first letter of the person's last name. He was given the letters M, N, O, P, Q, and U, which included "Unknown." For a body with a name, his job included finding contact information for the next of kin. For one without a name—that is, an "unknown"—he was tasked with determining the person's identity. Investigator Bristow's quest turned into a lifelong obsession that lasted for the next thirty-six years, until the day he died. His colleagues credited him with keeping the case open, and they acknowledged that without his personal crusade, the "Boy in the Box" might have been forgotten a long time ago.

Investigator Bristow had grown up in Oregon, the son of a mortician. He worked with his father for two years before enrolling in a two-year course at the Los Angeles College of Mortuary Science. After he graduated he joined the navy and served until the end of World War II. In 1947 he opened a funeral home in central California, where he also served as deputy coroner. In 1952 Investigator Bristow and his wife moved to South Philadelphia. After assisting several funeral directors, he joined the Philadelphia Medical Examiner's Office. He had been on the job for one year when case number 29109 (the "Boy in the Box") was assigned to him for identification.

As the years passed, Investigator Bristow began using his vacation time to follow leads, all at his own expense. "It just keeps gnawing at me," he told a reporter in 1963. "I can't stop searching for an answer." He put an advertisement in a Pennsylvania newspaper, asking for information leading to the boy's identity and offered a $1,000 reward. "I can't let the case alone," he stated. "I want to know who the boy is, and until I find out I'll never be satisfied." Bristow also softened the stated cause of death by theorizing that it may have been an accident, perhaps what investigators today would call "homicide by neglect." The investigator stated publicly that whoever placed the boy in the box and left him along the side of the road may have been afraid to come forward.

In February 1967, ten years after the boy's burial, Investigator Bristow stated the following to a Philadelphia newspaper reporter, although it may have been a ruse to encourage those responsible for the boy's death to come forward:

> I'm getting older now and more compassionate, I guess, and I'm convinced that this wasn't a murder. If it were homicide, they would not have put him in a box, cut his hair, bathed him, crossed his hands over his stomach gently and carefully. Maybe they were going to dig a little grave for him and were frightened off by a car. I'm convinced the parents were ignorant. The boy was dead. They had no money. Didn't know what to do. So they did all that in preparation for burial. There was definitely love there.

Investigator Bristow added that he often visited the grave and kept it clear of weeds and debris. He told a reporter that he hoped the boy's parents visited it too. If so, he wanted them to come up to him and introduce themselves. "I feel I know them already," he said. "They shouldn't fear me because, if nothing else, we've shared the experience of loving a boy—though it be in death." The investigator's colleagues visited, as well, offering their prayers and covering the boy's grave with roses. Investigator Bristow made a point of telling a reporter that their actions weren't solely for the unknown boy but for all of the unknown and unclaimed bodies in the city cemetery.

In February 1969, the twelfth anniversary of the boy's death, Investigator Bristow opened up to the press about his concern that police officers may have overlooked an insignificant clue when they inspected the crime scene. "Hundreds of cops were going over a field," he added, "but they didn't know what they were looking for." By 1973, the investigator explained that his office handled approximately 120 unidentified bodies per year. In the previous seventeen years, he stated that his office had identified all but twenty-eight of them. "That's about a 99 percent average," he told a reporter, "but it's not enough."

Other investigators kept up the search as well. The boy had no visible polio vaccination scar (then given to as many children as possible), which may have indicated that he was a recent immigrant. His features appeared Northern European, and, beginning in 1956, only a year before the boy's body was found, many Hungarian refugees had settled in Philadelphia. William H. Kelly, supervisor of the Philadelphia Police Department's Identification Unit, who had inked the boy's fingers and feet on the morgue table, personally checked more than eleven thousand passport photographs of young boys in the hopes of finding one that looked like the unknown child. When he finally did find a similar photo, he tracked down the child and found him alive and well in North Carolina.

Supervisor Kelly also spent hours, before and after work, day after day for nine long years, searching medical records for footprints of babies born in the Philadelphia area. By the end of his search, the impression of the boy's foot had been seared into his brain, but none of the footprints was a match. Other investigators followed reports of carnival workers thought to have neglected or disposed of their children while traveling from one location to another.

By the twentieth anniversary of the boy's death, in February 1977, Investigator Bristow, then two years into retirement, still had not given up his dream of identifying the boy. The investigator even continued after he suffered a stroke, in 1981. In his briefcase, he carried around with him, and often handled, the only tangible connection he had with the boy: the "death mask" of his face.

Throughout the investigator's search there was one lead that never left his mind. Back in 1961, only four years after the boy had been found, the investigator read of a self-proclaimed psychic, Florence Sternfeld. The New Jersey woman had a reputation for helping police solve crimes. When the investigator contacted her, she said that she had never been to Philadelphia, but she conjured up an image of an old house (with a log cabin on the property) where children were playing.

Investigator Bristow drove city block after city block until he found what he believed were the same house and cabin. Conveniently, they were located less than two miles from where the boy was found. The investigator talked with neighbors and learned that the properties belonged to a couple who kept foster children. When the house and cabin were put up for sale, he went to a preview of an auction of its furnishings. The investigator said that he never forgot what he saw then: a bassinet that, originally, had been packaged in a box like the one that had contained the boy, as well as blankets cut in half like the one in which the child was wrapped.

"I've been built up and let down many times," Investigator Bristow told a reporter. "When I eliminate one lead, I go on to the next." He died, however, in 1993, at the age of seventy-two, believing to the end that the answer lay with the foster family. This was in spite of the fact that during the initial days of the investigation, the police had contacted the family and had confirmed that no children matched the boy's description nor were any children missing. In 1984, at the investigator's request, police reinterviewed the former owners of the home. Once again, police were assured that they had no involvement in the case of the "Boy in the Box."

THE VIDOCQ SOCIETY AND A NEW BURIAL

Leads continued to come in, with many that turned into dead ends. As the long-term followers continued to visit the boy's grave, Detective Tom Augustine (of the Philadelphia Police Department) generated new interest in the case when he took charge of the investigation in 1998. Like Bill Fleisher, Detective Augustine also had seen the "Boy in the Box" poster in 1957. The detective had been eleven years old at the time and had no idea that he would grow up to investigate the murder himself. And now he had DNA, a new "tool in his toolbox."

Back in 1957 there was less reason for medical examiners to preserve samples of tissue or teeth or bone, as they do today. But in the early 1990s, as DNA became the legal means of human identification, medical examiners were encouraged to take samples from unidentified bodies and to keep the samples on file. The process worked well for recent deaths, but what about the bodies of unidentified persons who have been in the ground for years? An example, at the time, was the "Tent Girl," an unidentified young woman who had been found wrapped in a tent in Kentucky in 1968. She remained buried for nearly thirty years; then she was exhumed and her DNA extracted. In April 1998 her DNA (when compared with that of a family member who came forward) identified her as Barbara Ann Hackmann Taylor. Police, as well as members of the newly formed Vidocq Society, believed the "Boy in the Box" could be solved as well.

Bill Fleisher, as commissioner, had chosen the name Vidocq Society to honor Eugène François Vidocq, the world's first detective, a seventeenth-century French crook-turned-investigator. The notable historical figure has been described as a combination of Sigmund Freud, Giacomo Casanova, Harry Houdini, and J. Edgar Hoover. The Society is limited to eighty-two members, the number of years in Vidocq's life, although associate members and guests often round out their meetings. Vidocq Society members' specialties range from forensics to law, and they meet monthly at the Union League in Philadelphia for luncheons and presentations brought to them by law enforcement agencies. The organization's mission has always been to assist law enforcement with cold cases, so it was natural that they tackle one in their own backyard.

In 1998 the Vidocq Society arranged for a court order to exhume the boy's remains, and the FBI's Philadelphia Division Evidence Recovery Team assisted in the boy's exhumation. Using a backhoe and shovels, inmates opened the grave, raised the still-intact coffin, and then transferred it, with its fragile contents, to a waiting ambulance. At the morgue, the medical examiner found a small pile of degraded bones within the pieces of clothing that the boy had been dressed in so many years ago. Fortunately, one of the child's teeth was able to produce mitochondrial DNA that could be used for identifying the child.

On October 3, 1998, television host John Walsh profiled the boy's case on a segment of *America's Most Wanted*. The show generated 150 new "tips," but most were unsubstantiated. The most relevant, however, were from Detective Augustine's reinterview with the former foster home owners, as some of the tips came from viewers who, long ago, had been children living in the home. None, however, knew of any missing children or any boy matching the description of the "Boy in the Box."

A few weeks later, on Veterans Day, November 11, 1998, Commissioner Fleisher, Supervisor Kelly, and other members of both the Vidocq Society and the Philadelphia Police Department reinterred the boy in a more dignified setting, in the city's historic Ivy Hill Cemetery. With bagpipes playing, the men honored the boy with a new and larger headstone, carved with a lamb to symbolize innocence. They renamed him "America's Unknown Child." They also placed the boy's original gravestone at his new grave. Today, the joint memorials are immediately inside the stone gate at the cemetery's entrance.

JONATHAN, MAYBE?

The *America's Most Wanted* television program renewed interest in the case. In a recent interview, Commissioner Fleisher recalled one more tip that came in from the show. The call was from a woman who, as a child, lived on a specific street in a specific Philadelphia suburb. She was acquainted with another schoolgirl who had a young boy living in her house—a boy whom no one saw. The show's telephone operator wrote down the name of the street and the name of the suburb and gave the information to police, who filed it away.

Two years later, on February 25, 2000 (the forty-third anniversary of the boy's death), an Ohio psychiatrist called the Philadelphia Police Department to explain that one of his patients, a woman in her fifties, wanted to report a murder. The victim was a young boy who was killed, said the patient, by the patient's mother in Philadelphia in February 1957. When the police discussed the case with the psychiatrist, the patient appeared credible, but another two years went by before she was ready to talk.

In a 2003 interview for *Philadelphia* magazine, Supervisor Kelly explained that after verifying as much as he could of the woman's story, he, along with Detective Augustine and Investigator Joe McGillen from the Philadelphia Medical Examiner's Office, had driven to Ohio to visit her. Called "M" to protect her privacy, the woman remembered being twelve or thirteen years old at the time and driving with her mother to a house in another Philadelphia neighborhood. There, an unnamed woman opened the door and handed M a little boy in a soaked diaper, while M's mother gave the other woman an envelope of money. M and her mother took the boy home, where the mother shut the boy in the basement and never allowed him to be seen or to leave the house. According to M, the child was malnourished and abused, never spoke, and had something wrong with him, perhaps cerebral palsy.

M told the investigators that her mother had violently beaten the boy after he threw up baked beans in the bathtub. After the boy was dead, M's mother cut the boy's hair, wrapped him in a blanket and put him in the trunk of her car. M, tall for her age, with short hair and wearing a raincoat, went with them, and she remembered the route. When she and her mother stopped at what M called a "forlorn place," they got out of the car and stood by the trunk of the car. At the same time, a man stopped and asked if they needed help. They ignored him. Then her mother found an empty box and placed the boy in it. M never knew his real name, but she called him "Jonathan."

Supervisor Kelly confirmed that M had lived on the same street in the same suburb confidentially reported by the tipster after the *America's Most Wanted* show. The supervisor also reinterviewed the motorist who, shortly after the boy was found, had reported the woman and a "teenage boy" who had turned their backs on him when he offered help. From the back, the motorist could easily have mistaken the teenage "boy" for a girl.

If what M stated was true, then what investigators were told was a horrific story about a young boy purchased on the black market and then sadistically abused and killed. As stated in author Michael Capuzzo's book, *The Murder Room*, M also explained that her parents didn't have "normal" sexual desires. Instead, they both abused her, and her mother also abused the boy. As is the case with most sexual predators, M's mother's sexual gratification likely arose from a desire for power and control.

After Investigator McGillen (from the medical examiner's office) and the others met with M, McGillen worked up an extensive genealogy for her and her family in the hope that another family member would come forward. But M was an only child and, by the time of her interview, both of her parents were deceased. Still, M's story appears credible. Even if there were other family members, however, their DNA would be of no help in identifying the boy if it was true that the family and the boy were not biologically related. Meanwhile, according to Commissioner Fleisher, the police never believed M's story. At the time of this writing, the case is the longest actively worked homicide investigation in Philadelphia's history.

NEW HOPE FOR THE FUTURE

The passage of time may have helped in this case, as it allowed M, a new witness, to come forward. And new technology, specifically DNA, gave investigators a brand-new tool to use to try to find the boy's identity. In 1998, at the time the boy was exhumed, his DNA could only be used to compare with the DNA of an immediate family member, but none was found. Since technology has continued to evolve, however, today's investigators may be able to solve the case by using forensic genetic genealogy, discussed in chapter 9 on the "Hatbox Baby."

The word "forensic" simply means that the process has legal implications, such as identifying a person in a criminal case and obtaining evidence that will hold up in court. The phrase "forensic genealogy" became a household term with the 2018 arrest of the alleged "Golden State Killer," a serial killer-rapist-burglar in California. The unidentified assailant's DNA, taken from a rape kit, initially was uploaded to the personal genomics database GED-Match. According to a *New York Times* article from 2018, GED-Match identified ten to twenty of the suspect's distant cousins, all living and all sharing the same great-great-great-grandparents. A team of five investigators then worked with genealogist Barbara Rae-Venter to develop a composite family tree. They then worked their way through the tree (ruling out people along the way) to positively identify the suspect. (The "Golden State Killer" pleaded guilty in June 2020.)

For the "Boy in the Box," a similar strategy to identify the boy by identifying his relatives using genetic genealogy is the investigators' current best hope. In addition, the boy has been entered into the NamUs database, as well as the database of the National Center

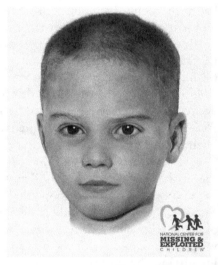

Figure 11.2. Facial reconstruction, "John Doe 1957."
This facial reconstruction for the "Boy in the Box" was prepared by an artist at the National Center for Missing & Exploited Children. COURTESY OF THE NATIONAL CENTER FOR MISSING & EXPLOITED CHILDREN

for Missing & Exploited Children. Both the police and the Vidocq Society still are very much involved.

Another reason for hope is that a new generation has embraced the boy, and this new generation involves the public. In June 2016, Boy Scout Nicholas Kerschbaum, from Troop 522 in Wilmington, Delaware, was in search of an Eagle Scout service project and turned to his father, Warren Kerschbaum, for advice. Warren, an Eagle Scout himself, as well as a retired Philadelphia police lieutenant, was familiar with the story of the boy's case and suggested the topic. Warren also put Nicholas in contact with Commissioner Fleisher at the Vidocq Society. Nicholas was the one, though, who came up with the idea to place a roadside historical marker at the site on Susquehanna Road where the boy's body was found. The marker is now on-site, but getting it there took a lot of determination.

The then-seventeen-year-old Salesianum High School senior petitioned the Pennsylvania Historical and Museum Commission for a state-sanctioned roadside historical marker. Although the state agency applauded Nicholas's research and preparation as "outstanding, well-presented and well-documented," its review panel turned him down, stating that, "Nominations seeking to simply commemorate those who died . . . are inappropriate for this program." Disappointed and disillusioned, Nicholas didn't take no for an answer. Instead, he persevered and arranged for a private marker to be placed at the site. In a recent interview, he reiterated, "The boy did not simply die. He was murdered or abused such that he died and then became a symbol of all murdered and abused children." He added, "My effort was to commemorate the location where the boy's body was found."

Nicholas then began to research private markers. He also reconnected with Commissioner Fleisher, who received permission from the Vidocq Society's Board of Directors to sponsor the project. To supplement the Society's financial assistance, Nicholas held a car wash and a bake sale. He also secured permission for the placement of the marker from the current landowner.

Dedication of the twenty-three-by-twenty-nine-inch roadside marker (on a pole six feet above the ground) was held on November 11, 2017, the year of the sixtieth anniversary of the boy's murder. Present that day was James Palmer, son of Elmer Palmer, one of the first Philadelphia police officers to arrive at the scene. James told a reporter that his dad always held out hope that before he died, the boy would be identified, and James credited Nicholas with tenacity and dedication. Also present was Officer Sam

Weinstein's widow, Sally. The dark blue marker, with gold lettering and gold border reads:

Vidocq Society, Philadelphia
AMERICA'S UNKNOWN CHILD
February 26, 1957, Police
Officers Elmer Palmer and
Samuel Weinstein responded to
the then rural Susquehanna
Road to investigate a report
of a body found in a box.
There they discovered the
naked, battered body of a small
boy believed to be 4 to 6 years
old. The unknown child became
known as the "Boy in the Box."
He has never been identified.
His case remains open.
He is now called
"America's Unknown Child."
Erected as an Eagle Scout Service Project by
Nicholas P. Kerschbaum, with the support of the Vidocq Society,
November 2017

Also at the dedication was Commissioner Fleisher, who stated, "It warms my heart to see a young man think enough of America's Unknown Child. It's a Herculean effort to get a plaque [marker]. I'm very proud of him. He makes the Boy Scouts and young men look good." In 2018, at the Vidocq Society's annual dinner, Commissioner Fleisher spoke of Nicholas's "sterling efforts" and presented him with his Eagle Scout Badge, along with letters of congratulations from Delaware's governor, senators, and a state representative.

As for Nicholas, he's hoping one day to become a pilot. He still lives in Wilmington, Delaware, and both he and his father continue to attend the annual November 11th memorial services at the Ivy Hill Cemetery as well as February services at the site of the marker on Susquehanna Road.

Figure 11.3. Grave of "Boy in the Box."
Nicholas P. Kerschbaum (left) posed in 2019 with Vidocq Society commissioner William L. "Bill" Fleisher (center) and Vidocq Society chaplain John Mullineaux (right) in Philadelphia's Ivy Hill Cemetery. The boy's new stone reads, AMERICA'S UNKNOWN CHILD, DEDICATED NOVEMBER 1998. PHOTO COURTESY OF WARREN KERSCHBAUM

And Nicholas will keep the local Boy Scouts involved as well. This younger generation is carrying the torch for the investigators and Vidocq Society members who preceded them. "America's Unknown Child" may never be identified, but he has found an extended family in those who have cared for and loved him throughout the many years ever since that day in 1957, when he had no more "little flame" to burn.

Connie Smith

Camper from the West

Unlike the "Boy in the Box," Connie Smith had an idyllic early childhood. When she was born in northeastern Wyoming on July 11, 1942, she and her three-year-old brother Nels J. lived with their parents on a large cattle ranch owned and operated by their father, Peter Smith. As the children got older, they shared chores, from gathering eggs to feeding the chickens and bringing in the milk cows. To the east were Wyoming's Black Hills, while the west opened up to the Powder River Basin dominated by one lone mountain, Inyan Kara, rich in history and sacred to the native people. The children were brought up with horses, and Connie loved to ride.

The children's grandfather, Nels H. Smith, was the state's governor at the time and was described in the local press as a "farmer, stockman, and businessman . . . with western ideas as to conservation and development." And the United States was involved in World War II.

Ten years later, in 1952, Connie, her brother Nels J., and their mother Helen Smith drove across the vast expanse of the Midwest and even north into Canada and then south to New England to visit relatives in Greenwich, Connecticut. While there, Helen enrolled her daughter for a month at Camp Sloane, in the foothills of the Berkshire Mountains of northwestern Connecticut. The boys and girls summer camp was, and still is, near Lakeville, within the town of Salisbury, in Litchfield County. Its tents and camp buildings are tucked into the rolling hills, fields, and woods, while canoes are neatly stacked on the shores of Wononpakook Lake. The camp experience was a first for Connie.

When Helen, brother Nels, and Helen's mother (Connie's grandmother) came for a visit on Sunday, July 13 (two days after the girl's tenth birthday),

Connie appeared to be enjoying the usual camp activities, which ranged from swimming and boating to horseback riding and square dancing. Her family then returned to Greenwich, approximately a two-hour drive. Five days later, Connie walked away from the camp. Despite intensive searches, both on the ground and in the air, all over the country, no trace of her or her whereabouts was found.

ROAD TO LAKEVILLE

At approximately 8:00 a.m. on Wednesday, July 16, 1952, Camp Sloane's gatekeeper watched as the ten-year-old girl turned onto Indian Mountain Road and then went north on the dirt road toward Lakeville. "I think she stopped to pick some flowers," the man later told police, adding that he didn't pay much attention to her, as he assumed she was one of the counselors.

Farther down the road, a man and woman out for a walk remembered seeing a girl later identified as Connie. Then, about a half-mile from the camp, a woman answered a knock on her door after a girl (also following Connie's description) asked for directions to Lakeville. The woman told her to continue up the hill and turn right. A day or two later, when interviewed by the police, the woman said she thought the girl had been crying, but she figured it was none of her business. "If only I had said something," she lamented when she found out that Connie had dropped completely from sight.

Two maids in a servants' residence were the next to give directions. Once Connie was on Route 44, the main road leading into Lakeville, a business-man and his wife passed her as she attempted to thumb a ride near the inter-section of Route 44 and Belgo Road. By then, she was approximately one and one-half miles from the camp and only a half mile from the Lakeville town center. It's likely she did get a ride, although where the driver took her may never be known. Hitchhiking in the 1950s was a lot more common than it is today, especially for a trusting young girl who was used to the wide-open spaces of her faraway home in Wyoming.

Obviously, something in Connie's world was wrong. When family and friends were interviewed in the days to come, some thought she had been homesick—a common occurrence for campers after a family visit. Apparently that wasn't the case, as she had asked her mother if she could stay longer but her mother said no. Did the western girl have an altercation with one, or more, of her eastern tentmates? Most of the campers came from East Coast states and, perhaps, were more sophisticated and citified.

Newspaper reports state that the night before Connie went missing, she had fallen down the steps of the wooden platform of her eight-person tent and bruised her hip. In the morning, a tentmate, whose legs hung over from a top bunk, was said to have kicked her, which gave her a bloody nose. And somewhere along the way, her glasses had become broken. The camp's telephone was off-limits to the campers, and maybe Connie hoped to make a collect call (on the closest pay phone, which, likely, was in Lakeville) to her mother or, perhaps, to her father back in Wyoming. Walking away from camp to make contact might have been tempting for the young girl.

The girls in Connie's tent, whether friendly or not, were the last people at the camp to see her. According to newspaper reports, all were questioned and none could offer a reason as to why she left the grounds. As the others were making their beds and readying their tent for inspection, Connie told them she was going to stop, before breakfast, at the camp's infirmary to return an ice pack. When her fellow campers returned from the mess hall, Connie's ice pack was still on her cot, and she was nowhere to be found.

Someone informed the gate-keeper (at Indian Mountain Road) that Connie was missing. The gatekeeper jumped in his car and drove to Lakeville and back, but he couldn't find her. Meanwhile, staff members frantically searched the camp, but they couldn't find her, either. Then, at 11:30 a.m., the camp director called the Connecticut State Police as well as Connie's mother, Helen, who received the news at her parents' home in Greenwich. She then telephoned Peter in Wyoming. By then, Connie's brother was back in Wyoming.

Although Peter Smith later theorized that maybe Connie had suffered from a touch of amnesia after her fall, the most likely scenario was that she accepted a ride

Figure 12.1. Connie Smith.
In July 1952, ten-year-old Connie Smith walked away from a summer camp in Connecticut. No trace of her has ever been found. PHOTO COURTESY OF NELS J. SMITH

by someone who did her harm. Still, her family maintained that it was out of character for her to ask directions several times as she made her way toward town. All that is known is that she was mature and independent for a ten-year-old, and she was wearing a bright red windbreaker, blue shorts with plaid cuffs, a halter top, and tan shoes and had her shoulder-length brown hair (with bangs) tied with a red hair ribbon.

INITIAL SEARCH

The Connecticut State Police was, and still is, responsible for law enforcement throughout the state of Connecticut, especially in areas not served by local police departments. Fortunately, one of the state police barracks was in the town of Canaan, less than ten miles from the camp. Police officers immediately searched the woods around the camp, then alerted radio stations and newspapers, and checked with local railroad stations, taxi services, and bus companies. The police also printed a missing-person flyer, with Connie's photo, and distributed multiple copies to law enforcement agencies in surrounding states.

Connie was five feet tall, weighed approximately eighty-five pounds, and was suntanned. Investigators believed that she carried no money, food, or extra clothes. She may, however, have had a black, zippered purse with photographs of friends. Mixed in with her physical description was a paragraph about her personality, which read,

> She loves all animals, especially horses; likes to swim and is a fair swimmer; likes to color with crayons and read funny [comic] books; makes friends very easily with youngsters; can handle a baton but is not very good at it; and has a vivid imagination, especially about her animal friends—some of her creations are about a rattlesnake pet and her horse "Toni" (a white mare) that can twirl a baton.

The Connecticut police stopped cars along the three-and-one-half-mile stretch of Route 44 between Lakeville and the New York state line. In the days before interstate highways, the two-lane, paved road was a major artery that connected Plymouth, Massachusetts (from the east), with several New York counties west of the Hudson River. Televised news was in its infancy, but word spread quickly through the newspapers.

On July 17, 1952, the day after Connie went missing, the Associated Press picked up the story and spread it all over the country, including in the *Casper Star-Tribune* in her home state of Wyoming:

Sundance, Wyo. (AP)—The father of a 10-year-old Sundance girl missing near a summer camp at Lakeville, Conn. left today to join in the search for his daughter. Relatives said Peter Smith, son of former Wyoming Governor and Mrs. Nels H. Smith of Sundance, left this morning for Lakeville after being advised of the disappearance yesterday of his daughter Connie. The child's mother and father are divorced. Mrs. [Peter] Smith telephoned the father of the child this morning to advise him of the little girl's disappearance. The father is a prominent rancher in northeastern Wyoming.

The *Hartford Courant* on Friday, July 18, ran an article titled "Father in Search for Missing Girl, Ex-Governor's Kin," explaining that Connie's father, Peter Smith, had flown from Wyoming to take part in the search. With his six-foot, seven-inch frame, he was immediately recognizable in a crowd. Unlike New Englanders, he wore a ten-gallon hat and "dungarees," long before blue jeans were fashionable. Connie's mother, Helen, also went to Lakeville immediately upon hearing the news.

Early newspaper reports made a point of emphasizing that Connie's grandfather (Peter's father) was a former governor of Wyoming, implying the prominence of the family and that Connie's search would be thorough and well financed. No one, however, demanded a ransom, but the family offered a three-thousand-dollar reward to anyone who could find her. In a move reminiscent of the 1942 film *Casablanca*, in which actor Claude Rains, as a Moroccan police captain, directed, "Round up the usual suspects," a reporter recapping Connie's case in July 1954 stated, "All of the known criminal suspects from miles around were gathered in by police. All were cleared."

Planes and helicopters belonging to the state police flew over roads, woods, and waterways. The first aerial search teams were quickly joined by search planes from the Connecticut wing of the Civil Air Patrol. Planes also flew in from Westover Field, Massachusetts, at the time the largest military air facility in the northeastern United States. Meanwhile, searchers with bloodhounds continued on the ground through the thick woods and underbrush, even speculating that Connie might have fallen into an abandoned, water-filled quarry or iron mine. Other searchers donned hip boots and waded through marshes. The ground-search teams kept in contact with the air searchers with portable two-way radios.

By Sunday, July 20, Connie's father, Peter, had chartered a plane of his own to supplement the searches already in place. But after two days, he called off the aerial part of his search, as thick foliage prevented him from seeing much of the ground below. Then he fruitlessly searched the woods on horseback. Five planes of the state police had already covered a twenty-square-mile area that included parts of northwestern Connecticut, southwestern Massachusetts, and eastern New York. When Connecticut State Police sergeant Richard Chapman, the first investigator on the scene, talked with a reporter, he said, "We just turned the place upside-down looking for her."

EARLY LEADS

Meanwhile (as the Philadelphia police did for the "Boy in the Box"; see chapter 11), the Connecticut police put out a "nationwide alarm" via teletype, which facilitated law enforcement agency communication. The police also prepared 1,100 circulars, which were distributed locally in stores, service stations, barber shops, and many other places of business. In addition, the circulars were mailed to police and sheriffs' offices all over the US as well as in Canada. Although the Connecticut State Police persevered, they soon found themselves faced with their own unsolved case as mysterious as that of eighteen-year-old Paula Welden, an art student missing from Bennington College, in Bennington, Vermont. In 1946 Paula was last seen thumbing a ride on Vermont Route 9 that connects with New York Route 22, a north-south road that parallels the eastern border of New York along Connecticut, Massachusetts, and Vermont.

As time went on, Connecticut State Police commissioner Edward J. Hickey was quoted in the *Courant Magazine* as he called for his men to work harder on the high-profile case. "I am not satisfied that this girl or any other young girl can disappear from the face of the earth for any long period, remain alive, and forsake all friendships long," he stated. "Dig a bit deeper in this case. Go into the woods again and go deeper. Search the waterways again and don't take anything for granted."

Newspaper readers, meanwhile, reported sightings of the missing child. One caller was sure he had seen Connie's face in a crowd at an Alabama football game. Another placed her with a New York band of gypsies who were working as itinerant barn painters and migrant laborers. A runaway from an Indian reservation in Massachusetts reportedly hitchhiked all the way to Texas. When police caught up with her, they found that she was not Connie. All leads, no matter how slim, were taken seriously and checked, without success. An anonymous caller who implied that Connie was dead told police to look in freshly dug dirt on top of someone else's grave. Connie's dental chart was published in the *Journal of the American Dental Association* in case it was needed to identify her remains.

Police undertook another aerial search in the fall, after the leaves were off the trees. In addition, three groups of six horseback riders from the Connecticut Trail Riders Association thoroughly covered a sixteen-square-mile area of brush and woodlands but turned up nothing. Connecticut game wardens, who patrolled the state's woods daily during hunting season, were given the missing-person flyers and told to be on the lookout for Connie's remains. Helen made a heartfelt appeal to the *Hartford Courant*, asking local hunters to search for any clothing that could be hers. "Each day is a little harder to face," she wrote. "We all know we might lose our children. But not to know what happened to her isn't human. Please do all you can."

Connie's missing-person case took an odd turn when the Smiths learned about Lady Wonder, a supposedly "clairvoyant" horse in Richmond, Virginia. For one dollar the horse's owner would allow three questions, and the horse would "reply" by pecking her nose on a crude typewriter. Supposedly, she had been asked the whereabouts of a missing four-year-old boy, and her answer, although not exact, led to the discovery of the boy's remains in a Massachusetts quarry. (Lady Wonder even fit into a Canadian case; see chapter 13.) Other communities also were known to have horses with psychic or similar abilities. Decades earlier, in Boulder, Colorado, "Mascot, the Educated Horse" entertained theatergoers by holding a piece of chalk in his mouth and then moving his head in front of a blackboard to write and "add" the numbers.

When Peter Smith asked Lady Wonder about Connie, the horse indicated that he look for her in Los Angeles, California. While there, Peter contacted police and reporters and even appeared with host Art Linkletter on his daytime variety television show, *House Party*. The show was a mixture of quizzes, musical groups, and celebrity interviews, but a well-known segment was "Kids Say the Darndest Things," in which the radio and television personality interviewed five- to ten-year-old children. While on the show, and assuming he had a sympathetic audience, Peter made a plea for help in finding his daughter. One viewer's reaction, however, threw the whole investigation into a tailspin.

FALSE CONFESSIONS

On April 8, 1953, a drunk man, Frederick Walker Pope, staggered into a police station in the town of Washington Court House, Ohio. Pope, a twenty-seven-year-old itinerant jewelry salesman, poured out a tale of murder. One of the victims, he said, was Connie. He explained that on July 16, 1952, he and his companion, Jack Walker, picked her up hitchhiking in Connecticut, and he offered to drive her to Wyoming. Then, after he deliberately went off course to Arizona, Pope said, his friend choked Connie to death, so he helped bury her.

Pope then said that he killed Jack Walker, sold his car, and ended up in a psychiatric hospital in Waco, Texas. When Pope showed up in Ohio, he told police, "I'm ready to go back to Arizona and point out the graves." Ohio and Arizona police were anxious to take him up on his offer, but the Connecticut police wanted more details and were skeptical when Pope couldn't remember a single town in Connecticut or the places he and the others stayed on their cross-country jaunt. One detail that Pope did talk a lot about was Peter Smith's height. "Connie was always talking about how tall her daddy was," he told a reporter. "She told me he was a real big man."

A police investigator then flew to Ohio and interrogated Pope for eight hours. Finally, when Pope emptied his pockets, the investigator noticed that he had a card from the Indiana Security Employment Division dated the day before Connie went missing. He couldn't have been in Connecticut when he said he had been. His story was proven to be a fraud, but it also was a cry for help. Pope said he had made up his confession in the hopes that he would be admitted to a hospital to help him overcome his alcoholism. He also explained that he had gotten most of his information on Connie from the missing-person flyer that he saw in a post office. When asked how he knew so much about Connie's father, Pope said he'd seen him on the Art Linkletter show. Of Peter Smith, Pope said, "He gave me my inspiration." And some have surmised that Pope's companion, "Jack Walker," was his whiskey.

Six years later, in 1959, the police received another "confession" from a Connecticut resident named George J. Davies. The garage mechanic had been on the police's radar since 1952, when he used a screwdriver to stab two young girls in the Waterbury, Connecticut, area. Both had refused his sexual advances, and both were found deceased. Initially, when Davies was asked about Connie, he denied ever seeing her. But in April 1959, while awaiting execution in the Connecticut State Penitentiary in Wethersfield, Connecticut, the "Screwdriver-Killer," as he was called, "confessed" to murdering Connie.

Whether Davies was just seeking attention or had actually committed the crime, however, was not known at the time. Again, as in the Pope case, the Connecticut State Police were skeptical. But the convicted felon did lead them to a sandy bank along a flood-prone river near Litchfield, Connecticut, where he claimed to have buried Connie in a shallow grave. A crew spent all day with hand and power shovels, as well as a bulldozer, but they failed to find any trace of her remains. A coroner told a reporter that if a body had ever been buried at that location, floods likely washed it away. Then, just as the killer was led to the electric chair, he asked to speak with state police lieutenant Wilbur Caulkins. "It was all a lie about Connie Smith," he told the lieutenant. "I raised the hopes of the girl's parents [for resolution] once before, and I don't want to do it again. I don't want to go with this lie on my conscience."

BACK TO ARIZONA

Although Frederick Walker Pope's long-winded tale of Connie being murdered in Arizona was a hoax, it did get the police, and also some family members, to realize the possibility that Connie could have been picked up and then driven across the country. In 1958, six years after Connie disappeared, the body of a teenage girl, estimated at between thirteen and seventeen years, was found north of Flagstaff, Arizona. She was believed to have been murdered and, when found, had been dead for approximately one year.

Called "Little Miss X," the girl's remains were buried in the Coconino County section of the Citizens Cemetery, in Flagstaff. The county section is a large, wide-open field ("full of bodies" say cemetery officials) with no gravestones or markers. At the time of this writing, the unknown girl still has not been identified.

In 1962, after a member of the public called in the suggestion that perhaps "Little Miss X" was Connie, the Connecticut police took a close look at the Arizona case. At the time, some of the unidentified girl's remains were exhumed so that a pathologist and a dentist could compare her teeth with Connie's dental records. Coconino County (Arizona) undersheriff Clark

Cole drove to Wyoming, with Little Miss X's skull and mandible in his car, to meet with Connie's father, Peter. The men continued on to Connie's former dentist in Spearfish, South Dakota.

According to a recent interview with Connie's brother Nels, Connie's dentist determined that four out of five points of identification matched. One filling did not match, but the dentist explained that an additional cavity could have been filled after Connie went missing and before the death of Little Miss X. On the undersheriff's drive home, he conferred with a pathologist in Denver, Colorado. Similarities were noted by both the dentist and the pathologist, but they said they were not enough to make a positive identification.

Newspaper reports from 1962 indicate that Undersheriff Cole returned to Flagstaff with the partial remains, but he neglected to leave records with either the Coconino County Sheriff's Office or the Coconino Superior Court as to the location of Little Miss X's grave. Perhaps, after he and his colleagues exhumed the partial remains, the men simply reburied them in the same grave. The undersheriff died in 1991 at the age of eighty. So far, no one has been found who can direct today's law enforcement officials to Little Miss X's burial site.

FAMILY STILL SEEKS RESOLUTION

Connie's mother, Helen Smith, died of a heart attack in 1961. Connie's grandfather, the former Wyoming governor Nels H. Smith, died in 1976. At the time, his grandson (Connie's brother), Nels J. Smith, was speaker pro tem of the Wyoming House of Representatives. Thirty-two years after Connie vanished, her father, Peter, was interviewed yet again regarding his search for his missing daughter. Peter always believed that she may have hit her head when she fell off the platform of her tent and kept open the possibility that she was still alive. "I think of her when I see a tall woman walk by who would be about her age," he told a reporter in 1984. "It's a perpetual hope that something will turn up." Peter Smith died in 2012, no doubt still hoping for his daughter's safe return.

According to the *Courant*, in a March 1988 article, the Connecticut State Police again reopened Connie's case after the arrest and conviction of a former Ferris wheel operator at a Pennsylvania carnival, in 1951, for the murder of an eight-year-old girl. When Connie's brother Nels was interviewed about the renewed interest in his sister's case, he stated, "The uncertainty of the disappearance is the worst agony that the family could go through. If this would resolve the case, it would be a relief." In 2004, Connie's brother gave his DNA to the Federal Bureau of Investigation. The agency entered it into CODIS, its national database, making it available for comparison with any remains thought to be Connie's, both then and in the future.

Hanging in brother Nels's Wyoming ranch home today is a painting by western artist Tim Cox that, to Nels, evokes his and Connie's childhood. Titled *Flowers for Mom*, a girl is seated behind a boy on a horse. The girl is clutching a bunch of yellow flowers, and both children are riding bareback. Although Cox created the painting in 1992 (forty years after Connie went missing), the poignancy of Connie's story and her relationship with her brother shines through. Added Nels, "The painting is so dead-on, even the halter is exactly the same type. It's just uncanny."

With today's advances in DNA technology, and an increasing number of unidentified remains being found, there's always the possibility that remains

Figure 12.2. *Flowers for Mom* painting.
Artist Tim Cox's painting hangs in Connie Smith's brother Nels J. Smith's home. For Nels it recalls memories of his childhood with his sister on a ranch in Wyoming. PHOTO COURTESY OF TIM COX AT TIM COX FINE ART (TIMCOX.COM)

yet to be unearthed could be Connie's. And with a more exact forensic analysis of Little Miss X's teeth (and also bones)—if they can be located in the cemetery in Flagstaff—there's also the possibility that the Arizona victim's remains could be identified as Connie's. But Connie would have had to have been alive for several years after she went missing, and the scenario, in the author's opinion, is unlikely.

Connecticut author Michael C. Dooling presented another theory in his book *Clueless in New England: The Unsolved Disappearances of Paula Welden, Connie Smith, and Katherine Hull.* In studying the cases of three young female hitchhikers, he surmised that both Paula and Connie, if not all three, may have been abducted and likely killed by the same perpetrator. If so, the abductor may have used New York Route 22 (a scenic route between Lakeville, Connecticut, and Bennington, Vermont) to his advantage in order to escape the local police. Perhaps someone with knowledge of the three disappearances may come forward.

There's also the possibility that, like "Boulder Jane Doe," who was buried for fifty years in a Boulder, Colorado, cemetery, Connie also could have been buried as a "Jane Doe" by a loving community. ("Boulder Jane Doe" was identified, in 2009, as Dorothy Gay Howard.)

So many questions remain as to why Connie left the camp and what may have happened to her on that fateful summer day. Her case remains open with the Connecticut State Police, and all agree that the independent young camper from Wyoming needs to be found and returned to her family in the wide-open spaces of the West.

PART 5

IN COLD BLOOD, AN
INTRODUCTION

This section covers three distinctively different murders. The first, in chapter 13, is the story of Marion McDowell, murdered and abducted from Toronto, Ontario. Next, in chapter 14, is the aerial sabotage of stunt pilot B. H. "Daredevil" DeLay, in Southern California. Also included in his chapter is mention of a sabotaged commercial airliner in Colorado in 1955. Chapter 15, set in Southern California, covers the Hollywood shooting death of silent film director William Desmond Taylor, also known by his birth name of William Cunningham Deane-Tanner.

In 1953 Marion McDowell's boyfriend watched in horror as a hooded man stuffed the bleeding seventeen-year-old into the trunk of the unknown man's car. No one ever found the young woman, either dead or alive. Although her case has gone cold (meaning there are no new leads), there's always the possibility that someone claiming knowledge of her disappearance will come forward or that her remains will be found and identified by DNA comparisons with her family members.

Proving who brought "Daredevil" DeLay's life of stunt flying to an end, however, may be next to impossible. The same holds true for identifying the man or woman who shot silent film director William Desmond Taylor. The murders of both men occurred in the early 1920s. For DeLay records are skimpy to nonexistent. As for the director, countless researchers and investigators have spent decades wading through tremendous amounts of Taylor-related documentation without identifying his assailant. A discussion of his case is not complete without including his brother's involvement—and a new twist.

Like journalists, investigators of cold case homicides try to answer the questions, Who? What? When? Where? Why? and How? In Marion's case, the answer to the "why" question—motive—may have been sexual assault. For DeLay someone (still unknown) must have acted on deep-seated resentment or hatred.

Investigators looking into director Taylor's cold-blooded murder need to figure out *why* he was killed and *who* had the means, opportunity, and motive to do so. That's easier said than done, although many have tried. Author and criminal justice professor R. H. Walton, in *Cold Case Homicides: Practical Investigative Techniques*, gives the main reasons for murder as "love, money or power, anger or rage, or retribution of a real or imagined wrong." Which one, or more than one, applied to Taylor's killer?

Marion Joan McDowell

Taken from Toronto

On a cold winter night near Toronto, Ontario, seventeen-year-old Marion Joan McDowell snuggled up to her boyfriend in his late 1940s model Plymouth coupe. The date was December 6, 1953, and the teens were parked off Danforth Road, north of Eglington Avenue East in Scarborough Township, now part of the eastern portion of the city of Toronto. The *Toronto Telegram*, one of the city's two major newspapers at the time, described the location both as a "lonely side road" and a "lovers' lane." A few other cars were parked nearby.

Suddenly, at 9:30 p.m. a hooded man with a gun yanked open the front door on the driver's side and ordered Jimmy Wilson, Marion's boyfriend, out of the car. Then the man struck Jimmy on the head, leaving him dazed and disoriented. When Jimmy regained consciousness, although still groggy, he realized he was sitting in the back seat of his own car with Marion, dead or unconscious, thrown on top of him.

The attacker climbed into the driver's seat and drove the couple, in Jimmy's car, to an abandoned farm one and one-half miles away. There, the man, still hooded and described by Jimmy as "short," lifted Marion from the blood-soaked car seat and stuffed her into the trunk of another car, "a black 1948 or 1949 model." Stunned, injured, and unable to be of any help, Jimmy saw the other car (with Marion in its trunk) drive away. When Jimmy was coherent enough to sit up and drive, he managed to get to his parents' nearby home. Together they went to the Scarborough Police Department.

Jimmy, a nineteen-year-old "rigger" for a scaffolding firm, was questioned at length. His two deep scalp wounds appeared to be from the handle of a pistol and required multiple stitches. As the last person to see Marion alive, he was considered a suspect, but it quickly became apparent to police that he couldn't have inflicted his head wounds on himself. Jimmy willingly agreed to take a lie detector test to help in the case and to clear his name. Police drove him to Buffalo, New York (two hours away), for the procedure. The polygraph technician at the Buffalo Police Department told a reporter that Jimmy "ran a good test" and that there was no reason to doubt his story. Despite massive searches throughout Canada, no trace of Marion ever has been found.

INITIAL INVESTIGATION

After the Scarborough police notified Marion's parents that their bleeding and apparently unconscious daughter had been abducted, the young woman's father, Ross McDowell, threw a coat over his pajamas and rushed out of the house to join police officers in their search. Marion's mother, Florence McDowell, was said to be nearly unconscious with grief. As in the disappearance of Connie Smith (see chapter 12), the girl's father worked alongside the police and aided in his daughter's search. In Marion's case, a dragnet extended from Toronto through most of Ontario and all across Canada.

For warmth, Marion had worn a headscarf. When investigators searched her boyfriend Jimmy's car, they found the scarf, bloody and with cuts in it, indicating that Marion had been struck on the head and, like Jimmy, pistol-whipped. In addition, police found a large amount of blood in the car but only later made public their belief that Marion had been murdered. According to a newspaper reporter, the police initially withheld that information from the teen's family (and the public) in order to spare the family additional grief. Marion's sweater, also left in Jimmy's car, was said to have "burrs" [prickly seeds or dried fruit] on the back. The early winter ground was dry and still free from snow, leading a Toronto *Telegram* reporter to write that the burrs on the sweater "led to the belief Marion was criminally assaulted [on the ground] while her companion was unconscious."

Apparently, there were other couples parked in the lovers' lane. What about them? What had they seen? It seems almost impossible that an attacker could have knocked out both Jimmy and Marion, and possibly assaulted the woman sexually, without anyone having witnessed something. After the police placed a plea in the newspapers for witnesses, reporters stated that two couples claimed that they hadn't seen anything, and a third couple never came forward. Could the attacker have knocked out Jimmy a second time and then assaulted Marion at the abandoned farm? Tragically, there was not enough evidence for anyone to figure out what type of weapon might have been used, let alone the likely sexual assault and what only can be described as, most likely, murder.

Marion's description was sent to all local newspapers and radio stations. The pretty seventeen-year-old with a roundish face wore her blond hair in bangs. Reporters also noted that she had blue eyes, good teeth, and was approximately five feet, three inches tall. She was wearing a black wool pleated skirt, a white blouse with blue or black trim, and black ballerina shoes. She also wore a silver-chain bracelet with a silver heart and a ring on her left hand with the initials "M. M."

Initial searches, the following day, were in the immediate area of the abandoned farm. Since police had not released the information about the amount of blood in the car, none of the searchers knew if they were looking for a body or for an injured woman held against her will. Marion's father joined police, firefighters, and volunteers as they searched farm buildings and shrubby streambeds. High school students and Boy Scouts were dismissed early from school. Under police supervision they searched, formed grid lines, and methodically walked across fields and climbed over fences looking on the still-dry ground for any clothing, clues, or even Marion's battered body. Police also appealed to service station and parking lot attendants to check the trunks of every car, just in case Marion was locked inside.

Meanwhile, local residents looked through barns and sheds and crawled under hedgerows. When advised of an approaching snowstorm, the searchers found themselves in a frantic race against time. Police brought in dogs and small airplanes and explored the area around the lovers' lane and the abandoned farm, but there was no evidence that Marion's body—if she was dead—would even be dumped nearby. She could have been driven miles away in any direction. Searchers were told to look for women's clothing, but the only items they found turned out not to be Marion's. The Scarborough police offered a thousand-dollar reward for either finding Marion alive, for finding her body, or for information leading to the arrest and conviction of her abductor and killer.

Marion's father, Ross, a factory foreman, also offered a thousand-dollar reward, although friends and family said that it was much more than he could afford. Quoted in the local newspaper, Ross told a reporter, "It's terrible. You want to find her, but you're afraid of what you're going to find." Meanwhile, as four-year-old Marjory West's mother had done in Pennsylvania (see chapter 10), Marion's mother appealed directly to her daughter's abductor. "Please,

please bring back Marion," she stated through the media. "I don't want any-
body punished. I just want her back."

ONGOING INVESTIGATIONS

The Ontario Provincial Police, like state police agencies in the United States,
also aided in Marion's case. Local police sent her bloodstained coat (also left
in Jimmy's car) to the provincial police laboratory for blood analysis. There
wasn't much that could be learned in the 1950s, other than whether or not
the blood was human and, if it was human, the blood type. Tests revealed that
the blood type was the same as Jimmy's. No one knew Marion's blood type,
but it may have been the same as her boyfriend's. If Marion had fought her
attacker, his blood also might have been on her coat. Brief mention was made
of dusting for fingerprints on the door handle of Jimmy's car, but no fingerprints were found, indicating that the attacker probably had worn gloves.

Reporters, and likely the police, too, compared Marion's abduction to the
unsolved disappearance in 1950 of Mabel Crumback, a nineteen-year-old
young woman who vanished, in the middle of the night, from her home in
another section of Toronto. Trying everything that might help them find their
daughter, Mabel's family did what Connie Smith's father did (see chapter 12)
and contacted the owner of Lady Wonder. The "clairvoyant" horse's typed-
out response to Mabel's whereabouts was that the young woman was living
in Maine. Mabel's mother made some inquiries, but, like Marion, Mabel has
never been found. Were the two cases related? No one knows.

Two days after Marion's abduction, the Scarborough police began
combing through Marion's address book. They systematically checked each
of her friends, including several former boyfriends, referred to by a reporter
as "motorcycle enthusiasts." Marion must have been a popular girl. Within
four days, police investigators interviewed two hundred of her friends and
acquaintances. When none could come up with any leads, the police interviewed some of the same people again. One of Marion's aunts even offered
to act as a confidential go-between for any of Marion's girlfriends who might
have something to say (especially about the boyfriends) but were too scared
to share with police. After clearing everyone, the police came to the conclusion that Marion's abductor was a total stranger.

Investigators also explored the possibility that the attacker had recently
been released from prison and/or a mental hospital. They checked and
rechecked their files on all known sex offenders but didn't come up with any

likely suspects. Finally, they settled on the premise that the stranger was a "sex maniac" and possibly a "drifter." Meanwhile, police held out hope for the third couple to come forward from the lovers' lane.

Marion and Her Family

Marion had attended East York Collegiate, a combination high school and vocational school. She dropped out of school to work in a bank before taking a job as a junior typist in the sales office of a Toronto photoengraving firm. Her coworkers called her a hard worker and stated that she was devoted to her family. According to news reports, Marion earned thirty-eight (Canadian) dollars per week, lived with her parents, and paid them room and board. Her twenty-one-year-old brother was married and had moved out of the house.

There were only four women who worked in Marion's office. Two weeks after her abduction, one of the remaining three young women, a friend of Marion's, was strangled. Police arrested the woman's husband and took him into custody. He may have been guilty of the coworker's murder but, after questioning, police were confident the two crimes were unrelated. The two very frightened women left in the office wondered who would be next. Meanwhile, cranks terrorized Marion's parents with telephone calls, cruelly causing them to live in fear but also giving them false hope. One caller said he had Marion and would kill her. Another demanded a ransom of fifty thousand dollars, an amount completely impossible for the family to provide even if they sold their modest house and everything they owned.

Interest from Abroad

Again raising the family's hopes, a Canadian psychic came forward and led police to a town northeast of Toronto where Marion's body was believed to be, but it wasn't there. An astrologer then claimed that Marion's body was submerged underwater near a stone bridge. The allegations sparked an editorial in the *Toronto Daily Star*, on December 18, 1953, that recalled the previous disappearance from Toronto of Canadian millionaire and theater magnate Ambrose Small. In December 1919, he (like Judge Joseph Force Crater; see chapter 1) completely vanished in a big-city crowd. Consulted at the time of his disappearance was Scottish author Sir Arthur Conan Doyle, creator of the greatest of all fictional detectives, Sherlock Holmes. In addition to writing books, Doyle also promoted spiritualism, the belief that spirits of the departed continue to exist in the hereafter and can be contacted by those still living. After Ambrose Small disappeared, Doyle held a séance in Toronto but was unsuccessful in reaching the missing man.

Psychic-inspired leads to find Marion proved fruitless, so the police reverted to traditional investigations, but suddenly they were forced to compete with an independent and flamboyant investigator, an Englishman named Robert Fabian. The fifty-five-year-old retired detective from London's famed Scotland Yard (headquarters of the London Metropolitan Police) was hired by the Toronto *Telegram*. He flew to Canada, publicly stating his intention to solve Marion's disappearance. Already on tour for his recent book, *Fabian of the Yard: An Intimate Record*, newspapers in both the United States and Canada announced that the "world's greatest detective," as he was called, was promoting a British television series of the same name.

Fabian, who insisted that he solely be called by his last name, landed in Toronto in August 1954, eight months after Marion's abduction. The whole front page of the August 11, 1954, issue of the *Telegram* featured the dapper but stern-faced investigator, photographed in his bowler hat and overcoat. Readers soon learned that he had joined the famed London police force in 1921, solving cases in England that included the "Black Butterfly" and the "Witch of Meon Hill." He was considered "a devil to work for" and his motto was, "Keep your eyes and ears open and use your brain."

So how was his involvement going to help Marion's family and provide new information to the Scarborough and the Ontario Provincial Police? According to reporters at the *Toronto Star* (the *Telegram*'s main competitor at the time), both police agencies saw Fabian as an interference and predicted that he would not be able to find any new leads. He didn't, but his presence, along with sensationalized reporting, did result in increased newspaper sales for the *Telegram*. "If anyone can do it, Fabian can," announced one of the August 1954 headlines for an article that summarized Marion's disappearance, heralding the renowned investigator as the "champion of champions." His slightly more modest comment was, "Perhaps I'll be lucky."

Reportedly, Fabian visited and reconstructed the crime scenes and then, oddly, differed from local police by concluding that no stranger to the area had been responsible for Marion's attack and abduction. The possible suspect, according to the famed detective, was someone Marion had known, described as "a man about 30 years of age, five-feet-eleven inches tall, about 168 pounds, good-looking, fair, with a tanned face and a powerful physique." No one like that was found, and Fabian did not state any basis for his description.

Fabian then pondered a motive, but he finally agreed with police that the perpetrator, in his words, was a "sex fiend." Then he upped the *Telegram*'s circulation and countered the police's still-under-wraps murder conclusion by theorizing that Marion might still be alive. "There are a good many indications she is dead," he said, "but the time has not yet come for me to make up my mind that I am looking for a murderer." Instead, he announced that he was eager for new information.

A reporter for the *Telegram* wrote that, from 12 noon to 1:00 p.m. and from 7:00 p.m. to 8:00 p.m., Fabian himself would answer a special phone line: Empire 3-4516. "Somebody knows a lot about this case," Fabian told the press, "and I'm ready to listen to anonymous phone calls or any other kind." One came from a "Mr. H.," who said that his son had been parked behind the car containing Marion and "he had taken the license number of the car in which she was said to have been abducted." Mr. H. didn't say if his son was at the lovers' lane or at the abandoned farm, but police still were anxious to hear from any possible witnesses. If Mr. H's lead was credible, and if his son did have the abductor's license plate number, that information might very well have led to finding Marion as well as her killer. But nothing came of it, for reasons that only surfaced more than three decades later.

In the 1980s, the former reporter for the *Telegram* (who had been assigned to Fabian in 1954) made a confession. When the reporter was interviewed, he said that he had made up the comments attributed to Fabian, calling the famed detective's investigation "facts from a Scotch bottle." As the reporter explained, he had been a young writer at the time, and his editor had asked him to come up with two stories per day on Fabian's progress. He and Fabian quickly fell into a routine. "Each day he [Fabian] advertised that he would be by the phone for two hours," stated the reporter. "The rest of the time, he and I, in a chauffeured limo, would wander about Scarborough or the red-light district or the vicinity of the Don Jail [a provincial jail in Toronto], setting up pictures for the next day. In the evening, we would retire to his hotel suite, pour a couple of scotches, order in steaks and invent stories for tomorrow's edition."

Fabian, with his eager reporter at his side, put on quite a show and probably sold lots of books while upping the readership of the *Telegram*. Surrounded by youthful admirers, he signed their autograph books and was photographed with pipe in hand. Portrayed as the embodiment of Sherlock Holmes, he insisted that he was checking every detail and definitely was on track to solve the case. Then, suddenly, on September 4, 1954, less than a month after he arrived, Fabian quit the case and flew away.

LATER YEARS

By the time Fabian left Toronto, Marion's family had been put through an emotional roller coaster. Her mother was hospitalized and in seclusion following a nervous breakdown, and her father had moved in with his mother-in-law. Meanwhile, Marion's brother, Ross McDowell Jr., joined the East York Police Department (a division of the Toronto Police Service) in what would, for him, become a lifelong career and a lifelong, but fruitless, search for his sister. In recent years, a family member related that Marion's father never spoke of her until fifty years later when he broke down in tears and said the worst part of the ordeal was that he probably would go to his grave without ever knowing what had become of his beautiful daughter.

Articles published decades after Marion's abduction reinforced the fact that the likelihood of its resolution had faded into the past. A 1986 obituary of Sergeant Norman Brickell, the officer on duty the night Marion was abducted, stated that her case was the one case of his career that haunted him most of all. Inspector Harold Adamson, who had organized what then was the largest search in Toronto's history, died in 2001. With his passing, the Toronto newspapers again reflected on the lack of any clues whatsoever in the then nearly half-century-old mystery.

Today, Danforth Road has become a four-lane paved thoroughfare. With its share of businesses, schools, libraries, and parks, it is surrounded by tidy residential neighborhoods of mostly single-family brick homes. As the landscape changed from rural to urban, Scarborough Township became absorbed into the larger metropolitan area and now occupies the eastern portion of Toronto. Few residents even recall the name of Marion McDowell, much less Ambrose Small and Mabel Crumback, except, of course, descendants of their families and readers of true crime.

Ambrose Small may have walked away and started a new life, or he may have been murdered. Judging from the amount of blood found in Jimmy Wilson's car, Marion *was* murdered. But why was she struck and abducted, and where are her remains? No one knows, except her attacker, who was free to walk the streets and kill again. As for Mabel, her disappearance was less publicized, but mystery still surrounds her as well. The abduction of Marion McDowell, as well as these other Toronto-area residents, remains unsolved.

14

"Daredevil" DeLay

Aerial Sabotage

Also unsolved is the murder of Beverly Homer DeLay, but he wasn't beaten or shot. Instead, his airplane was rigged, causing him to fall to his death. "Daredevil" DeLay, as he was known in the silent-film era, was an aviator and actor who thrilled audiences in air shows and in Hollywood films. On the Fourth of July 1923, a stunned crowd watched as DeLay flew to an altitude of two thousand feet and then started a series of long graceful loops, a stunt he had performed many times. Suddenly, his plane nose-dived. When it hit the ground, both DeLay and his passenger were dead.

Fliers from nearby Clover Field (now the Santa Monica, California, airport) jumped into their automobiles and rushed to the scene, where they pulled the men's bodies from the wreckage just before it burst into flames. The next day, horrified spectators read in their newspapers that what they had witnessed was an "air murder." In examining what was left of the wreckage, investigators from the Los Angeles Police Department found that substandard-size pins (three-eighths of an inch) had replaced the standard one-half- or three-quarter-inch pins used to hold the wings of DeLay's Curtiss "Jenny" biplane to its frame. The plane had been flown many times by its seasoned pilot.

Perhaps DeLay's claim—and climb—to fame and fortune came too quickly. But in the beach communities near Los Angeles, the Roaring Twenties had begun and "Daredevil" DeLay, both before and after his death, held a certain mystique.

FORMATIVE YEARS

In 1891, at the time of Beverly Homer DeLay's birth, "Beverly" was considered a man's name. Shortly after the turn of the twentieth century, the name came into common use for women. In fact, when the aviator's second daughter was born in 1919, he named her "Beverley," with an extra "e." In this chapter, to eliminate gender and generational confusion, we'll refer to Beverly Homer DeLay by his last name. He grew up in the San Francisco, California, area and was the son of Charles Young DeLay, a mining engineer. Initially, the boy followed in his father's footsteps, until his aerial interests took him from under the ground to up in the air.

When young DeLay was a boy and the aviation and automobile industries were in their infancies, he grew up fascinated with both. In 1903, when he was twelve years old, he no doubt read about Orville and Wilbur Wright's invention of the world's first motor-operated airplane. That same year, Henry Ford incorporated the Ford Motor Company and assembled his first automobile. Then in 1908, Ford began producing Model Ts. Meanwhile, the Stanley Motor Carriage Company developed several steam-powered automobiles, including race cars for competitions at Daytona Beach, Florida.

With rapidly changing advances in transportation going on all around him, DeLay developed a taste for speed before he was twenty years old. Between 1909 and 1911, he competed in stock-car road races based in Oakland, California. Each race lasted for approximately four hours as the race cars wound up, down, around, and through 254 miles of Alameda County communities. DeLay crashed his car in one of the races, but it didn't slow him down, even as he broke multiple bones and suffered a broken leg that resulted in a slight limp.

In 1914, after the advent of World War I (then called the Great War), aviation advancements really took off. Around this time, DeLay learned to fly. Also, he married Juanita Smythe, another Bay-area native. By 1917 the couple and their first daughter, Patricia, had moved to Vicksburg, in southwestern Arizona, where his father managed a gold and copper mine. There, perhaps because he needed the work to provide for his family, DeLay got a job as an assayer.

According to DeLay's World War I draft registration card, which he filled out in June 1917 while still in Arizona, he described himself as twenty-six years old, medium in height, and with a slender build, black hair, and gray eyes. In answer to a question that asked whether he had any disabilities, he wrote, "Yes, left leg crippled." Although he registered, he did not serve in the war. DeLay didn't stay long at the mine, as the promising new field of aviation pulled him back to California.

Flying High

At the war's conclusion, in November 1918, US Army brigadier general Billy Mitchell gave the aviation industry a boost by stating, "The day has passed when armies on the ground or navies on the sea can be the arbiter of a nation's destiny in war. The main power of defense and the power of initiative against an enemy has passed to the air." The public, too, looked to the air and excitedly entered a new transportation age. Without a war to fight, the federal government found itself owning a surplus of airplanes, particularly single-engine two-seater Curtiss "Jenny" biplanes. Anyone with three hundred dollars could get one, and buyers like DeLay snapped them up.

By this time, DeLay had been flying for five years, having started prior to his year or so in Arizona. He became a skilled pilot, landing jobs in the

Figure 14.1. B. H. "Daredevil" DeLay.
"Daredevil" DeLay is shown here, in the cockpit of his Curtiss "Jenny" biplane, probably before one of his stunt-flying performances. PHOTO COURTESY OF SHAWNA KELLY AND WIKIMEDIA COMMONS

middle of the silent-film era. As the words "silent film" imply, the motion pictures had no spoken dialogue, although they often were accompanied by live piano music. Scenes were separated by a sentence or two of written dialogue, but the plot needed action to hold the audiences' attention. Along with several of his contemporaries, DeLay had taken up stunt flying and kept his audiences on the edges of their seats.

DeLay and his contemporaries also raked in the money from their fans. He charged forty dollars per hour for "wing walks," previously the specialty of his colleague, Ormer Locklear, who died when his plane exploded into a fireball during the filming of *The Skywayman*. Another stunt was called "loop-the-loops," in which DeLay flew his plane in complete vertical circles, sometimes including a chimpanzee as his passenger. Not to be outdone, another aviator, Roscoe Turner, flew from Canada to Mexico with a pet lion cub named Gilmore. When the big cat outgrew Turner's cockpit, he was retired and pampered with fine food for the rest of his life.

Before long, DeLay accepted the position of manager for the Ince Airfield in Venice, California. Owner and movie producer Thomas H. Ince, described by film historian Marc Wanamaker as the "Father of the Western," already had made a name for himself writing and directing films at the outdoor-movie-set town that he named Inceville, located up the coast from Venice, between Santa Monica and Malibu. It was there, in 1913, that Ince had given stage actor William Desmond Taylor his first taste of movie acting, prior to Taylor also becoming a director (and a murder victim) in the motion-picture business (see chapter 15).

In 1920 DeLay moved up in the flying community and purchased the Ince Airfield. After renaming it the DeLay Airfield, he turned the location into the premier headquarters for Hollywood movie aviation. Between 1919 and 1922, air show attendees and thrill seekers demanded even more action. In addition to the shows, DeLay starred in more than fifty films, some of which were produced by Ince and filmed at the DeLay Airfield. In the 1922 film *Skin Deep*, seventeen years before the invention of the helicopter, an actor portraying an innocent convict escaped from the roof of a moving train by climbing a rope ladder that DeLay lowered from his plane, while in flight.

DeLay, in other films, also scooped up an actor from a running horse as well as from a moving automobile. He even rescued a heroine from the top of a burning building. And in an eerie foreshadowing of the 2001 attack on New York's World Trade Center, he was the first to be filmed using an airplane to knock down a building.

The 1920s movie theater audiences also craved newsreels, the true-life short films of news events that were shown before the beginning of feature films. Often, the newsreels started with DeLay and other adventurous aviators "buzzing" crowds at air shows. Many in the crowd had never been in a plane, much less flown in one, and they were awestruck by what they saw. The shows turned into nail-biters when DeLay and the other pilots looped, rolled, pulled out of tailspins, and, sometimes, even hung from the wings. With beacons lighting up the night skies and cinematographers pushing hand-cranked movie cameras on large dollies, the excitement and expectations of the audiences were lifted higher and higher into the sky.

DANGERS AND DISCONNECT

With all of the dangers associated with stunt flying, someone needed to look out for the safety of the aviators, and it appears that DeLay led the way. In 1921 he made the DeLay Airfield (the former Ince Airfield), in Venice, California, the first airport in the country to install lights on the field. He also established a movie-stunt-pilot training school. Meanwhile, the city of

Figure 14.2. *Skin Deep* film advertisement.
This excerpt from the publication *The Silver Sheet* advertises the 1922 film *Skin Deep* in which "Daredevil" DeLay rescues an escaped convict from a moving train. PHOTO FROM WIKIMEDIA COMMONS

Venice received the distinction of being the first municipality in the country to establish a "life-saving aerial corps." As a reporter for the *Pasadena Post* explained, an aviator in the shorefront town was on duty at all times "with a plane equipped with life buoys to go to the rescue of any bather [swimmer] in distress."

According to the same newspaper reporter, Venice also was the first community to prohibit, above its city limits, the transportation of liquor in airplanes (as well as in balloons and dirigibles and even with parachutes). Only a year earlier, the United States had enacted the National Prohibition Act, banning the manufacture and sale of alcoholic beverages. Even though illegal liquor still flowed, Venice's new law extended the federal government's anti-liquor sentiment to the air.

DeLay may have promoted a safe airfield, with trained and sober pilots who looked after the welfare of others, but his management didn't satisfy the California State Legislature. In 1921 the lawmakers prohibited stunt flying over all California cities and towns. An editorial writer in a Quincy, California, publication in November 1921 stated that the new regulation was a step in the right direction, but he wanted to see stunt flying eliminated altogether. "Sane flying is one of the safest of sports, and an airplane flown in an upright position by a competent pilot offers one of the safest modes of transportation," stated the writer. "The great trouble is that one never reads of aviation in the newspapers except of an instance where fliers are killed."

Ormer Locklear's crash in *The Skywayman* in 1920 had been just one of several accidental aerial deaths that made the press. A few months before the editorial writer took pen to paper, a stunt pilot in Huntington Beach (south of Los Angeles) went into a nosedive and slammed his "Curtiss machine" into a bathhouse on a crowded beach. Instantly killed was a twenty-one-year-old man who was struck by flying debris from the plane's propeller. A witness stated that several women fainted, and others were thrown to the ground by the panicked crowd. According to another newspaper reporter several weeks later, neither the pilot nor his passenger was expected to live.

Behind all the fascination of the masses for Hollywood's aerial movie productions, hostilities arose at the DeLay Airfield, possibly over the ownership of DeLay's expanding assets. Brief mention in the press alluded to DeLay having "a number of enemies." If so, what better way was there for one of them to commit murder than to make the pilot's death appear as an accident?

Murder and Its Aftermath

Stunt flying, or "aerobatics," as the practice sometimes was called, was a dangerous profession, particularly in its early days. Accidents weren't frequent, but, tragically, they happened. The phrase "aerial sabotage," however, was a brand-new concept when DeLay's plane went down.

The day after the crash of DeLay's plane, a reporter for the *Los Angeles Daily News* wrote, "Murder plot is seen in crash of plane and death of two." The statement had been made, to police, by a friend of DeLay's, and it initiated an investigation to determine whether DeLay and his passenger, Ruel I. Short, were victims of a murder conspiracy. The friend told police that hostilities had been building for some time, and other attempts had been made on DeLay's life. Allegedly, an unknown man previously had tried to ambush and shoot the pilot while he walked alone near his airfield. On July 7, 1923, another reporter, in an article titled "Air Murder Seen in Tragic Smash of Flyer's Plane," explained that after DeLay dived into a loop, one of his plane's wings collapsed "with the first real strain upon the machine."

According to author D. D. Hatfield, in his book, *Los Angeles Aeronautics 1920–1929*, DeLay and his lawyer had confronted a man in court in 1921 with regard to an ownership dispute of the DeLay Airfield. Allegedly, the man had "a couple of his thugs plant posts in DeLay's airport so that planes could not take off." After DeLay and his crew removed the posts, the gang dug trenches. DeLay's new ownership of the former Ince Airfield (including hangars and airplanes) must have created jealousies and conflicts among those with whom he interacted on a daily basis.

In a much more recent article in the *Los Angeles Times*, in 2010, Shawna Kelly, a great-granddaughter of DeLay and the author of *Aviators in Early Hollywood*, agreed that DeLay's murder may have been related to the "ruckus" (likely the airfield property dispute) that broke out between DeLay and the man, or men, who disputed his ownership. Shawna also speculated that the killer may have had a more personal connection. Repeating what was likely passed down through family lore, she stated that DeLay had engaged in several extramarital affairs and, "on one occasion, he faced down the gun of an angry wife." (Whether she was his wife or a jilted lover is not known.) It's also possible that movie plots had blended into real life, making it difficult to separate fact from fiction.

But what about DeLay's passenger, an automobile accessory manufacturer who appeared to have only been along for the ride? Did he have any enemies? The press barely mentioned him. Both men were only thirty-one years old, and both left behind wives and young children. As to who was responsible for their deaths, no one knows. No known suspects were brought forward, and no one ever was charged.

After the crash that ended the two men's lives, the DeLay Airfield was dismantled and redeveloped. Most of the aviators moved their hangars to Clover Field. According to DeLay's family's wishes, he was cremated and given what the *Long Beach Telegram* termed an "aerial burial." On Memorial Day, in 1924, another pilot flew DeLay's mother, Matilde DeLay, over the Pacific Ocean, where she scattered her son's ashes.

Many changes would come to Hollywood in the years following DeLay's death. The year 1928 saw the first productions of "talkies," films with soundtracks that included spoken dialogue. But DeLay was not forgotten, especially by Dick Grace, a friend, fellow pilot, and stunt flier. He also was a novelist who highlighted aerial murder in his book, *The Lost Squadron,* which he adapted into a fictional film that featured four pilots who all took up stunt flying at a California airfield.

The film's plot centered on the murder of one of the pilots after a jealous husband (none other than a tyrannical film director) tampered with the safety of one particular pilot's airplane by applying acid to the plane's control wires. In the movie, the pilot was alerted, but before he could get to his plane, another of the pilots unknowingly took off in the sabotaged plane. He crashed and died.

Was the author and screenwriter of *The Lost Squadron* making a veiled accusation against a former film director, perhaps even Thomas H. Ince? The film is still available, so heed, if you wish, this spoiler alert that concludes with some additional intrigue. In the film, yet another of the four stunt-fliers shoots the director and then stuffs the man's corpse into the cockpit of a fully functional plane. The fourth of the stunt pilots (screen idol and star Richard Dix) then flies the plane into the night sky in an attempt to save his fellow pilots by willingly taking the blame for shooting the director. Then he deliberately crashes the plane.

ANOTHER AERIAL MURDER: UNITED AIRLINES FLIGHT 629

Readers interested in aerial murder can fast-forward thirty-two years from the sabotage of DeLay's biplane to 1955. That year saw the first case of aerial sabotage of a commercial aircraft, when forty-four passengers and crew perished on a Douglas DC Mainliner, United Flight 629. On Tuesday, November 1,

1955, the passenger plane left Chicago, Illinois, for Seattle, Washington, with a stop in Denver, Colorado. There, only one passenger, Daisie King, boarded the plane. Eleven minutes after takeoff from Denver's Stapleton Airport, a bomb (planted in Denver by her son, John Gilbert Graham) exploded in her luggage, bringing down the entire plane in an empty field north of Longmont, Colorado, and killing everyone on board.

Graham had disguised twenty-five sticks of dynamite, two blasting caps, and a timer in a box that looked like a Christmas present. At the airport he took out a $37,500 life insurance policy on his mother and even paid an additional baggage fee when Daisie was told that her bag was overweight. Then, Graham and his wife waved good-bye to the unsuspecting woman as the airliner pulled out from the gate. Graham eventually confessed, and, in an effort to speed up his trial, he was only charged with the premeditated murder of one person, his mother. His motive was a combination of deep-seated resentment along with greed for money. In January 1957, he was executed in the gas chamber at the Colorado State Penitentiary. His last words were, "I will see my mother tonight."

Air travel had drastically changed between the 1920s and the 1950s, yet the mindsets of these aerial saboteurs were very much the same. Apparently, both had only one victim in mind when the killers caused the planes to crash, having complete disregard for the others they knew would die. There's no reason to believe that whoever tampered with DeLay's plane had any grudge against DeLay's passenger, yet he also became a victim. And Graham obviously didn't care about the forty-three other people (and their families) or his mother.

The tragedy was referenced in *The FBI Story*, a 1959 film starring James Stewart, but there's never been a memorial to those who died. Graham's mother and others on her plane have been forgotten by the public. Also swept into the past is DeLay's passenger. Meanwhile, the murder of the daring and seemingly fearless pilot known as "Daredevil" DeLay remains a mystery, while his murderer simply walked (or flew) away.

William Desmond Taylor and His Brother

Double Blood Bond

Hollywood movie director William Desmond Taylor shot more than sixty silent films, but none of the plots on the silver screen had the lasting intrigue that surrounded the drama of his own murder. A servant found the forty-nine-year-old lying on the floor of his home on February 1, 1922. William had been shot in the back, but the last moments of his life were overshadowed by the glitz and glamor of Hollywood, California, celebrities, many of whom became suspects. Their opulent lifestyles included an excess of drinking, drugs, and romantic intrigues that comingled with a sensationalized press and an incompetently run investigation. In reality, fiction got so mixed up with facts that the press, at least, could no longer differentiate between the two and reported on both.

Now, a century later, there still are multiple theories as to who fired the fatal shot, including a whole parade of Hollywood characters and even the mother of a lovesick actress. Taylor's murder isn't likely to be solved, as no evidence—not even the .38 caliber revolver that killed him—ever was found. Was the murderer his lover or a jealous spouse, or did the butler do it? The cast of players from this long-ago crime also are dead, but the whodunit mystery lives on.

Lost in the seemingly endless parade of multiple suspects, however, was the dashing and debonair man himself: the director who seemed a perfect fit within the Hollywood scene. But he had led a double life, and only in death was his true identity revealed to the public.

Behind the Scenes: Act I

William Desmond Taylor was the assumed name of William Cunningham Deane-Tanner, the eldest son of a wealthy British army officer. Born in 1872, William was a young man when he emigrated from his native Ireland to the United States, eventually settling in New York City. In 1908 he left his wife and daughter and mysteriously disappeared—only to burst upon the silent screen a few years later, under the name of William Desmond Taylor. His brother, Denis Gage Deane-Tanner, would follow him to New York City, where he, too, would ultimately disappear. From then on, Denis lived in William's shadow, and their lives became uncannily intertwined.

As a child, William was expected to follow in his father's footsteps. By the age of eighteen, however, he had developed an interest in acting and performed onstage in England, in a play. According to Robert Giroux, author of *A Deed of Death: The Story Behind the Unsolved Murder of Hollywood Director William Desmond Taylor*, William's acting so angered his father that in 1890, the father banished his son to an Irish-run "colony," in faraway Kansas. Called Runnymede, the pseudo boarding school in midwestern America was a place for wealthy British families to send their sons to begin careers as gentlemen farmers. Years later, when a reporter interviewed William, he mentioned his one and one-half years on the frontier and said he enjoyed the time he spent riding horses. But horses couldn't compete with acting, and Runnymede, as an outpost for compatriots, was near collapse anyway.

Cut off from his father's support at age twenty, William struck out on his own and bounced around the central and western United States from one job to another. He may have traveled back to Ireland in 1893. A "William Tanner" showed up that year on a ship passenger list. In the mid-1890s, however, he definitely was in New York, where he signed a three-year contract with an acting company.

Perhaps money from working onstage financed round-trip passage to his homeland in style, as he returned to New York, again, in 1897. By today's standards, the SS *Mongolian*, the British steamship on which he traveled, was small. Its engines, with one smokestack, were supplemented by two-hundred-foot masts for sails. William was twenty-five at the time, his listed occupation was "gentleman," and he was one of only eight people who traveled in cabin, also called first, class. He and his fellow first-class shipmates could move freely on the ship's only deck. In contrast, fifty-seven men and women, self-described as merchants, farmers, domestics, and others, along with their children, were cooped up below, in steerage.

In 1901 William lived, and possibly acted, in the borough of Manhattan, in New York City. That same year, he married Ethel May Harrison. Four months later, "New York's prettiest chorus girl" was pregnant and gave up the stage altogether. William and Ethel's daughter, Ethel Daisy Deane-Tanner, was born in 1902. William's wife's rich uncle set him up in business, working in an antique furniture store. As Giroux stated, William's "knowledge of art and antiques, combined with his British accent, genteel manners, and elegant wardrobe, quickly won the confidence of a wealthy clientele."

Meanwhile, in 1899, William's brother Denis Gage Deane-Tanner had left Ireland for South Africa and served with the British during the Second Boer War. Then in June 1903, he showed up in Toronto, Ontario, and entered the United States through Buffalo, New York. In September 1907, Denis married Ada C. Brennan, in Manhattan, and they had two daughters. According to the 1910 US Census, where he's listed as a "salesman," he (like his brother) also worked in an antique store. Whether they were the same or different stores is not known.

William then made another trip to England in 1906, perhaps on a buying trip for antique furniture. Still traveling as a gentleman, he retained his Irish citizenship and was first in a list of "foreigners" in cabin class. Back in New York he played golf and was an active member of a yacht club. William and his family seemed to be living the good life until a day in October 1908 when he took off, as usual, for his store. He never returned home.

Figure 15.1. William Desmond Taylor. The murder of William C. Deane-Tanner, aka William Desmond Taylor, in 1922, has never been solved. The photograph shows the Hollywood film director in 1917. PHOTO BY ALBERT WITZEL, FROM WIKIMEDIA COMMONS

What *was* unusual was that William left his wife five hundred dollars. Again relying on research by Giroux, William sealed the cash in an envelope and had a clerk from his store personally deliver it to his wife. Had William committed a crime, was there another woman, or did he just want to change his life? According to the 1910 US Census, Ethel May Deane-Tanner had obtained a divorce by that year, reportedly on the grounds of adultery. (This date conflicts with an interview, after William's murder, in which Ethel May told a *New York Times* reporter that she was divorced in 1912.) Ethel described his departure as "just like a man picking up his hat to leave the house." But where did he go, and would he resurface?

BEHIND THE SCENES: ACT II

What little is known about William's location between 1908 and 1913 can best be explained by his friends. After William's murder, in 1922, they popped out of the woodwork in an attempt to fill in the gaps of the Hollywood director's mysterious missing years. The following is a rough timeline.

1908. According to several of William's "old acquaintances," he surprised them at their homes in Los Angeles, claiming that he had been "shanghaied" [taken against his will] at night on lower Broadway, in Manhattan, and then placed aboard a sailing vessel bound for Cape Horn, South America. William added that, several months later, he reached a port on the Pacific Northwest coast (identified in another source as San Francisco). Whether he really was taken against his will or made up the story to cover up the possibility that he chose to leave his home and family voluntarily is not clear. But it was obvious that the Deane-Tanner paper trail had stopped abruptly, and a new chapter in William's life had begun. From 1908 on, and using his same initials, he went by the name William Desmond Taylor.

A conflicting scenario was given by actor George Alan Cleveland, who stated that after leaving New York, "William Desmond Taylor" showed up in a theatrical stock company a lot closer to home—in New Jersey. One would think that William would have been recognized or that someone would have tracked him down, but apparently, that wasn't the case. By 1909 actor-friend George was working onstage in Vancouver, British Columbia. Perhaps William crossed the country with him, as William then showed up in the Klondike gold region of Yukon Territory, Canada, although his arrival was a decade later than the famous Klondike Gold Rush. Interspersed with life in the Yukon, he took frequent trips to the United States to act in various stage productions. (Many years later, in the 1950s, George would make a name for himself as "Gramps" in the television series *Lassie*.)

1909. An employment application for William shows that in May 1909, he began working on dredge and hydraulic operations as a timekeeper for the Yukon Gold Company in Dawson City, Yukon Territory. Previously, according to the application, he had worked for the Grand Trunk Pacific Railway, a western Canadian railway under construction at the time. William would continue to work, off and on, in the gold fields through 1912. The goal of most prospectors was to strike it rich, but perhaps to him it was an escape.

A man who worked with William in the Yukon referred to him as "the Dude of Dawson." He also called William a "mysterious man" who had confided that he had left New York City because of an overwhelming burden of debt he had contracted as an art dealer. According to the coworker, "He [William] wore tweeds, a soft crush hat, tasteful haberdashery, and was immensely popular with the women. He played crack tennis, was a card expert and attended most of the big functions in a dress suit, one of the few dress suits in the town," adding that he used to wonder why a man of his personality and culture should spend his time there at such meager pay.

1910. William left the Yukon for periods of time to work on the stage, acting in plays in Seattle and Bellingham, Washington, where he performed in leading roles. The *Bellingham Herald* praised him in January 1910, stating, "Mr. Taylor is a man of commanding appearance and charming manner, finely educated and of excellent English parentage. He has traveled the world over, and carries with him the air of a man who knows life in all its phases." In February 1910, William was a witness at his friend George Cleveland's wedding, also held in Bellingham.

William's residence at the time of the 1910 US Census (usually taken in April) is unknown. He may have been in Canada, where that country's federal census was taken in 1911. But in May 1910, William, along with George and his bride, was performing in a stage play in Denver, Colorado. Then William took a job as a night clerk in a hotel in the mining town of Telluride, in the southwestern portion of the state. According to a Telluride newspaper reporter who interviewed the hotel proprietor after William's murder (in 1922), William had, in 1910, come from Alaska (bordering the Yukon Territory), where he had lost a fortune and was said to have been "down and out."

In December 1910 William suddenly left his job at the hotel, stating that he had been called to California due to the illness of his brother. If true, what was his only brother Denis doing so far from New York City *before* Denis was known to have disappeared? (In April 1910, federal census records show

Denis and his family still living together in Manhattan, where Denis continued to work at the antique store.)

1911. Presumably, William was back in the Yukon, working for the Yukon Gold Company and/or prospecting on his own, perhaps in Alaska. But he doesn't show up in the 1911 Census of Canada either.

1912. From January through March, William was in Hawaii, where he played a leading role in another stage play. According to remarks made by a fellow actor who tried to talk William into traveling with him to Australia, William was anxious to get back to prospecting for gold. "All his mind was focused on his old mine in the Klondike," the actor told a reporter, "and every cent he got went up to brother Dennis [*sic*] to develop it. I left him at the boat for San Francisco, headed back toward the Arctic."

This reference to Denis seems to affirm that the brothers were, in fact, in contact between the time that William lived and worked in Manhattan and when he became a film director in Hollywood. But how, and when, did William's brother Denis leave his obligations as a husband, father, and antique salesman and travel to Yukon Territory—more than four thousand miles from New York City—even if he went the fastest route, by train? According to a September 1912 article in the *New York Times*, Denis was living in New York City until August 1912, when he walked away from his home, family, and shop, just as William had done in 1908. The police speculated that the clean-shaven, five-foot, eight-inch man with a broken nose "suffered an attack of aphasia [brain injury/amnesia] and had wandered off somewhere."

Both brothers were said to have left their store accounts in perfect order. Both also appeared to have been in good spirits and did not take any luggage. Certainly their wives, and likely the police, would have realized that their nearly identical disappearances (William in 1908 and Denis in 1912) couldn't have been a coincidence, but if members of the press picked up on it, they didn't write about it. One would think that the police would have, at least, sent out requests to other law enforcement agencies to be on the lookout for William and then Denis, as they recently had done for Dorothy Arnold in 1910 (see chapter 2).

1913. After leaving the Yukon again, William picked up another acting job, in San Francisco. There, onstage in 1913, he was discovered by Thomas H. Ince Sr., director of the Motion Picture Company at Santa Monica. (See "Daredevil" DeLay, in chapter 14.) The director cast William as "Don Jose" in the silent film *The Iconoclast*, a Western, filmed at the studio town of Inceville on California's rocky coast. There, perhaps reflecting on his days at the

Irish-run ranch in Kansas, William was back on horseback. He loved anything and everything about the film industry and was hooked after his first movie. Fifteen movies later, he would make the transition from actor to director.

IN FRONT OF THE SCREENS: ACT I

In 1914, during the early days of the Great War (World War I), Britain declared war on Germany and many appeals were made for British citizens living abroad to return home and fight. At the time, instead of fulfilling his patriotic duty in real life, William took the leading role in *Captain Alvarez*, a melodrama advertised as "a thrilling story about war," starring a revolutionary leader battling evil government spies in Argentina. A few years later the movie was rereleased and shown all over the country. Far away, in New York, William's former wife, Ethel May (then remarried), and William and Ethel May's daughter, Ethel Daisy, then age sixteen, went to see the film. Suddenly, when Captain Alvarez's image was flashed upon the screen, Ethel May exclaimed to her daughter, "That's your father!"

Figure 15.2. Taylor in *Captain Alvarez*.
Taylor (in the white shirt) starred in the silent film *Captain Alvarez*, a melodrama advertised as "a thrilling story about war." PHOTO FROM WIKIMEDIA COMMONS

According to a later interview given by Ethel May, the day that she and her daughter saw William in the film was the first time either of them knew that William had assumed the name William Desmond Taylor. His wife and daughter may not have even known that he was alive. Ethel Daisy wrote to her father in care of his employer, and they began a regular correspondence. William even traveled to New York to meet Ethel Daisy and said he would make her his heir, which he did.

In July 1918 William traveled to Chicago to enlist and then proceeded onward to Newfoundland for training before arriving in England in November 1918. There, like his father and brother Denis (in the Second Boer War) before him, he was commissioned an officer in the British Army. He could have signed up earlier, but, in retrospect, his dashing off near the end of the war and making an appearance were similar to the actions of his former film character, Captain Alvarez.

Between July 1918 and May 1919, some newspapers ran photographs of William in uniform, but reports of what he did and where he went are open to question. So, at least, says Kevin Storey of Durham, England, a researcher into William Taylor's army unit. He speculates that "Lieutenant W. D. Taylor, Royal Army Service Corps" (as he had become) could have been given a role at "Army leave clubs, theatres and cinemas in France, the operation of which were his unit's responsibility and would make the most of his celebrity status." He adds that William's official service records likely were lost to fire in the London Blitz of World War II.

All this time, brother Denis seemed to have remained in William's shadow. The original film reel from *Captain Alvarez* no longer exists, but Denis (under an assumed name) was rumored to have played a minor part—that of a blacksmith. Meanwhile, his wife, Ada Deane-Tanner, and children had moved to California. After Ada learned about the film, she contacted William at his studio and asked him about Denis. According to a later police interview, William either wouldn't, or couldn't, tell her Denis's location. But William did send Ada fifty dollars per month until his death in 1922.

Was William's financial support to his brother's wife and family based on a sense of duty, or was he acting on behalf of Denis, who didn't want to be found? Or was there an even deeper reason for the brothers' secrecy? In 1930, eight years after William's murder, Ed C. King, a special investigator in the Los Angeles District Attorney's Office at the time of the murder, wrote a long magazine article titled "I Know Who Killed William Desmond Taylor."

The article originally was published that same year in two subsequent issues of *True Detective Mysteries*.

Special Investigator King, who wrote the only known substantial account by one of the officers actually involved in the investigation, stated that a few days after William's murder, his office received a letter from a man in Denver, Colorado, who claimed to have known both brothers. According to the investigator, "This letter stated that one Edward F. Sands, former secretary [valet] to Taylor, was none other than the missing Denis Gage Deane-Tanner; that at one time William, the older boy, had won the love of his brother's fiancée, and for many years the younger brother had hunted the older, swearing vengeance."

In Front of the Screens: Act II

On February 2, 1922, William's then-current valet, Henry Peavy, came early in the morning, as usual, to his employer's home. There he found William's body. The police arrived, but they neglected to fingerprint any of the items or furniture in the room. And the first "doctor" on the scene concluded that William (lying flat on his back) died of a stomach ailment. After the doctor left (and never returned), a medical examiner turned over William's body and found a gunshot wound and blood on the floor. As soon as word got out, newspaper reporters called in hastily written stories to their newspaper offices.

As a then-prominent film director, William's murder garnered a lot of attention. Nationally syndicated stories splashed the news all over the country. Los Angeles investigator King, in his 1930 article, set the scene as follows:

> *Hollywood, ordinarily serene, playful and carefree, was no longer calm. The atmosphere of make-believe that has always seemed to hover over that portion of Los Angeles, where lived and worked so many of those whose careers and fortunes were centered in the world of finer arts, was gone. One of its most dearly loved members had been brutally done to death—not a man with a past—not one at whom a finger of even the remotest suspicion had ever been cast. Rather, one who represented the very highest in the manly types of manhood.*

Story after story emphasized that William had been a ladies' man, stating that he may have been "shot by the discarded suitor of some woman with whom he had been friendly," or that he was "shot by a woman who, for some unknown reason, had been enraged at him." Then the plot thickened, and it thickened so quickly that it curdled.

The Los Angeles District Attorney's Office apparently was motivated to keep the case under wraps. Unlike Special Investigator King's sugarcoating of the Hollywood scene, William's murder came immediately on the heels of a scandal. The district attorney had dragged another actor-director, Roscoe C. "Fatty" Arbuckle, through three trials until he eventually was acquitted for the rape and manslaughter of a silent-screen actress. It didn't help that the public, and those in the public eye, seemed to be drinking a lot, even though the country was two years into national Prohibition. The post–World War II use of drugs had surged, too, especially among the Hollywood elite. In addition to a fed-up district attorney, there was speculation that the "movie bosses" controlled the police. The consensus was that they needed to either make a quick arrest or make the whole case go away.

William had lived in the exclusive Alvarado Court Apartments on Los Angeles's South Alvarado Street. The residential complex, since demolished, was composed of sixteen apartments, in eight two-story, white stucco bungalows, in a bucolic setting overlooking Westlake Park. At the time, the park district was the favorite neighborhood for motion-picture movers and shakers, who later moved farther away from the city center to Hollywood and Beverly Hills.

Among William's neighbors was Faith MacLean, wife of silent-screen actor Douglas MacLean (known as the "Man with the Million-Dollar Smile"), who claimed to have heard the gunshot. She told police she then had seen a "funny looking man" leave William's apartment. The person was wearing a heavy coat, a cap, and a muffler around his (or her) neck. Three days after the murder, the coroner held an inquest. Faith was subpoenaed and was in attendance, but, oddly, she was not called to testify.

At the inquest, actress Mabel Normand was the only subpoenaed screen star called to the witness stand. Other than the killer, she had been the last person to see William alive. She had visited with him the evening before his death, and the two reportedly had an affection for each other. Mabel was addicted to cocaine and was said to have appealed to William, as a father figure, to help her get off the drug. Giroux theorized that William's murderer was "a hired hit man" and implied that he was a "narcotic peddler" who roamed Hollywood at the time.

Henry Peavy, William's valet, had been in the apartment for part of the time that Mabel was there but had left before Mabel did. Of discovering William's body the following morning, the valet stated at the inquest, "The first thing I saw was his feet. I looked at his feet a few minutes and said, 'Mr. Taylor.' He never moved. I stepped a little further in the door and seen his face, and turned and ran out and hollered." The valet also testified that William was dressed just as he had been the previous evening and still was wearing his diamond ring. According to the valet, nothing in the house, except the slight movement of a chair, had been disturbed, and nothing was missing.

The inquest for William Desmond Taylor's murder was very short, less than an hour. The only conclusion made by the six businessmen who sat on the jury was that the director had "come to his death from a gunshot wound inflicted by an unknown person with homicidal intent." As soon as the verdict was read, the police rushed off to continue their search for their then number-one suspect, Edward F. Sands, who had been implicated by the anonymous writer in Colorado. Police still believed this *former* valet was none other than William's brother, Denis Gage Deane-Tanner.

In addition to being a valet, Edward F. Sands's duties had included those of butler, secretary, and chauffeur. But he had proven to be untrustworthy. Several months before the murder, Edward had stolen items from William's home and then pawned them under the name of "William Deane-Tanner." How would Edward have known William's real name? What was the relationship between William and this former valet? And what was the real relationship between William and his brother? The police raised a lot of questions.

Another player at the time was actress Mary Miles Minter. Nearly everyone who has written about the murder seems to agree that Mary was a lovesick teenager who was unabashedly taken with William, a man who was old enough to be her father. Meanwhile, Mary lived with, and financially supported, her fiercely protective mother, Charlotte Shelby, who *also* was thought to have been in love with the director. One theory is that Charlotte (dressed as the "funny looking man" observed by the neighbor) had walked into William's apartment and shot him in a jealous rage.

Substantiating the theory about Mary, William was said to have confided (on the day before his murder) to a friend that he didn't know what to do about the overt affections of a "sweet young girl." According to Giroux in *A Deed of Death*, the friend told police what William had told him and explained that Mary had visited William during the night of January 30, two nights before his murder. As William's friend stated, Mary had hoped to spend the night, and William "had great difficulty in finally persuading her to let him take her home." Later, when an undertaker was preparing William's body for burial, the undertaker found three long blond hairs on the collar of William's coat. When they were compared to hair found in the dressing room of Mary Miles Minter, they were said to have matched.

After that came conflicting reports that Mary's lingerie and love letters also were found in his home. It had also been speculated that even though women had swooned over him for years, William may have been bisexual or gay, and his knowing female friends (who combed through the crime scene shortly after the murder) planted Mary's items in order to hide the truth about his sexuality and, thus, not "tarnish" his image.

If the life and death of William Desmond Taylor were made into a movie, it would need a conclusion. And even before trying to figure out who pulled the trigger, there would need to be an explanation for why William, and then Denis, disappeared from New York. Was there a dark secret from their past that tied them together? Was Denis quietly living in William's shadow waiting patiently to seek revenge?

POSTMORTEM

On February 7, 1922, many questions plagued the estimated ten thousand people who tried to attend William's funeral in St. Paul's (Episcopal) Cathedral, in downtown Los Angeles. Most in the crowd were left waiting on the street. Some had gone to pay their respects, while others merely hoped to catch a glimpse of Gloria Swanson, Rudolph Valentino, and the other movie stars who showed up.

Among the elaborate floral displays was a small bouquet of violets and lilies of the valley with a note that read, "With Ethel Daisy's love." She was still in New York and unable to attend her father's funeral. Also missing at the funeral was William's brother, Denis. Mary Miles Minter was absent as well, and there was no mention of her mother, Charlotte Shelby. Actress Mabel Normand made a dramatic entrance, cried throughout the service, and then collapsed.

Figure 15.3. Plaque on Taylor's/Tanner's crypt.
William C. Deane-Tanner's remains lie in crypt 594 in the Cathedral Mausoleum in Hollywood Forever Cemetery in Hollywood, California. PHOTO COURTESY OF EDWARD MELTSER

The funeral procession of more than a hundred upscale automobiles escorted William's body to crypt number 594 in the Cathedral Mausoleum in the Hollywood Forever Cemetery. Today, William is among nearly fifty thousand other burials, including many from the era of the silent screen. His name, "William Desmond Taylor," was written on his director's chair, but Ethel Daisy felt that, in death, it was important that her father be given back his birth name. She chose the words for his plaque, which simply reads, "In Memory of William C. Deane-Tanner, Beloved Father of Ethel Deane-Tanner. Died February 1 1922."

No one ever was indicted for William's murder, and the disappearances of William and Denis remain long-standing mysteries. Although the special investigator who came forward in 1930 began his article by stating that he knew the name of the killer, he admitted, at the end, that he didn't have proof.

He did, however, leave open the possibility that Charlotte Shelby, mother of Mary Miles Minter, was involved. In his conclusion, he stated:

> *Today [in 1930], the Taylor case is listed among the great unsolved crime mysteries of the world, the chances being good that it will stay there. Dope, love, jealousy, revenge, blackmail—all have entered into our investigations. There was never a particle of real evidence to connect Taylor with a dope ring. The only way love and jealousy entered into the case was through the admission of Mary Miles Minter, who confessed unashamedly that she loved William Desmond Taylor. Never, for one moment, have I suspected Mabel Normand of knowing anything about the murder. I questioned her many times when she was completely off her guard. If she had known anything, the truth would have come out. The revenge motive was found only in connection with Sands. Taylor had threatened his arrest and filed charges against him.*

After William's murder, no trace of his brother Denis ever was found. According to Charles Higham, author of *Murder in Hollywood: Solving a Silent Screen Mystery*, Ada had Denis legally declared dead in 1924 but without any proof. (For more on "Legal Presumption of Death," see chapter 7, on Lawrence Joseph Bader.) Recent correspondence with the Los Angeles County Register-Recorder/County Clerk also failed to provide documentation, as did a search for Denis's death certificate with the California Department of Public Health, Vital Records. Higham speculates that Denis was still alive in 1924 but living under an assumed name in Riverside, California. Higham also mentions that there were "reports" indicating that Denis had died, perhaps from tuberculosis, in New York's Bellevue Hospital in 1930. (*If* that was the case, and *if* his body was unclaimed, he may have been buried on Hart Island; see chapter 3.)

Oddly, Denis's wife, Ada, a party to the court proceedings, waited until February 1937 (thirteen years later) for a hearing with the Los Angeles district attorney to try to clear her husband's name. She brought with her an old letter and two faded envelopes that, she claimed, showed Denis's handwriting. According to the *San Francisco Examiner*, "an internationally known handwriting expert" stated, "I am unable to find any handwriting characteristics which would suggest that [Denis] Deane-Tanner and Edward F. Sands were the same writer."

Meanwhile, fifteen years had passed since police received the "Colorado letter" that led them to believe that Denis was Edward F. Sands. And eighteen years had passed when a retired broker named Alfred A. Wright also appeared in 1937 before the district attorney. Wright testified that prior to William's murder, he had met a man on a train who went by the name of "Sandy Tanner." According to Wright, Sandy Tanner (was he Edward F. Sands?) said he was going to work for William Desmond Taylor.

On July 8, 1986, fifty-five years after William's murder, television correspondent Connie Chung with *Newsmagazine* interviewed long-retired detective William Cahill for an episode titled "Shot in Hollywood." Detective Cahill, then one hundred years old, was the last living detective on the case, and he said he remembered it as clearly as if it had happened yesterday. He was sure that Mary's mother, Charlotte, was the killer, but that's not where he cast the blame. "The case was never solved because the police weren't allowed to do their job," he said. "The district attorney's office kept pulling investigators off the case, because they were being paid off by Charlotte Shelby."

Amid all the speculation and theories, the connection between William's brother Denis and William's valet Edward F. Sands remains unresolved. The man in Denver, Colorado, who claimed to have known both William and Denis and wrote to the Los Angeles police in 1922, believed that the brother and the valet were one and the same. Yet they were said to have had major differences in looks, mannerisms, age, and, as previously noted, even their handwriting. What if one of them wished for William's murder and the other pulled the trigger?

Further research has uncovered a February 10, 1922, *Denver Post* interview with the anonymous "Denver man." Whether he told the truth is up for debate, but the article adds more fuel to the supposition that William had won the love of Denis's fiancée. The "Denver man" stated,

> *I knew the Tanner brothers in Dublin years ago. At that time, the younger one we call Sands was engaged to a beautiful girl who was a visitor at his mother's home near Dublin. William, we'll use this name, was evidently as attractive to women then as in the last hour of his life, for somehow he won the trust of his brother's fiancée. Later this girl committed suicide.*
>
> *It was eighteen years after this tragedy that Sands entered my office in Portland, Oregon, to find if I had heard anything or knew*

anything about the whereabouts of his brother. He told me in a brief way that he was hunting for his brother and had to get him. I suggested he go into northwest Canada and make a search. He did so, but returned later to report failure. He then went to Alaska, where the two men, one hiding, the other a revenger, met. [William] Taylor returned to the United States and in Seattle joined a company of players. There he was joined by [Edward] Sands.

Knowing as I do of the double blood-bond between Sands and Taylor, the stories of Taylor's leniency toward Sands, who was charged with forging his name and stealing his goods, was not surprising to me. Taylor was in the absolute power of Sands, and while Sands was out to revenge what he called the defilement of the woman he loved— and had taken more than eighteen years to turn thumbs down—he was having a living off of Taylor and knew himself to be safe from legal action.

If William's brother Denis, or William's valet Edward F. Sands, had walked into the "Denver man's" office in Portland, Oregon, in 1911, then the "tragedy" that occurred eighteen years earlier in Ireland would have been in 1893. In the fall of that year, William would have been twenty years old and Denis seventeen—not too young for young love. According to Giroux, a coworker who knew William while he was working at the Chicago World's Fair in the winter of 1893 said that William "carried a picture of a girl with whom he had been in love in England" and "always seemed worried."

Clearly, the curtain came down on William in a most untimely fashion. If Denis and Sands were not the same man, perhaps Denis had hired Sands as his hit man. After William's murder, both men remained missing. The "Denver man" concluded his *Denver Post* interview by stating, "Revenge of a dead love, not because of any living screen star, is the motive behind the murder of William Desmond Taylor. . . . The old Irish Faey [foreboding of death] held them in bond."

PART 6

THROUGH THE LENS OF TIME

What if, in 1922, a home-security camera had been located outside the residence of William Desmond Taylor? What if, in 1930, there had been a surveillance camera on the Manhattan street where Judge Joseph Force Crater hailed a cab? What if, in 1952, residents in and around the Berkshire Mountains of Connecticut had received notifications, called AMBER alerts, on their cell phones during the search for ten-year-old Connie Smith? We take our law enforcement resources for granted today, but we should remember that detectives in the early and mid-twentieth century could only work with the evidence-gathering and investigative methods then available.

In order to review the cases of several of the victims featured in this book, investigators (including you, the reader) need to be able to place them under a lens of time, that is, to put them in historical perspective. Then, using the deductive reasoning skills of Sherlock Holmes, try to put yourself at the scene of a crime or in the middle of a missing-person investigation. In the process of reflection, it's helpful to consider the following:

- Did police and sheriff officials cover the basics?
- Did they leave any clues unexamined?
- Did they consider every conceivable option and make use of the technology then available?
- What would law enforcement officials do differently today?

As we will see, the answers to these questions vary greatly from case to case. First, let's travel back in time so that we can better understand the investigative methods and procedures available to our predecessors.

EARLY FORENSICS

A good place to start is with Eugène François Vidocq (1775–1857), the French detective for which the Vidocq Society is named (see chapter 11, on the "Boy in the Box"). Considered by historians and members of law enforcement as the "Father of Modern Criminal Investigation," Vidocq was known for introducing the science of ballistics and an index-card system for record keeping as well as then-innovative techniques that included plaster-of-Paris casts of foot and shoe impressions.

In the mid-nineteenth century, three decades after Vidocq's death, British author (and also physician) Sir Arthur Conan Doyle contributed to the public's crime-solving interests with his creation of Sherlock Holmes. In *A Study in Scarlet*, published in 1887, Doyle (through Holmes) displayed an uncanny ability to describe scientific methods of detection before they officially were implemented by police. For instance, Doyle wrote about the detective's use of a reagent as a preliminary indicator of the presence of blood several years before the inception of serology—the scientific study or diagnostic examination of blood serum.

During this same time, law enforcement agencies developed the use of fingerprints as a form of identification. After a British officer in India required thumb or palm prints instead of signatures from his illiterate laborers, Sir Edward Richard Henry, the head of the London Metropolitan Police, created a print-classification system based on fingertips. His method of analysis, called the Henry System, was based on the assumption that no two persons have exactly the same arrangement of raised skin surfaces, or ridges, and that the patterns of these ridges of any one individual remain unchanged throughout life.

By the early 1900s investigators in both Europe and North America manually classified every fingerprint into three types: loops, whorls, and ridges. Also during this time period, French criminalist Dr. Edmond Locard formulated what was called "Locard's Exchange Principle," a theory relating to the transfer of trace evidence between objects. The perpetrator of a crime, for instance, will bring evidence such as blood, fingerprints, hair, and fibers into the crime scene and will leave with similar evidence from the victim.

In 1908 US president Theodore Roosevelt's administration created the Bureau of Investigation, which would, in 1935, be renamed the Federal Bureau of Investigation (FBI). In 1924 J. Edgar Hoover was the director of the Bureau, where he established an Identification Division to register rolled finger and thumb impressions in ink. Each set was on its own index card within a master file. Law enforcement agencies all over the country apprehended and fingerprinted criminals and then sent their fingerprint cards to the Bureau to add to its ever-expanding collection of files.

EARLY TWENTIETH-CENTURY MISSING: DOROTHY ARNOLD AND JUDGE CRATER

Not even fingerprints, however, would have helped in finding Dorothy Arnold (missing in 1910) or Judge Joseph Force Crater (missing in 1930). In fact, both cases were hampered by delayed police involvement. As we've seen in chapters 1 and 2, Dorothy's father and Judge Crater's wife, respectively, were concerned with avoiding scandals and preventing publicity, so for weeks, they relied solely on private investigators. That's not to say that the private investigators weren't doing their jobs, but they may have missed out on the personal connections that police officers of their eras formed with neighborhood residents as they walked their beats. Weeks later, when the Arnold and Crater families did contact law enforcement, Dorothy's and Judge Crater's trails had gone cold.

The good news was that once the police were involved, so, too, was the press, although sensationalism could, and did, get mixed in with investigative journalism. In New York City, newspaper reporters competed for stories, each one hoping for an exclusive scoop. During briefings or court hearings, these reporters would scribble their stories by hand and then rush to pay telephones to read their "copy" to newspaper office typists. By the 1920s, large, bulky console radios had made their way into many of America's living rooms, allowing the news of Judge Crater's disappearance in 1930 also to be broadcast on air.

Telephones had come into use in the late nineteenth century, although not everyone had one. In 1910 Dorothy Arnold's family did, however, as well as the New York City police. By 1930 a patrol officer who needed to report a crime or required backup would go to a call box (like an emergency telephone) on the street. Also available was the telegraph. When Dorothy was thought to have left New York City on a ship, a police investigator telegraphed a recently departed ship at sea to ask whether Dorothy was a passenger on board.

One major improvement in communications by the time Judge Crater disappeared was the invention of the teletype machine. According to *The History of Policing in the City of New York*, by Pascal Storino Jr., the first use of teletype machines by law enforcement was in 1922, making it possible for police to quickly and efficiently send and receive typed messages over dedicated telephone lines to police in other locations. In Manhattan, communication by teletype quickly allowed police to summon help in 1928, when a subway train jumped its tracks under Times Square. Presumably, teletype machines were used in sending Judge Crater's missing-person information to law enforcement agencies throughout the country.

Incomplete, missing, and destroyed case reports, however, make it impossible to know if these early twentieth-century police investigations covered the basics and/or considered every option. Sadly, since the police were not involved right away, they never had the chance to adequately do their jobs. But when they finally were involved, did they go back and thoroughly interview everyone Dorothy and the judge had come in contact with on the day of (and the days leading up to) their disappearances? How well trained were the investigators? How sharp were the memories of the interviewees?

If Dorothy and/or Judge Crater were reported missing today, their high-profile and possibly suspicious disappearances would have been handled very differently, due to technological advances and new investigative tools. Credit cards (Diner's Club is said to have been the first) came into use in the 1950s, leaving, for some, a paper trail. A few businesses began using surveillance cameras in the 1970s and they, possibly, could have picked up a missing person's movements. Now that we're well into the internet age, police still rely heavily on surveillance equipment while also analyzing credit card and bank transactions, downloading call history from landlines and cell phones (with geotracking capabilities), and searching missing persons' social media postings.

As retired Boulder County (Colorado) Sheriff's Office Operations Division Chief Phil West adds, "Computer forensics and the ability to mine an individual's computer or phone for information about recent activity, personal habits, relationships and history of personal contacts is a real boon to today's investigator."

1920s Murders: William Desmond Taylor and "Daredevil" DeLay

Lack of adequate police work also contributed to the cold-case status of William Desmond Taylor, murdered in 1922. According to Giroux, in *A Deed of Death*, the police never were given the opportunity to solve the crime. Giroux quoted a *Chicago Tribune* reporter, on the day after Taylor's inquest, as follows:

> *The murder may never be solved, say the police. Twenty people are said to be under suspicion. Twenty theories of the crime are being aired, but there has been not one arrest and not one clue. It is believed the movie interests would spend a million* not *to catch the murderer, to prevent the real truth from coming out.*

Apparently, the "real truth" involved rampant drug use among the Hollywood elite, along with protecting the ability of the movie industry to make a living. Giroux also explained that when the *Tribune* reporter defended his responsibility to tell the truth as he saw it, a Los Angeles, California, undersheriff replied, "That isn't the point. The industry has been hurt. Stars have been ruined. Stockholders have lost millions of dollars." Meanwhile, rumors were circulating that the Los Angeles District Attorney's Office was being paid to pull its investigators off the case. One detective (as quoted by Giroux) stated, "We were doing all right and then, before a week was out, we got the word to lay off."

As to the "aerial sabotage" of "Daredevil" DeLay, the public doesn't even know if the police who sifted through the wreckage of DeLay's airplane were able to retrieve any fingerprints. Did they identify and interview the so-called thugs who allegedly interfered with takeoffs on the airfield's runway? Did the news reports bring forward any additional witnesses?

Obviously, in the cases of both Taylor and DeLay, if video surveillance had existed during their times, most of the people who approached or left Taylor's house on the night he was shot likely would have been documented and, perhaps, identified with facial recognition technology. In addition, a camera could have caught a suspicious person tampering with DeLay's airplane. If either of these deaths occurred today, the law enforcement agencies involved would lose no time conducting full-scale murder investigations. And, for DeLay, the Federal Aviation Administration (FAA) and the National

Transportation Safety Board (NTSB) would send in their investigators to give their opinions on the exact cause of the plane crash.

MISSING ADVENTURERS OF THE 1930S

The disappearances of Everett Ruess, Glen and Bessie Hyde, and Joseph Halpern, all missing in wilderness locations, differ from the above-discussed victims, who went missing and/or were murdered in urban settings. The searches for the adventurers evolved from attempts to rescue them to attempts to recover their remains—assuming they died from accidental deaths, as was likely. Aerial surveillance for Glen and Bessie Hyde did spot their boat, and a pilot in a small plane searched for Everett Ruess, but searching abilities were limited.

As Division Chief West states, "Today's search-and-rescue entities have access to a much broader array of technology, including helicopters that can hold a static position and deploy thermal imaging equipment that can detect heat signatures." West adds that drones (unmanned aerial vehicles) can provide live-video footage while accessing remote and/or enclosed areas that would be otherwise inaccessible. No aerial surveillance was used in the search for Joseph Halpern in Rocky Mountain National Park, but imagine what a difference it would have made if today's equipment and expertise had been available.

Bones that may well be Everett's were found in the 1970s, but they now are lost or missing. If they were to be located again, it might be possible to compare Everett's DNA profile with the profile or profiles of one or more of Everett's family members. (Unfortunately, in the 1970s, DNA identification had not been discovered.) The young man was last seen in 1934, in Garfield County, Utah, but a recent check with its Sheriff's Office has not revealed any new information about his disappearance.

MISSING IN THE 1950S

Readers who have lived through or read about the 1950s will recall that the era was a time when children were taught that "the police are your friend." Capturing this attitude in popular culture was the *Andy Griffith Show*, a situation comedy television series in which Sheriff Andy Taylor (played by Griffith) interacted with residents in the slow-paced, fictional town of Mayberry, North Carolina. As in the 1920s and 1930s, most police and sheriff officials got to know the residents in their neighborhoods, whether they were in big cities or rural towns and communities. (In all fairness to today's law enforcement, some patrol officers still form these relationships, particularly with local business owners and the homeless population.)

Of the missing persons discussed in this book, the only one we know of who disappeared on her own—that is, voluntarily—was Twylia May Embrey. She was from Maywood, Nebraska, not Mayberry, North Carolina, but the small towns were similar. In 1955 the Social Security Administration (SSA) issued clear instructions stating that when applicants married and requested new cards, they had to keep their same SSA numbers. When Twylia filled out her new application, she simply wrote that she had no prior card or number. Without a computerized database, there was virtually no chance of being caught. In today's world, the charge would be criminal fraud. People still disappear, but to do so they have to completely go off the grid and disconnect with their former identities.

There's no doubt that the 1950s was a simpler time. But it also was the decade in which Steven Damman and Freddie Holmes were abducted and Connie Smith walked away from her summer camp. In each case, the police did what they could by communicating via telephone and sending teletype messages as well as canvassing door-to-door and distributing missing-person flyers. Helicopters had come into use during World War II, but it's not known whether the Connecticut Civil Air Patrol used them (instead of fixed-wing aircraft) in its search for Connie.

In Connie's case, one wonders, too, how much cooperation there was between the local and state police in Connecticut and agencies just over the Connecticut/New York state line. Did the police in Connecticut conduct their searches within a radius of where Connie was last seen, or did they limit their efforts solely to their own localities? Even today, law enforcement agencies have jurisdictional disputes that can become barriers to effective case investigations.

If Steven, Freddie, and Connie had gone missing today, the likelihood of successful reunions with their families would be much greater. This increased probability is due in part to today's AMBER alerts, along with the rapid dissemination of the news of an abduction through social media. The AMBER Alert System began in 1996 when Dallas–Fort Worth, Texas, broadcasters teamed with local police to develop an early warning system to help find abducted children age seventeen and younger.

AMBER stands for "America's Missing: Broadcast Emergency Response" and was created as a legacy to nine-year-old Amber Hagerman, who was kidnapped while riding her bicycle. The alerts interrupt regular programming and primarily are broadcast on radio, television, and cell phones, as well as on Department of Transportation highway signs. There are several criteria, one being that the law enforcement agency overseeing the case believes that the child is in imminent danger of serious bodily injury or death. Since the inception of the system, AMBER alerts have been credited with the successful return of more than one thousand children.

Helping implement AMBER alerts is the National Center for Missing & Exploited Children, the NCMEC. According to its website, the Center is "a private, non-profit 501(c)(3) corporation whose mission is to help find missing children, reduce child sexual exploitation and prevent child victimization." The organization was founded in 1984 by child advocates including John Walsh (creator and host of the longtime television show *America's Most Wanted*) and Revé Walsh, whose six-year-old son, Adam, was abducted from a department store and murdered. As in the old days of missing-person flyers, the NCMEC prepares missing-person posters, as shown for Steven Damman, in chapter 10.

MURDERED IN THE 1950S
In the search for Marion McDowell in 1953, the police performed similar ground and aerial searches as their contemporaries. They also brought in dogs. But in examining what additional efforts they could have implemented, the most obvious questions revolve around the assaults of Marion and her boyfriend. Didn't anyone in the lovers' lane see a suspicious person who could have been the attacker? The police interviewed Marion's friends, but did they question students in local high schools or canvass nearby homeowners?

What about tire tracks at the abandoned farm where Jimmy saw Marion being stuffed into the trunk? If Eugène François Vidocq could make foot and shoe impressions in the nineteenth century, wouldn't the police in Toronto have made an attempt to take a tire impression of the abductor's car? If they did, no newspaper reported their efforts, but even a partial impression might have led to the tire type, its manufacturer, and, in some cases, even the make and model of the car.

The case of the "Boy in the Box" (see chapter 11) elicits similar questions. A witness reported seeing two people unloading what could have been the boy's body from the back of a car. As in the investigation into Marion's disappearance, did the Philadelphia police record any tire impressions? Did the witness get even a partial plate number? As noted in chapter 11, Investigator Bristow told a newspaper reporter, "Hundreds of cops were going over a field, but they didn't know what they were looking for." Likely, the police did leave some clues unexamined, but the case is still an open homicide investigation and, thus, is not available to the public.

The boy is listed, however, in the NCMEC as "John Doe 1957" (see figure 11.2). His DNA profile also is in the Combined DNA Index System (CODIS). Maintained by the FBI, this database includes DNA samples from close relatives of missing persons, as well as samples collected from unidentified remains, convicted offenders, and crime scenes. The new field of genetic genealogy, however, offers a different approach to identification that relies on matches to both close and more distant relatives. If the boy is not identified through a CODIS match, genetic genealogy offers an alternative.

TECHNOLOGICAL ADVANCES

Colleen Fitzpatrick, a pioneer in the field of genetic genealogy as well as a Vidocq Society member, is hopeful that the police soon will be able to apply genetic genealogy to identifying the Boy in the Box and, thus, return his remains to his family. In a recent interview, Colleen stated, "The use of this advanced technology illustrates how we are moving from the era of forensic identification into an era of investigative intelligence. While we will still depend on CODIS for legal identification, genetic genealogy has proven itself capable of providing so much more—ethnic admixture, geographical origins, and deep family pedigrees—that can lead up to that identification."

Other new technological advances include the Integrated Automated Fingerprint Identification System (IAFIS), launched in 1999. Now, instead of investigators needing to tediously compare the FBI's manual fingerprint cards, they can, on their own computers, easily search prints, which resemble digital photographs. Division Chief Phil West adds that in addition to having better tools, today's investigators are better trained than in previous years: "That's not meant to denigrate our forebears," he states, "but today's cops frequently are college-educated, have greater exposure and access to experts in a variety of fields and are technically more savvy that their counterparts of years' past. They also receive specific training in interview and interrogation techniques."

After recounting horror stories of missing and destroyed case files, West hopes that computerized record keeping will keep sloppy documentation and investigations in the past. And as we have seen, yes, there were clues left behind—lots of them. But, again, we really do have to view these and other unsolved cases through the lens of time. Will they, one day, be solved? They are included in this book in order to keep them in the public eye or, perhaps, the public's eyes. Sometimes, all that is needed is a fresh pair of eyes, and they just might be yours.

Acknowledgments

Special thanks go to my husband and my best critic, Ed Raines, for reading draft after draft of individual chapters long before I would share them with anyone else. Then, when I did, I welcomed feedback from my sister Marilyn Mildrum as well as friends and fellow researchers Sandy Bausch, Dina Carson, Linda Fulmer, and Micki Lavigne. And I appreciated the efforts of R. H. Walton, EdD, professor of criminal justice at Utah State University Eastern, for brainstorming with me on cases to include, especially those of Judge Joseph Force Crater and William Desmond Taylor.

Thanks, too, to my publisher, Rick Rinehart, for suggesting the topic of *Cold Case Chronicles*; to his former associate editor Stephanie Scott, who helped me shape the manuscript; to Helen Subbio, who did an excellent job of copy editing; and to senior production editor Meredith Dias, who readied it for publication. Kudos, too, to cover designers, proofreaders, graphic designers, and others who work behind the scenes.

I couldn't have asked for a better foreword writer and manuscript reviewer than longtime friend and colleague Phil West, retired division chief from the Boulder County Sheriff's Office, in Boulder, Colorado. In addition to his writing skills, he provided an invaluable law enforcement perspective during the preparation of the manuscript.

Halfway through the research and writing of this book, the country and the whole world suddenly was forced to live under the restrictions brought on by the COVID-19 pandemic. Instead of the travel and in-library research I had planned, I corresponded with historians, librarians, and individuals in various parts of the country. Like me, most were working from home, but they still gave my questions their careful attention.

Beginning with the chapter on Judge Crater, I'd like to thank the reference staff at the Irma and Paul Milstein Division of United States History, Local History and Genealogy, at the New York Public Library. In researching the chapter on Dorothy Arnold, I enjoyed corresponding with Mary Combs and Preston Arnold, fellow genealogical researchers who shared their interest in, and insights on, the socialite. Mary also provided me with some British records on George Griscomb Jr. that came from The National Archives in the United Kingdom.

Linda M. Mackey, with the New York State Office of Parks, Recreation and Historic Preservation, provided historic preservation documentation for the chapter on Hart Island. Patrick Raftery shared pages of his research that gave me an insight into the early burial process at Potter's Field. Melinda Hunt filled me in on events in recent years and kindly read my draft for accuracy, while Lori Reese assisted me with a photograph from Redux Pictures LLC.

In writing about Everett Ruess, I appreciated talking with Denise Dastrup, of the Garfield County (Utah) Sheriff's Office, and also with Dustin Driscoll, regional program specialist with the National Missing and Unidentified Persons System (NamUs). Photo archivists Sara Caroline Davis and Lorraine Crouse, from the Special Collections Department of the J. Willard Marriott Library at the University of Utah, went out of their way to locate images of Everett Ruess in their Everett Ruess Family collection. Ana Daraban, from the *Salt Lake Tribune*, was helpful in answering my questions about a map, published in the *Tribune*, of "Indian Country."

For the chapter on Glen and Bessie Hyde, thanks go to Peter Runge and Cindy Summers for finding a specific photo I requested from the Special Collections and Archives at the Cline Library at Northern Arizona University.

I couldn't have written the chapter on Joseph Halpern without his family's correspondence and photographs as well as the recent and extensive research provided by Joseph's nephew, Roland Halpern. Roland and I have kept in contact for several years, and I welcome his willingness to share his family's story with the public. Thanks, too, to Alice de Sturler, author and founder of the research website defrostingcoldcases.com, for helping to publicize Joseph's missing person case.

In writing the chapter on Lawrence Bader, I'd like to thank the anonymous family member who corresponded with me. As for Twylia May Embrey, her grandniece, Jennifer Kitt, introduced me to Twylia's sister Mildred "Midge" Garner and also provided me with decades-old Nebraska family correspondence and photos. The research skills of Micki Lavigne provided the vital link that led to Twylia's second family in Massachusetts.

Credit on the "Hatbox Baby" chapter is due, first of all, to fellow researcher Sandy Bausch who shared with me the still-unfolding story, as published in the *Arizona Republic* in recent years by reporter John D'Anna. Throughout three decades of perseverance and hard work, D'Anna fine-tuned his research and writing skills to become the saga's lead detective, raising the bar for all investigative journalists. Readers can look forward to his continued reporting on the "rest of the story," a phrase made famous by the late radio broadcaster Paul Harvey. I'd like to also thank Kim Reis, at Imagn (part of the USA Today Network), who assisted me in obtaining Sharon Elliott's photograph.

Gavin Portnoy and Christine Barndt, of the National Center for Missing & Exploited Children, provided me with the poster for Steven Damman in the chapter on child abductions as well as the facial reconstruction image in the chapter on the "Boy in the Box": "John Doe 1957."

Several others also contributed to the chapter on the "Boy in the Box." First, I was pleased to have the opportunity to continue my correspondence with former Vidocq commissioner William L. "Bill" Fleisher, with whom I had worked in the past on the Boulder Jane Doe case. Warren Kerschbaum, also a Vidocq Society member as well as a retired Philadelphia police lieutenant, contributed the cemetery photograph. Warren's son, Nicholas P. Kerschbaum, has taken the cause of abused children into the next generation.

In illustrating the "Boy in the Box" chapter, I also wish to thank Josue Hurtado, Kim Tully, and Brenda Galloway-Wright at the Special Collections Research Center, Charles Library, at Temple University in Philadelphia. A product of our correspondence is the photo of the scene where the boy was found, as shown on the cover of this book (and also figure 11.1).

One of the few people I had the honor of meeting in person was Nels J. Smith, brother of Connie Smith. Nels gave me his family's perspective on Connie's disappearance, filled me in on her home surroundings in Wyoming, and contributed her photo. I also would like to thank Jennifer Schwartz, of the Scoville Memorial Library in Salisbury, Connecticut, for corresponding with me on the New England landscape where Connie was last seen. Fellow researcher Sandy Bausch and I have corresponded on this case for years, and her knowledge was very helpful as well. I also appreciate the insights provided by fellow author Michael C. Dooling. Lastly, I'm grateful to artist Tim Cox for sharing his very poignant painting, *Flowers for Mom*.

In years past, while assembling information on the abduction of Marion McDowell, I exchanged several emails with one of her cousins. Although we have not had recent contact, I often think of the McDowell family and the heartache they have lived with for so many years. I have not had personal contact with the family of B. H. "Daredevil" DeLay, but I came across his photograph in the public domain and want to thank one of his family members, Shawna Kelly, for making the photo available.

For the chapter on William Desmond Taylor, a big thank you goes to Bruce Long both for answering my questions and for assembling his extensive database and website, Taylorology (taylorology.com). Also, I very much enjoyed my correspondence with British military researcher Kevin Storey, who provided new insights on William Taylor's service in the British military. Thanks, too, to Edward Meltser, whom I "met" through FindAGrave.com. He kindly photographed (especially for this book) Taylor's/Tanner's crypt. Several other photos in this book came from the public domain. The Library of Congress and its staff deserve thanks and praise for preserving and providing these historic photos for all of us to use.

In "Through the Lens of Time," I appreciated the insight of both Division Chief Phil West and his wife, Patti West, as they helped me compare and contrast investigative methods of today with the procedures of our predecessors. In addition, I'm grateful to fellow Vidocq Society member Colleen Fitzpatrick, for her careful attention to detail in reading the manuscript, her much-appreciated editorial suggestions, and her expertise in the field of genetic genealogy. Yes, there is hope for the future.

And, thanks, too, to my daughter, Clara Thomas, for taking my author photo.

For Further Reading

In an ideal world, researching historical cases starts with primary sources, when, and if, they still exist. With cases such as the ones in this book (from 1910 through the 1950s), however, digging through all pertinent case files and/or court transcripts for each story was unrealistic and would have been impossible. Fortunately, in the missing-persons cases of Joseph Laurence Halpern and Twylia May Embrey, previous generations provided today's family members with correspondence that they, in turn, generously shared with the author.

Some of the older cases, including those of Dorothy Arnold and William Desmond Taylor, cite documents that are accessible through genealogical websites such as ancestry.com. In addition, newspaper accounts acquired through newspapers.com and similar databases reveal events and information as they became known to the public. As any good researcher knows, newspapers are not primary sources (and it's no surprise that, sometimes, they are sensationalized and inaccurate), but they often are the best record available. Newspaper accounts can also provide insights, such as colorful details and quotes, that make the people in the stories come alive. See the following pages for selected newspaper and other references, both historic and as recent as this century.

CHAPTER 1: JUDGE JOSEPH FORCE CRATER: CABS AND CABARETS
Research for Judge Crater's case began with dozens of newspaper articles from September 4, 1930 through 1931. The newspapers included the *Brooklyn Daily Eagle*, *Brooklyn Times Union*, *New York Daily News*, *New York Post*, *New York Sun*, *New York World*, and the *Standard Union*. Since Judge Crater's disappearance was high profile, many of the stories in these newspapers were syndicated and republished by the Associated Press, United Press, and United Press International for publication all over the country. Several books have been written on Judge Crater, as well.

A couple of selected newspaper references from later dates include:

Staff. "Claim Is Accepted." Associated Press, January 10, 1940.
Staff. "Obituary for Stella Crater Kunz." Associated Press, September 25, 1969.

Selected twenty-first-century newspaper and website references include:

Bryk, William. "The Missingest Man in New York." *New York Press*, June 25, 2002 (as reprinted on the website "City of Smoke: New York in History and Anecdote," cityofsmoke.com/archives/300).
Celona, Larry. "Cops Map Out Dig for Judge Crater." *New York Post*, October 13, 2005.
Celona, Larry. "Crater Vanish 'Solved'—Dead Woman's Note: My Hubby & Cop Pal Killed Judge." *New York Post*, August 19, 2005.
Rashbaum, William K. "Cold Case Heats Up Again—75 Years Later." *Chicago Tribune*, August 21, 2005.
Rashbaum, William K. "Judge Crater Abruptly Appears, at Least in Public Consciousness." *New York Times*, August 20, 2005.

CHAPTER 2: DOROTHY ARNOLD: AS THOUGH SHE NEVER EXISTED

Newspaper articles on Dorothy Arnold, beginning with those on January 26, 1911, were found in the *Boston Globe*, *Brooklyn Citizen*, *Brooklyn Eagle*, *Daily News*, *Evening World*, *New York Daily News*, *New York Times*, *Seattle Star*, and the *Sun*, as well as other newspapers syndicated nationwide. Additional references were found in the *Norwich Bulletin*, *Passaic Daily News*, and the *Washington Post*.

Selected newspaper, book, and website references include:

Bell, Ernest A. *Fighting the Traffic in Young Girls or War on the White Slave Trade*. Privately published by Ernest A. Bell, 1910.
National Archives and Records Administration, accessible via Ancestry (ancestry.com) for George Griscomb Jr.'s 1918 passport application.
Staff. "Dorothy Arnold Made Secret Visit to Boston." *Boston Globe*, February 22, 1911 (reprinted in the *Seattle Star)*.
The National Archives (United Kingdom), for George Griscomb Jr.'s British "Naturalisation Certificate."

CHAPTER 3: LOST SOULS AND A BURIED PAST: HART ISLAND

Several newspapers as well as a magazine referencing Hart Island's early days included the *Brooklyn Daily Eagle, Evening Sun, Harper's Weekly, New York Daily Graphic, New York Times, New York Tribune,* and the *New York World.* Federal census records from the National Archives and Records Administration are accessible via ancestry.com.

Selected book and website references include:

Hart Island Burial Records, data.cityofnewyork.us/City-Government/ DOC-Hart-Island-Burial-Records/c39u-es35.

Hart Island Project, hartisland.net. (Includes "Search burials since 1980.")

Hunt, Melinda, and Joel Sternfeld. *Hart Island.* Berlin, Germany: Scalo, 1998.

National Missing and Unidentified Persons System, namus.gov.

New York City Department of Health and Mental Hygiene, www1.nyc.gov/site/doh/ index.page.

New York City Department of Records and Information Services, www1.nyc.gov/site/ records/index.page.

New York City Human Resources Administration, Office of Burial Services, www1.nyc .gov/site/hra/about/about-hra.page.

New York Parks, Recreation and Historic Preservation. *Resource Evaluation, Hart Island Historic District.* New York Parks, Recreation and Historic Preservation, October 4, 2016.

Raftery, Patrick. *Cemeteries of the Bronx.* New York: Westchester County Historical Society, 2016.

Staff. *A Historical Resume of Potter's Field, 1869–1967.* New York: Department of Correction, 1967.

Selected twenty-first-century newspaper references include:

Brady, Emily. "A Chance to Be Mourned." *New York Times,* November 12, 2006.

Buckley, Cara. "Finding Names for Hart Island's Forgotten." *New York Times,* March 24, 2008.

Chan, Sewell. "Searching for Names on an Island of Graves." *New York Times,* November 26, 2007.

Santora, Marc. "City Introduces Online Database for Its Potter's Field." *New York Times,* April 10, 2013.

Chapter 4: Everett Ruess: He Kept His Dream

As Everett's story unfolded, it, too, was followed in the newspapers. References documenting the early days of the search included the *Salt Lake Telegram, Salt Lake Tribune, Los Angeles Times, Los Angeles Daily News, Ogden Standard-Examiner, New York Times,* and the *Deseret News.*

Selected book and twenty-first-century newspaper references include:

Fradkin, Philip L. *Everett Ruess: His Short Life, Mysterious Death, and Astonishing Afterlife.* Berkeley: University of California Press, 2011.
Gulliford, Andrew. "Putting Everett Ruess to Rest: Perhaps a Final Conclusion to a 1934 Desert Mystery." *Durango Herald,* May 13, 2017.
Roberts, David. *Finding Everett Ruess.* Broadway Books, 2011.
Thybony, Scott. *The Disappearances: A Story of Exploration, Murder, and Mystery in the American West.* Salt Lake City: University of Utah, 2016.
Verne, Jules. *Twenty Thousand Leagues under the Sea.* France: 1870.

Chapter 5: Glen and Bessie Hyde: Grand Canyon Honeymoon

Newspapers cited in Glen and Bessie Hyde's story included the *Deseret News, Ogden Standard-Examiner, Twin Falls Daily News, Needles Nugget, Salt Lake Tribune, Charlotte Observer,* and *Arizona Daily Sun.* In addition, both the United Press and the Associated Press spread news reports all over the country.

Selected book references include:

Dimock, Brad. *Sunk Without a Sound: The Tragic Colorado Honeymoon of Glen and Bessie Hyde.* Flagstaff, AZ: Fretwater Press, 2001.
Krakauer, Jon. *Under the Banner of Heaven: A Story of Violent Faith.* New York: Anchor Books, 2004.

Chapter 6: Joseph Laurence Halpern: Reaching for the Stars

Publications and newspapers covering the search for Joseph Laurence Halpern include a Rocky Mountain National Park newsletter, the *Denver News, Denver Post,* and several articles published by the Associated Press. Most of the documentation on Joseph, along with correspondence among members of his family, friends, and the Federal Bureau of Investigation (FBI) was passed down through the Halpern family and provided by Joseph's nephew, Roland Halpern.

Selected book, correspondence, and website references include:

McLaughlin, John S. "A Report on the Disappearance of Joe Laurence Halpern." August 23, 1933. Included in a file titled "Accidents in National Parks," preserved by the National Archives and Records Administration.

Moomaw, Jack C. *Recollections of a Rocky Mountain Ranger*. Denver: YMCA of the Rockies, 1994.

Pettem, Silvia. *Cold Case Research: Resources for Unidentified, Missing and Cold Homicide Cases*. Boca Raton, FL: CRC Press, 2013.

Pettem, Silvia. *Joseph Halpern Part 1*. defrostingcoldcases.com. March 5, 2012.

Pettem, Silvia. *Joseph Halpern Part 2*. defrostingcoldcases.com. March 5, 2012.

Pettem, Silvia. *Joseph Halpern Part 3*. defrostingcoldcases.com. March 5, 2012.

Rogers, Edmund B. Letter to Bernard Halpern, September 18, 1933.

US Department of the Interior. *The Rocky Mountain National Park Motorists Guide Map*. 1933.

Verne, Jules. *From the Earth to the Moon*. France: 1865.

Chapter 7: Lawrence Joseph Bader: Gone Fishing

The Bader story was followed, as it made the news, in both Ohio and Nebraska newspapers, primarily the *Akron Beacon Journal*, *Cincinnati Enquirer*, and the *Lincoln Star*, with United Press International and the Associated Press syndicating their stories nationwide.

Chapter 8: Twylia May Embrey: Don't Fence Me In

Newspapers referenced in Twylia's story include the *North Platte Telegraph*, *Omaha World Herald*, *Boston Globe*, *McCook Gazette*, and the *Denver Post*. The author also met several times with Twylia's grandniece, Jennifer Kitt, and with Twylia's sister, Mildred "Midge" Garner, who provided insight into Twylia's background as well as the Embrey family's correspondence with Bill Wederski. In addition, the author and Micki Lavigne interviewed, by email and telephone, several of the family members and friends of "Theresa Naimo."

Selected references include:

Florida Department of Health. Marriage record for Theresa Trende and William R. Keeley. 1954.

Pettem, Silvia. *Someone's Daughter: In Search of Justice for Jane Doe*. Lanham, MD: Taylor Trade, 2009.

Social Security Administration. "Application for Social Security Account Number for Theresa Jonne Keeley." August 12, 1955.

Twenty-first-century newspaper and website references include:

Hammel, Paul, "Nebraskan Used a New ID to Craft Life Far from Kin." *Omaha World-Herald*, May 7, 2006.

Merritt, George. "'54 Cold Case Helps Solve a 2nd Mystery." *Denver Post*, April 29, 2006.

Staff. "Theresa J. Naimo Obituary" (online). Gately Funeral Home, April 2, 2006.

Staff. "Theresa J. 'Teri' Naimo Obituary" (print). *Boston Globe*, April 2, 2006.

CHAPTER 9: THE HATBOX BABY: A CHRISTMAS MIRACLE

Newspaper articles on this story came from the *Arizona Daily Star*, *Arizona Republic*, *Davenport News*, *Kansas City Star*, *Los Angeles Times*, and the *Tucson Citizen*, as well as many articles reprinted in additional newspapers by the Associated Press.

Selected historical newspaper references include:

D'Anna, John. "Mystery of 'Hatbox Baby' Solved Half-Century Later." *Mesa Tribune* (reprinted by the Associated Press), December 26, 1988.

Dedera, Don. "State's Christmas Miracle Baby of the Desert." *Arizona Republic*, December 25, 1961.

LeBaron, Alan D. "Where Is the Hatbox Baby Today?" *Parade, the Sunday Newspaper Magazine*, December 24, 1951.

Staff. "Find Abandoned Babe in Hatbox on Desert." *Arizona Republic*, December 25, 1931.

Selected twenty-first-century newspaper and website references include:

Ancestry, ancestry.com.

D'Anna, John. "Adoptive Parents of the 'Hatbox Baby' Had a Short-lived Marriage." *The Republic*/azcentral.com, December 26, 2018.

D'Anna, John. "An Old Note Provides a Clue to Possible Birth Mother of the 'Hatbox Baby.'" *The Republic*/azcentral.com, December 27, 2018.

D'Anna, John. "A Trip to Iowa Gives More Answers—and More Questions in the 'Hatbox Baby' Mystery." *The Republic*/azcentral.com, January 1, 2019.

D'Anna, John. "Could DNA Tests Unlock Clues in the 'Hatbox Baby' Mystery?" *The Republic*/azcentral.com, December 28, 2018.

D'Anna, John. "DNA Sleuth's Labor of Love Uncovers New Leads in 'Hatbox Baby' Mystery." *The Republic*/azcentral.com, December 30, 2018.

D'Anna, John. "Libraries and Librarians Were Essential in Solving the Mystery of the 'Hatbox Baby.'" *The Republic*/azcentral.com, December 25, 2018.

D'Anna, John. "Meet the Couple Who Found the 'Hatbox Baby' in the Arizona Desert." *The Republic*/azcentral.com, December 25, 2018.

D'Anna, John. "Miracle Baby Found on Roadside Is One of Arizona's Great Mysteries. Will New Clues Solve It?" *The Republic*/azcentral.com, December 23, 2018.

D'Anna, John. "New DNA Connections Finally Provide Answers in the 'Hatbox Baby' Mystery." *The Republic*/azcentral.com, December 31, 2018.

D'Anna, John. "Sharon Elliott Found Out She Was the 'Hatbox Baby' Just before Her Mother Died." *The Republic*/azcentral.com, December 24, 2018.

D'Anna, John. "Storytellers Event Brings Another Sleuth to Help Solve the 'Hatbox Baby' Mystery." *The Republic*/azcentral.com, December 29, 2018.

Reddit, reddit.com.

CHAPTER 10: YOUNG CHILD ABDUCTIONS AND BLACK-MARKET BABIES

Newspaper references for this chapter include the *Des Moines Register*, *New York Post*, *The Tennessean*, and the *News Journal*.

Selected references include:

Gardner, Mona. "Traffic in Babies." *Collier's Magazine*, September 16, 1939.

Poppy, Nick. "This Woman Stole Children from the Poor to Give to the Rich." *New York Post*, June 17, 2017.

CHAPTER 11: THE BOY IN THE BOX: AMERICA'S UNKNOWN CHILD

The initial days of the "Boy in the Box" investigation were covered in many newspapers, including the *Philadelphia Inquirer*, *Indiana Gazette*, *Kane Republican*, *Pocono Record*, *Latrobe Bulletin*, *Philadelphia Daily News*, *South Bend Tribune*, *The Mercury* (Pottstown, Pennsylvania), and the *Republican* and the *Herald* (Pottsville, Pennsylvania). The author also corresponded with Vidocq Society members William L. "Bill" Fleisher, Colleen Fitzpatrick, and Warren Kerschbaum, and interviewed, by email, Nicholas P. Kerschbaum.

Selected newspaper references include:

Belle, Marisol. "Who Is This Boy? Haunting Case Has Stumped Sleuths for More than 40 Years." *Philadelphia Daily News*, October 2, 1998.

Rubinkam, Michael. "Boy Killed 41 Years Ago Reburied after Testing." Associated Press, April 20, 1994.

Sabatini, Richard V., and Bill Price. "To Give the Child a Name . . . a Life." *Philadelphia Inquirer*, October 23, 1988.

Staff. "Beaten Boy's Body Found in Box: Seek Clues to Identity of Youngster." *Philadelphia Inquirer*, February 27, 1957.

Staff. "Pair Seen Unloading Car Trunk." *Philadelphia Inquirer*, February 28, 1957.

Several twenty-first-century book, newspaper, and magazine references include:

Capuzzo, Michael. *The Murder Room: The Heirs of Sherlock Holmes Gather to Solve the World's Most Perplexing Cold Cases*. New York, NY: Gotham, 2010.
Dale, Maryclaire. "50 Years Later, Still No Name for 'Boy in the Box.'" Associated Press, February 27, 2007.
Erdely, Sabrina Rubin. "Who Is the Boy in the Box?" *Philadelphia*, November 2003.
Kolata, Gina, and Heather Murphy. "The Golden State Killer Is Tracked through a Thicket of DNA, and Experts Shudder." *New York Times*, April 27, 2018.
Rowan, Tommy. "Some Can't Forget Unsolved 'Boy in the Box' Case." *Philadelphia Daily News*, March 6, 2017.

Chapter 12: Connie Smith: Camper from the West

Newspapers referenced for the early days of Connie Smith's case include the *Casper Star-Tribune*, *Courant Magazine*, and the *Hartford Courant*, as well as the Associated Press. The author also interviewed and corresponded with Connie's brother, Nels J. Smith.

One selected book reference is:

Dooling, Michael C. *Clueless in New England: The Unsolved Disappearances of Paula Welden, Connie Smith and Katherine Hull*. Connecticut: Carrollton Press, 2010.

Chapter 13: Marion Joan McDowell: Taken from Toronto

The primary newspapers that covered the Marion McDowell case were the *Toronto Telegram* and the *Toronto Daily Star*.

Selected references also include:

Fabian, Robert. *Fabian of the Yard: An Intimate Record*. New York: British Book Centre, 1953.
Pettem, Silvia. *Someone's Daughter: In Search of Justice for Jane Doe*. Lanham, MD: Taylor Trade, 2009.

Chapter 14: "Daredevil" DeLay: Aerial Sabotage

Newspapers referencing DeLay's aerial sabotage include the *Pasadena Post*, *Los Angeles Daily News*, *Los Angeles Times*, and the *Long Beach Telegram*. DeLay's World War I draft registration card is accessible on Ancestry, ancestry.com.

Selected book, periodical, newspaper, and film references for both DeLay and United Airlines Flight 629 include:

Breen, Richard L., and John Twist. *The FBI Story*. Burbank, CA: Warner Bros. Pictures, Inc., 1959. Film.

Grace, Dick. *The Lost Squadron*. New York: Grosset & Dunlap, 1932.

Hatfield, D. D. *Los Angeles Aeronautics 1920–1929*. Hatfield History of Aeronautics. Inglewood, CA: Northrop Institute of Technology, 1973.

Kelly, Shawna. *Images of America, Aviators in Early Hollywood*. Charleston, SC: Arcadia Publishing, 2008.

Pettem, Silvia. "Longmont Plane Explosion Left 44 Victims." *Boulder Daily Camera*, May 8, 2016.

Smith, Wallace. *The Lost Squadron*. New York, NY: RKO-Radio Pictures, 1932. Film.

Staff. "Action and Thrills Support Dramatic Theory in *Skin Deep*." *Silver Sheet*, September 1, 1922.

Chapter 15: William Desmond Taylor and His Brother: Double Blood Bond

Many of the early newspaper references came from the *Bellingham Herald*, *Chicago Tribune*, *Denver Post*, *New York Times*, and the *San Francisco Examiner*. Selected book, magazine, and website references include:

Chung, Connie. "Shot in Hollywood." *Newsmagazine*, 1986.

Giroux, Robert. *A Deed of Death: The Story Behind the Unsolved Murder of Hollywood Director William Desmond Taylor*. New York: Alfred A. Knopf, 1990.

Higham, Charles. *Murder in Hollywood: Solving a Silent Screen Mystery*. Madison: University of Wisconsin Press, 2006.

King, Ed C. "I Know Who Killed William Desmond Taylor." *True Detective Mysteries*, 1930.

Taylorology, taylorology.com.

Through the Lens of Time

Doyle, Sir Arthur Conan. *A Study in Scarlet*. Ward Lock & Co., 1888.

Storino, Pascal, Jr. "The History of Communications: Part 1." *The History of Policing in the City of New York*, 2016. nypdhistory.com.

Walton, R. H. *Cold Case Homicides: Practical Investigative Techniques*. 2nd ed. Boca Raton, FL: CRC Press, 2017.

Index

Note: Page numbers of figures are in italics.